70 Hebrew Words Every Christian Should Know

70 Hebrew Words Every Christian Should Know

Matthew Richard Schlimm

Nashville

70 HEBREW WORDS EVERY CHRISTIAN SHOULD KNOW

This book is printed on acid-free paper.

Library of Congress Cataloging-in-Publication Data has been requested.

978-1-4267-9996-9

19 20 21 22 23 24 25 26 27—10 9 8 7 6
MANUFACTURED IN THE UNITED STATES OF AMERICA

Contents

Acknowledgments

Every book worth reading results from many people working together. In this case, I want to thank Michael Stephens and Paul Franklyn of Abingdon Press for approaching me with the idea and helping it reach completion.

My students over the years have inspired my work. In particular, I think of the students I taught at Duke Divinity School in 2003–4, when I first started discussing why Hebrew words are worth learning. I also want to thank more recent students like Joan Naraghi, Katrina Richardson, Jennifer Hardin, Marilyn Panco, Heather Libich, and especially Christina Ennen, who have sharpened my manuscript in various ways.

Many of my teachers and colleagues inspired me over the years with a passion for Hebrew, including Victor Hamilton, Ellen Davis, James Crenshaw, Jacob Stromberg, and Travis Bott. In their own way, each has transmitted their love of Hebrew to me, and I hope to transmit it to my readers here.

I also want to thank several people at the University of Dubuque, including the trustees, Jeffery Bullock, Mark Ward, Annette Huizenga, and my colleagues. I can't imagine a more supportive place to work. Dean Huizenga took the time to read a draft of my manuscript and offer very useful feedback.

Lastly, I want to thank my family for all their support and love. My children and wife bring me immense joy, even amid stressful times. My dad and sister always cheer me on and know how to make me laugh. My mom, Sheila Bluhm, read a draft of this book and offered constructive comments, even while battling cancer. I dedicate it to her.

Introduction

English isn't God's first language. The Bible's native tongue is Hebrew. Three quarters of the Bible was originally written in that language.

No translation is perfect. Translators inevitably fail to capture everything taking place in the source language.

Many Bible translators even talk about the violence of translation.[1] In the fourth century, Saint Jerome translated the Bible into Latin, the most common language of his day. He said that translators acted like invaders who went inside foreign lands, stole thoughts, and brought them back home.[2] More than a thousand years later, Martin Luther translated the Bible into German. Under heavy fire from critics, Luther said he had to choose whether to "demolish" the German language or "depart from" the biblical word. In passages of greatest importance, he insisted he deformed German rather than harm the Bible.[3]

In recent times, biblical scholar Robert P. Carroll picked up on this metaphor:

> The need to transform . . . the ancient languages of the Bible (Aramaic, Hebrew, Greek) into a modern language, thereby modernizing the language, thought, and culture of the Bible by means of such translation does unimaginable violence to the text. It wrenches the text from its home in the ancient cultures and languages, deports that text and exiles it in foreign languages and cultures. The cultural transformations required to make the translation work in its new language and culture often involve serious violations of the text. Radical changes between cultures are not easily accommodated by translation techniques and each cultural translation shifts the text further away from its roots in ancient culture.[4]

The imagery and its implications are striking: translation is war. Loss and destruction inevitably occur.

The purpose of this book is to help readers find what's lost in Bible translation. It helps them locate nearly forgotten prisoners of war and remains of the dead. This book allows readers to rebuild the rubble left by Bible translations, or at least imagine the glory of the structures that once stood in their splendor before translations demolished what lay in their path. This book is an important first step in seeing the riches of God's word in its original language.[5]

A Useful Resource for...

I write this book for three primary audiences. The first is Christians of all types of who never took a Hebrew class but want new tools to dig more deeply into the Bible. Learning Biblical Hebrew—even snippets of it—helps us understand how the writers of the Bible expressed their experiences, thought about reality, and viewed the world.

The second audience is seminary students. Many people preparing to become pastors don't know why they should take a course in Hebrew. Or, they're in a Hebrew class but can't see why it matters. As they memorize verb conjugations and cram vocabulary words into their already full brains, they struggle to connect their studies with the life of the church.[6] By reading this book alongside their grammars, students can see in fresh ways the vast importance of what they are learning.

The third audience is pastors who once took Hebrew but have since forgotten it. Ministry is extremely demanding, and few pastors have time to review class notes from seminary. This book serves as a refresher focused on features of Hebrew that matter deeply to understanding the Bible.

A few additional notes about my intended audiences: readers of this book need no prior knowledge of Hebrew. If you would like to learn the Hebrew alphabet, I've provided an explanation in the appendix. However, you don't need to know that material to enjoy this book.

This book isn't comprehensive. I've stuck to examples that have moved me, and I hope they'll strike you as interesting, too. Most people who know Hebrew have favorite examples, and space limitations unfortunately don't allow me to treat every significant word.

Nevertheless, many of these Hebrew words are very popular.[7] In fact, these seventy words appear over thirty thousand times in the Bible. They show up in nearly fifteen thousand verses. More than 60 percent of the verses in the Old Testament contain at least one of the seventy words mentioned here.

This Book and Biblical Scholarship

In the first half of the twentieth century, many biblical scholars perceived a fundamental connection between biblical Hebrew and biblical theology.

Unfortunately, they sometimes did sloppy work that later received criticism. In 1961, in his book *The Semantics of Biblical Language*, James Barr vigorously attacked previous work.

For several decades, his ideas held sway. However, more recent scholars have realized that while many insights can be gained from Barr, one can also go too far and fail to see the important links between language and thought. This book is part of this more recent stream, heeding Barr where necessary but also moving beyond his limitations.

As Enio Mueller puts it, "Barr's work represented a major development in modern Biblical interpretation, one from which nobody can safely turn back. His criticisms were in order. . . . Nevertheless, the main tenet of Barr's view, the absence of correlation between thought and language, has itself proved inadequate."[8]

My specialties as a scholar pertain to the Bible's first five books, so you're likely to see a fair amount of them here. A book by a specialist in Obadiah would look quite different.

To help as broad an audience as I can, I've minimized technical jargon. However, I recognize that some readers might use this book as a springboard to deeper studies. So, I've included various textboxes that provide important quotes, explain more academic work, and define technical terms for those who are interested. When you see a parenthetical remark like the one at the end of this paragraph, feel free to check the textbox if it interests you. (See **This Book and Biblical Scholarship**.)

This book isn't an introduction to biblical Hebrew vocabulary. Such an introduction would include Hebrew words for "the," "on," and the like. On a related note, this book doesn't treat Hebrew grammar at all. Naturally, more can be unlocked from the Bible by learning how sentences are put together. However, grammar is too big a topic to cover here.[9] (See **Sentence Versus Word**.)

Sentence Versus Word

Many people working with languages have argued that studying words alone isn't worthwhile, that meaning truly resides on the level of sentences. A more balanced position is advocated by John C. Poirier:

> The claim that meaning resides in the sentence rather than in the word is naïve and simplistic. . . . To say meaning resides in the sentence rather than the word is like saying flavor resides in the recipe rather than in the ingredients. In short, it is [a] hasty and unjust exclusion of a middle position.
>
> It is far better to think of meaning—that is, the codified aspect of transcribed meaning—as a bifocal field, mapped through the give-and-take between words and the sentences they comprise. Meaning resides in the sentences, but it also resides in both larger and smaller loci.[10]

My website www.MatthewSchlimm.com provides several additional resources:

1. A concordance listing verses in which the words discussed in this book appear in the Bible. This concordance is especially important for those wanting to apply insights from this book to other biblical texts.

2. Sound files explaining how to pronounce the words.

3. Various reading schedules. While it makes sense to read this book from beginning to end, it's also possible to read the introduction and then read about particular words as they are memorized for a course. The reading schedules on the website explain how to read this book alongside popular Hebrew grammars.

The Necessity of This Book

Some might object to the premise behind this book. After all, Christianity has always been comfortable translating the Bible into other languages. Many of Jesus's followers used a Greek translation of their Hebrew scriptures. The Gospel writers even wrote in Greek, despite the fact that Jesus spoke Aramaic most of the time. So, since its inception, Christianity has embraced God in translation.[11] Islam, in contrast, prides itself on maintaining its holy book in Arabic.[12] Most Muslims today would insist that any translations of the *Qur'an* are only approximations, not the *Qur'an* itself.

So, why is this book, which introduces Christians to Hebrew words, ultimately necessary?

The basic message of the Bible can be understood in any language. At the same time, many biblical texts are hard to understand. They don't quite make sense when translated into English. Something is missing. Quite frequently, what readers miss has been lost in translation. (See **Translation: A Beginning**.) The original language allows various parts to click together like well-constructed puzzle pieces.

Translation: A Beginning

"Translation is of course the beginning of an exegetical argument—and one of which many monolingual readers in the West are entirely unaware."[13]

—*Ellen Davis*

So, given the Bible's sacred status, there's immense value in studying it as carefully as possible. In many ways, it's the difference between an old-fashioned television and a new high-definition one. With Hebrew in mind, interpreters see new details they didn't realize were missing before. They make new connections. They immerse themselves in scripture more fully.

What's Lost in Translation?

Throughout this book, we'll see that English cannot capture everything the original biblical languages convey. The next chapter looks at cases in which the sound of the original Hebrew is very important, but English translations give readers no clue what's taking place audibly in the text. The Bible is filled with puns and wordplays that cannot survive translation. This chapter shows some of these missing connections. It examines ten Hebrew words worth knowing because of how they shed new light on various texts:

- the story of Adam, Eve, and their children (Gen 2:4b–4:16)
- the tower of Babel (Gen 11:1-9)
- a parable Isaiah tells (Isa 5:1-7)
- one of the prophet Amos's visions (Amos 8:1-3)
- a well-known part of Numbers (Num 6:24-26)

Learning these words allows readers to see these scriptures in fresh ways.

Chapter 2 shows how English translations sometimes convey the sound of Hebrew words without explaining what those words mean. This problem arises most commonly with [1] names and [2] words such as "hallelujah" that have leapt from Hebrew to English (also known as "loanwords"). In these cases, it's nice that English readers hear echoes of Hebrew sounds (unlike the words in the previous chapter). However, it's unfortunate that Hebrew meaning is lost. So, this second chapter recaptures meanings lost from names and loanwords:

- names in Genesis 2:4b–4:16
- a sampling of other names in the Bible
- amen
- hallelujah
- Sabbath
- Satan

This chapter helps readers learn what these words mean.

Chapter 3 looks at Hebrew words worth knowing because they don't have precise equivalents in English. Sometimes, English words can only approximate Hebrew meaning. Readers don't see all the nuances of what's in the original text. So, we'll learn the richer meanings of words that are often translated as:

- create
- heart
- soul
- the LORD
- Sheol
- ban

As we'll see, the Hebrew words behind these English words have dimensions uncaptured in translation.

Chapter 4 turns to Hebrew words that have more than one meaning. When English translators encounter such words, they have to pick a single English word to replace the Hebrew. However, the Hebrew sometimes carries overtones that convey more than just that one meaning. So, we'll examine Hebrew words that mean:

- hear and obey
- evil and disaster
- justice and judgment
- breath, wind, and spirit
- hoping and waiting
- law and instruction

Many texts make use of these words' various meanings, so these words are well worth our study.

Chapter 5 looks at Hebrew words that have lost their concrete meanings in translation, being replaced by abstract concepts that are more difficult to understand than the original text. We'll see how there are vivid images conveyed by the Hebrew behind the following words:

- vanity
- transgression
- keep (as in "keeping the law")
- sin and forgiveness
- repentance
- blessing

The Hebrew equivalents to these words evoke concrete images that can help people enormously in learning the basics of faith.

Chapter 6 examines cases in which translators have replaced Hebrew words with outdated English words. It provides useful alternatives to the following translations:

- behold
- woe
- alas
- atone
- deliver
- redeem
- host

People today tend either to avoid using these words or to use them in a different sense than the writers of the Bible had in mind. By looking at the Hebrew, we can learn what's really taking place in the text.

Chapters 7 and 8 turn to the fact that words have both dictionary and encyclopedia definitions. When translating Hebrew to English, it's relatively easy to find words that align in terms of dictionary definitions. However, encyclopedia definitions are obviously much longer, and it's precisely here that we find grand differences between Hebrew words and the English typically used in translation. Chapter 7 focuses on three practices and three objects that differ in biblical Hebrew and modern English:

- remember
- covenant
- walk
- horses
- gates
- houses

Then, chapter 8 examines cultural values understood in very different ways by the Bible and modern readers:

- peace
- love
- cleanliness
- holiness
- glory
- wisdom
- fear

By learning the encyclopedia definitions of the Hebrew behind these words, readers can imagine new ways of thinking about practices, objects, and values.

The final concluding chapter summarizes the book's findings, showing how biblical Hebrew can enrich our knowledge of God and enable faithful living.

Chapter 1

Losing Hebrew Sounds

Every word has both sound and meaning. Usually, translation means we lose the sound of Hebrew words:

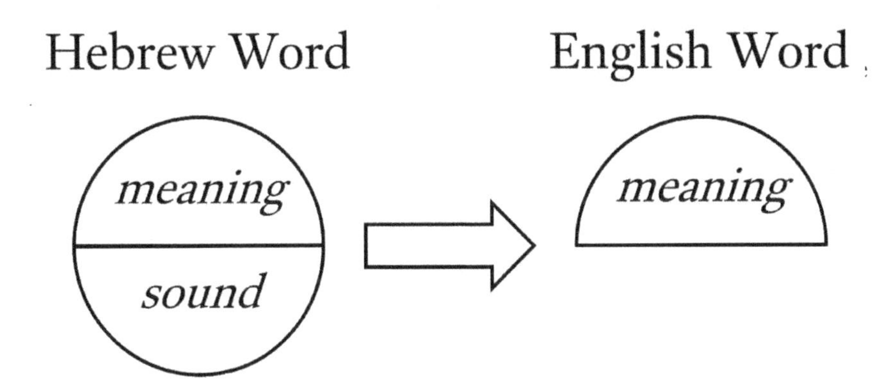

Figure 1

This point seems very obvious. Of course, words sound different when translated! We could even ask, does the loss of sound matter? People who study languages have maintained for a long time that most words' sounds are arbitrary.[14] In English, we talk of "blood." In the Old Testament, it's called *dam*. As different as "blood" and *dam* sound, they refer to the same red substance that flows through our veins. Nothing innate about this liquid requires that it be called "blood" or *dam*. (See **Signifier and Signified**.)

So, at first thought, it might seem that the loss of sound has relatively little significance for Bible translation. It doesn't seem to matter what sounds are used, as long as the audience understands what's in mind.

> **Signifier and Signified**
>
> Signifier: how a word sounds and appears.
> Signified: what a word refers to, its meaning.[15]

The Bible, however, comes out of an oral culture that placed high priority on how words sound. Even today, thousands of years later, we can still find many cases in the Bible in which the sounds of Hebrew words actually matter a great deal. The writers of the Bible often draw connections between different words that sound alike but mean something different. This is called "wordplay." (See **Wordplay and Other Terms**.) Although wordplay doesn't show up in every verse of the Bible, it's hardly a rare occurrence. According to one scholar, there are more than five hundred cases in which the Old Testament text plays with how

> **Wordplay and Other Terms**
>
> Wordplay: an umbrella term that usually encompasses artistic uses of words' sounds and meanings.
> Paronomasia: a wordplay when two or more words sound alike but have different meanings.
> Alliteration: a wordplay when words start with similar sounds.
> Rhyme: a wordplay when, aside from initial sounds, words sound similar.[16]

words sound in order to drive home a larger point.[17] That means sound plays an important role, on average, more frequently than once every other chapter. In these cases, when the sound of the Hebrew is muted, we lose a key component of the passage. (See **The Irony of Not Hearing**.)

> **The Irony of Not Hearing**
>
> R. Murray Schafer writes, "The sense of hearing cannot be closed off at will. There are no earlids. When we go to sleep, our perception of sound is the last door to close and it is also the first to open when we awake."
>
> Ironically, those who want to hear the original sounds of scripture usually cannot, no matter how hard they strain. It's only through learning Hebrew and Greek (or using resources like this book) that the Bible's original music begins to tickle our ears.[18]

Genesis 2–4

The opening chapters of Genesis overflow with wordplays that are lost in translation. Consider Genesis 2:7: "The LORD God formed the human from the topsoil of the fertile land" (CEB). In terms of the meaning of the Hebrew words in this verse, the Common English Bible does an excellent job. However, the Hebrew words for "human" and "fertile land" are remarkably similar:

	English	Hebrew	Hebrew Transliteration
1.	human	אָדָם	*adam*
2.	fertile land	אֲדָמָה	*adamah*

A few brief notes about this chart: First, the Hebrew letters are explained in the appendix at the end of the book. Second, I've also transliterated the Hebrew, meaning I've put Hebrew letters into their closest English equivalents in the right column. Third, my website www.MatthewSchlimm.com provides sound files explaining how to pronounce these words.

Both *adam* and *adamah* are very popular: *adam* appears about 550 times in the Bible, while *adamah* shows up over 230 times. Twenty verses feature both words, including Genesis 2:7, which says that God formed the *adam* from the *adamah*. It's easy to see—even in terms of the letters and sounds themselves—how *adam* comes from *adamah*: "The LORD God formed the *adam* (human) from the topsoil of the *adamah* (fertile land)" (CEB, alt.). Scholars have tried to capture the wordplay by going alternate routes. Some have suggested translating *adam* as "human" and *adamah* as "humus." While this translates *adam* correctly, few people today talk about the ground as "humus." In fact, we might get things confused with what we put on pita.

Others, including myself, have translated *adam* as "earthling" and *adamah* as "earth." However, people today tend to talk of "earthlings" only when they're impersonating aliens. Capturing all the nuances and connections of the Bible's original language is notoriously difficult—even when these connections are immensely important to the text itself. In Genesis 2:4b–4:16, the words *adam* and *adamah* appear fourteen and twenty-five times, respectively, as the text artfully interweaves the two words together to drive home the key message that humanity is intricately connected with the soil. (See **Humans and Land**.)

Many other wordplays exist in Genesis 2–4. The following examples involve Hebrew words that aren't very popular and don't need to be learned at this point. However, they illustrate the literary artistry of these opening chapters of the Bible:

- The Hebrew word for "stream" or "mist" is *ed* (2:6), which sounds like a shortened form of *eden*, the name of the garden (2:8, 10, 15; 3:23-24; 4:16). The *ed* gives life to *eden*.
- The text describes the human beings as "naked" in 2:25 (see also 3:7, 10-11), and the next verse describes the snake as "crafty" (3:1). The Hebrew words for "naked" (*arom*) and "crafty" (*arum*) are nearly identical. The *arom* humans are vulnerable to the *arum* snake.[20]
- In Genesis 4:12, 14, Cain is called a "vagrant and a wanderer" (NASB). The Hebrew words behind those terms are very similar (*na* and *nad*). They are also akin to the Hebrew for Nod (*nod*), the land where Cain settles in 4:16. Cain is a *na* and *nad* left to the land of *nod.*

As these examples begin to illustrate, the opening chapters of Genesis are rich in meaning and wordplay. The Hebrew of this text reveals textures that cannot be captured in translation.[21]

Humans and Land

"There is a kinship between humans and the earth: 'And YHWH God formed the human being [*adam*], dust from the fertile soil [*adamah*]' (Gen. 2:7). Although the wordplay is captured surprisingly well by the English pun 'human from humus,' the Hebrew is more fully descriptive of their family resemblance. Both words are related to *adom*, 'ruddy'; in the Levant, brownish red is the skin tone of both the people and the earth. *Terra rossa*, 'red earth,' is the geological term for the thin but rich loam covering the hill country where the early Israelites settled. Thus *adam* from *adamah* is localized language; it evokes the specific relationship between a people and their particular place."[19]

—*Ellen Davis*

Babbling at Babel

In Genesis 11, readers learn of people's attempt to stay in one place and become famous by building a huge tower. The name of their city is usually translated "Babel," which matches the Hebrew fairly well:

	English	Hebrew	Hebrew Transliteration
3.	Babel, Babylon	בָּבֶל	*bavel*

This word appears over 250 times in the Bible. Aside from Genesis 10:10 and 11:9, it's always translated "Babylon." That's the name of the kingdom that conquered Jerusalem in 587 BCE and scattered segments of its population into exile where they were forced to learn new languages. Babylon was also home to a massive towering temple to the god Marduk.[22]

When readers know the Hebrew, the connection between this story and Babylon is hard to miss: it presents God as scattering the very people who scattered Israel (See **Mocking Babylon**.)

Mocking Babylon

"In Babylonian eyes, Babylon is invincible and eternal because it was founded by the gods, for their own purposes. In contrast, the biblical story quashes this notion and presents the city's construction as the result of human action, with no divine corroboration; and many have interpreted the builders' words, to 'make a name for ourselves,' as a kind of rebellion against God. . . .

"Babylon is famously characterized as a political monolith: they oppress and dominate their subjects—their 'language' is enforced upon everyone. This portrait of Babylon is undermined by the biblical portrait of Babylon's founding: rather than unite humanity under its own language and beliefs, Babylon is the source of universal dispersion and divergence."[23]

—*Jonathan Grossman*

The Hebrew *bavel* sounds similar to this Hebrew word:[24]

	English	Hebrew	Hebrew Transliteration
4.	mix up, confuse	בָּלַל	*balal*

In Genesis 11:7, God uses this verb to talk about confusing the people of *bavel.* For that reason, 11:9 reads as follows: "Therefore it was called Babel [*bavel*], because there the Lord confused [*balal*] the language of all the earth; and from there the Lord scattered them abroad over the face of all the earth" (NRSV). The NRSV contains a footnote on the word "confused" explaining the wordplay taking place here. Footnotes, however, never receive as much attention as the main text. What's most striking about this verse in the Hebrew only constitutes a footnote in English.

In fact, in this particular passage, the text as a whole builds to the moment when the name *bavel* and word *babel* are used: in only nine verses, the text contains twenty-two appearances of a Hebrew letter that can be pronounced as "B" or "V," as well as thirty-seven appearances of the Hebrew letter pronounced "L." The earliest audiences of this text would have heard a chorus of "B," "V," and "L" sounds growing until the passage's last verse when they learned that the place was named Babel because there God "babbled" the people's languages.[25] This artful construction of sounds does not appear in English renderings of the story.

The Parable of the Vineyard

The beginning of Isaiah 5 tells a parable.[26] A farmer plants a vineyard, takes perfect care of it, and does everything to ensure the growth of delicious grapes. Instead, the grapes smell awful and cause nausea.[27] At a climactic moment, God says, "For the vineyard of the LORD of hosts is the house of Israel, and the people of Judah are his pleasant planting" (Isa 5:7a NRSV). Why does God draw this comparison?

God has done everything for the people of Israel and Judah—transforming them from a motley group of slaves into a royal kingdom. And yet, the people don't bring forth what God expects. The passage explains: "[God] expected justice, but saw bloodshed; righteousness, but heard a cry!" (Isa 5:7b NRSV). Nothing that God wants comes to fruition.

Word-for-word, the NRSV (shown above) does a decent job translating the meaning of 5:7b. We have two pairs of opposites. Bloodshed suggests a violation of justice.[28] Meanwhile, the Hebrew word for "cry" here isn't a sad sob but a life-threatening cry for help. It's used when talking about things like mass slaughter (Exod 11:6; 12:30) and rape (Deut 22:27). Obviously, that type of outcry shows that everything is not right.

While this sort of translation captures the basic meaning of the Hebrew words, it completely misses something present in the Hebrew. In the original text, the words for "justice" and "bloodshed" look and sound nearly identical:

	English	Hebrew	Hebrew Transliteration
5.	justice	מִשְׁפָּט	*mishpat*
6.	bloodshed	מִשְׂפָּח	*mispakh* (the "kh" sound is a hard *h*, similar to a hacking sound, like the end of Bach)

The Hebrew words for "righteousness" and "cry" are also nearly identical:

	English	Hebrew	Hebrew Transliteration
7.	righteousness	צְדָקָה	*tsedaqah*
8.	cry	צְעָקָה	*tseaqah*

What we have in the Hebrew text of Isaiah 5:7 are two pairs of words closely related in terms of appearance and sound. That's important because in the parable, the vineyard's grapes initially look good, but close inspection reveals they are repulsive and nasty. It's like buying berries that look good at the grocery store, only to open the box at home and find white, fuzzy mold hiding behind the label.

The NRSV and similar translations do nothing to communicate how the expectations for fruit were both so close and yet so far from what was actually produced. Yes, the NRSV captures the basic meanings. But there's nothing about the English word pairs *justice-bloodshed* and *righteousness-cry* that communicates how the grapes should have been perfect but instead disgusted people. However, it's nearly impossible to capture the precise meanings while still coming up with two pairs of words related visually and audibly.

The NJPS translation comes closest. Here's how it renders the text: "And [God] hoped for justice, But behold, injustice; For equity, But behold, iniquity!" (Isa 5:7b NJPS). Here, we see a play on "justice" and "injustice," as well as a play on "equity" and "iniquity." Such a wordplay does reflect parts of the Hebrew quite nicely. However, what's captured in terms of appearance and sound is lost in terms of meaning: the Hebrew word *mispakh* literally means "bloodshed," not "injustice." Meanwhile, the word *tseaqah* means "outcry," not "iniquity."

So, either way, something is lost. The NJPS captures the audible bond between the word pairs in the Hebrew, but it deviates from the meaning. The NRSV and most other English translations capture the meaning, leaving readers clueless about the auditory and visual connections, which make an important point about how Israel turned out so close and so far from what God intended. The English fails to capture exactly what's going on with the Hebrew.

The Horror of a Fruit Basket?

The book of Amos rages with disturbing images. Because of Israel's harsh treatment of poor people, God's judgment is coming with furious destruction.

Toward the end of the book, just before describing a new round of horrors, God shows the prophet Amos a basket of summer fruit. Without explaining the fruit basket, the text jumps to God's coming judgment. Here's the passage:

> This is what the Lord God showed me: a basket of summer fruit. He said, "Amos, what do you see?"
> I said, "A basket of summer fruit."
> Then the Lord said to me,
> "The end has come upon my people Israel;

> I will never again forgive them.
> On that day, the people will wail the temple songs,"
> says the Lord God;
> "there will be many corpses,
> thrown about everywhere." (Amos 8:1-3 CEB)

Most English readers of this text are left confused. Why did God show Amos the summer fruit? How could *that* be terrifying? What on earth does it have to do with what follows?

The text actually makes perfect sense in Hebrew. Here's the Hebrew word for "summer fruit":

	English	Hebrew	Hebrew Transliteration
9.	summer fruit	קַיִץ	*qayits*

This word is associated with the last crop to be picked during the agricultural calendar. In fact, one of the oldest inscriptions from Israel is a tenth-century BCE calendar that lists what farming activities take place during the year. The last word in this inscription is what we have here: "summer fruit." This word sounds similar to the Hebrew word for "end" that God uses to talk about Israel's demise in this passage[29]:

	English	Hebrew	Hebrew Transliteration
10.	end	קֵץ	*qets*

This word evokes ideas of death not only here but also when it's used to describe Noah's flood (Gen 6:13) and the destruction of Jerusalem (Lam 4:18; Ezek 7:2-3). So, although in English the words "summer fruit" and "end" look and sound nothing alike, in Amos the two are closely related. God shows Amos a basket of *qayits* as an ominous sign of Israel's *qets*. English readers wonder what's horrifying about a fruit basket, but Hebrew readers see the ominous potential in Amos's vision. Together, *qayits* and *qets* make over one hundred appearances in the Bible.

A Famous Benediction

It's helpful to close this chapter by examining a case in which sound plays a key role in a passage, even if we don't need to know the particular Hebrew words at hand.

The book of Numbers isn't popular. Yet, it contains a blessing that priests would give in ancient Israel. Archaeologists have found this blessing, in part or whole, on jewelry from ancient Jerusalem and on a jar in northern Sinai, dating from seven hundred to five hundred years before Jesus. Even today, many pastors use this blessing at the end of worship services. Here it is: "[v. 24] The LORD bless you and protect you. [v. 25] The LORD make his face shine on you and be gracious to you. [v. 26] The LORD lift up his face to you and grant you peace" (Num 6:24-26 CEB). Unbeknownst to most English readers, the three lines of the blessing build phonetically upon one another. In Hebrew, there are clear patterns:

- Verse 24 has three Hebrew words, twelve syllables, and fifteen consonants.
- Verse 25 has five Hebrew words, fourteen syllables, and twenty consonants.
- Verse 26 has seven Hebrew words, sixteen syllables, and twenty-five consonants.

We have in the words of one scholar "a rising crescendo."[30] Furthermore, there are three references to "the LORD" with twelve Hebrew words remaining, possibly a reference to the Lord being present with the twelve tribes of Israel.[31] The first half of the first line ("The LORD bless you") has seven syllables in Hebrew, just like the last half of the last line ("and grant you peace").[32] All in all, the Hebrew sounds more poetic than the English, akin to limericks and haikus with their own rhythms.

In the context of Numbers, the people are presented as an army that will soon go forth from Mount Sinai to the promised land. The rhythm and cadence of this blessing inspire the Israelites to march with metered precision, assured of God's presence. Unfortunately, English readers miss the poetic sounds of the blessing.

Conclusion

At first glance, the loss of Hebrew sound seems minor, a necessary casualty of any Old Testament translation. However, in many passages, readers lose something quite important. The text often drives home larger points through how words look and sound. It's one thing to read that God formed the first human from the ground. It's another thing to hear that God formed the *adam* from the *adamah* so that our eyes and ears reinforce what our brains process. With knowledge of Hebrew sounds, other passages come to life as well. Too often, translations can capture mental ideas but lose sound in the process. It's as though we have the lyrics to a song without the accompanying music.[33] Knowing key Hebrew words, we recover missing parts of important passages.

Chapter 2

Losing Hebrew Meaning

As we just saw, translation means abandoning Hebrew sound and letters, replacing them with sound and letters in English. However, sometimes in our English Old Testaments, we actually hear an echo of Hebrew sounds but lose the meaning. This chapter looks at cases where our English Bibles retain Hebrew sound but let go of meaning:

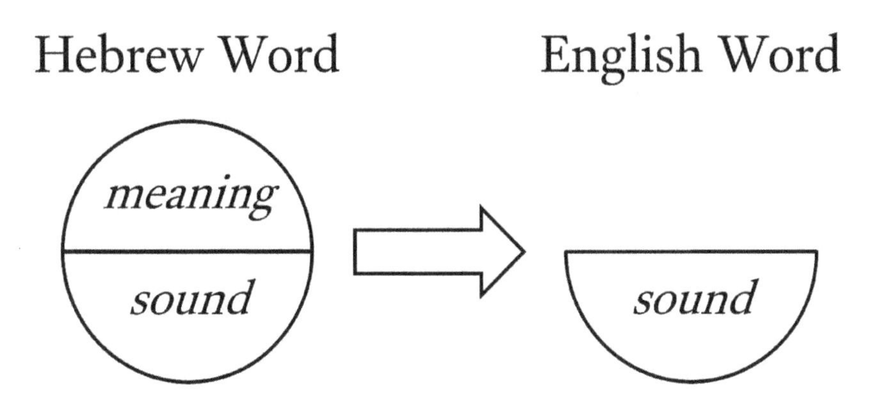

Figure 2

Adam and Eve

English readers hear something of how Hebrew sounds when they encounter names.[34] Our English Bibles talk about a couple named Adam and Eve who live in the garden of Eden. They are the parents of Cain and Abel. Each of these names comes close to the sound of the Hebrew:

	English	Hebrew	Hebrew Transliteration
1. (see above)	Adam	אָדָם	*adam*
11.	Eve	חַוָּה	*khavvah*
12.	Eden	עֵדֶן	*eden*
13.	Cain	קַיִן	*qayin*
14.	Abel	הֶבֶל	*hevel*

As the Hebrew Transliteration column shows, vowels might change, and the letter "h" doesn't always transfer across languages. Nevertheless, connections surface between how the Hebrew and English are pronounced.

While it's nice to hear the Hebrew approximated, each Hebrew name in these chapters is loaded with meaning that does not translate into English:

- The Hebrew for Adam means "Humanity."
- The Hebrew for Eve means "Life."
- The Hebrew for Eden means "Delight."
- The Hebrew for Cain means "Spear."
- The Hebrew for Abel means "Fleeting Breath," like what we see on cold mornings. It's there one second and gone the next.

Translators could have gone with meanings instead of sounds when translating these Hebrew words. In fact, an ancient Greek translation of the Bible does just that with Eve in Genesis 3:20, calling her "Zoe"—which matches the Hebrew meaning of "life" but is far removed from the Hebrew sounds.

Our English Bibles could be summarized as follows:

> *Adam and Eve initially live in the garden of Eden. After God kicks them out, Cain kills his brother Abel.*

However, if we focus on the meaning rather than the sound of these names, Genesis 2–4 looks a bit different. The Hebrew could be summarized like this:

> *Humanity and Life initially live in the garden of Delight. After God kicks them out, Spear kills his brother Fleeting Breath.*

The English translation sounds like an account of ancestors the farthest removed from us. The Hebrew sounds more like an account of human nature: what we're like. The names' meanings suggest we may have less a historical account and more a parable about God, humanity, our world, and the loss of innocence. (See **Symbolic and Literal**.)

Symbolic and Literal

"My point, once again, is *not* that those ancient people told literal stories and we are now smart enough to take them symbolically, but that they told them symbolically and we are now dumb enough to take them literally."[35]

—John Dominic Crossan & Richard G. Watts

Names alone don't determine whether a story is symbolic or historical. However, Genesis 2–4 has other clues that it's more symbolic in nature. There's a talking snake—with no explanation of why the snake can do more than hiss (3:1). The directions to the garden in Genesis 2:10-14 describe the world as a whole, rather than a single location. No one has ever found angelic beings guarding the entrance to the forbidden garden (3:24). The Hebrew text has poetic qualities, and Hebrew poetry is filled with symbolism. These factors, combined with highly meaningful names, suggest that the story as a whole should be seen as symbolic.[36]

Sometimes when I tell my students what these names in Genesis mean, they become angry that no one told them that earlier. Throughout their lives, they've felt an enormous tension between science and faith. They've felt like they needed to choose between Darwin on the one hand and Adam and Eve on the other. But when we see what the Hebrew names actually mean, then Genesis 2–4 appears less about science or history and more a symbolic story that helps us understand who we are, who God is, and why the world works the way it does. The words behind "Adam" and "Eve" are invitations to see ourselves in these characters.

When translators kept the Hebrew sounds for "Adam," "Eve," and their children's names, they also surrendered the rich meanings of these names that allow us to see what the opening of Genesis is really all about.

Other Names

Most names in the Bible have been rendered according to their sounds, rather than their meaning. Sometimes, the meanings of these names have relatively little significance to the text itself. For example, an important prophet during the time of David is called "Nathan." His name means simply "he gives." (A related biblical name is "Jonathan," meaning "the Lord gives.") Knowing the meaning of Nathan's name doesn't add a new layer of meaning to the stories involving him.[37]

Untranslated in English Bibles

"There are about 3500 words in the Bible that most of us can't understand because their meaning is not translated into English. These are biblical names."[38]

Some names, however, do unlock the meanings of stories, or at least add fresh insights to them. (See **Untranslated in English Bibles**.) Here are some examples:

	English	Hebrew	Hebrew Transliteration
15.	Deborah, bee	דְּבוֹרָה	*devorah*

Deborah served as a military and judicial ruler over Israel before it had kings (see Judg 4–5). Her name means "bee." While it may be coincidental, bees can be threatening (Deut 1:44), more so than their size would suggest. Deborah was also threatening, more so than ancient readers might assume, given that women didn't serve in combat roles to the same extent as men in the ancient world. Israel's queen bee packs a powerful sting.

	English	Hebrew	Hebrew Transliteration
16.	Hannah, gracious gift	חַנָּה	*khannah*

"Hannah" means "gracious gift." For much of her life, she has no children and is mocked by a rival wife (1 Sam 1:1–2:21). However, she fervently prays for a child at the tabernacle. Eli the priest has a conversation with her, which ends as follows: "Eli answered, 'Go in peace, and may the God of Israel grant you what you have asked of him.' She said, 'May your servant find <u>favor</u> in your eyes'" (1 Sam 1:17-18 NIV). The Hebrew word for "favor" there is *khen*, which is closely related in Hebrew to "Hannah." Just two verses later, Hannah receives the gracious gift she so desperately wanted, becoming pregnant with Samuel. *Khannah* finds *khen*.

	English	Hebrew	Hebrew Transliteration
17.	David, beloved	דָּוִד	*david*

"David" means "beloved." David was loved by his people, even before he became king (see 1 Sam 18:5-9, 16). David also had a special place in God's heart (2 Sam

7:8-16). Some scholars think that "David" might even be a throne name assumed by Jesse's son when he took power.[39]

	English	Hebrew	Hebrew Transliteration
18.	Solomon	שְׁלֹמֹה	*shelomoh*

"Solomon" is related to the Hebrew word *shalom*. Shalom is discussed later in this book, but it means "peace, wholeness, well-being, and prosperity," all of which have connections with Solomon's reign (see 1 Kgs 3:13; 10:7, 14-29; esp. 1 Chron 22:9). This word can also carry overtones of retribution and just deserts, something Solomon also faces (see 1 Kgs 11:1-43).

	English	Hebrew	Hebrew Transliteration
19.	Jonah, dove	יוֹנָה	*yonah*

The prophet Jonah certainly was one given to flying away (Jonah 1). Further, Israel is sometimes compared to a dove (e.g., Hos 7:11; 11:11), suggesting that Israelites should consider ways they are similar to Jonah.[40]

If you're wondering what a biblical name means, good commentaries and study Bibles can be useful.[41] Even internet searches can reveal what names originally meant in Hebrew, though it's good to check multiple sites for reliability.

Theophoric Element

Theophoric Element: the part of a name referring to God.

Some names have God's name included in them. (See **Theophoric Element.**) These names include:

1. Names ending in "-iah," which means "the LORD." So, the name "Isaiah" means "salvation of the LORD."

2. Names beginning with "Jeho-" or sometimes "Jo-," which also means "the LORD." So, the name "Jehoshaphat" means "the LORD judges," while "Joab" means "the LORD is [my] father."

3. Names beginning with "El-" or ending with "-el," which means "God." So, the name "Ezekiel" means "God strengthens." Or, the place name "Bethel" means "house of God." It's no coincidence that Jacob falls asleep at Bethel, dreams of a ladder reaching to heaven, then wakes up and thinks, "This sacred place is awesome. It's none other than God's house and the entrance to heaven" (Gen 28:17 CEB).[42] Two verses later, it says that Jacob named the place "Bethel." It's nice that English readers know he named it "Bethel," but the passage makes better sense when they know that "Bethel" means "God's house."

Biblical names often give readers an echo of Hebrew sounds, but the meaning that's lost can be significant.

Amen

A few other Hebrew words circulate in modern English. Several of these relate to worship.[43] While we talk of "contemporary worship" today, there's a tendency to preserve the past when it comes to religious ceremonies.[44] Sometimes, we find ancient Hebrew words preserved in present-day English services.

Perhaps the most common example is "amen." We say it at the end of almost every prayer. Functionally, it means, "The prayer is over. We can all open our eyes now." The Hebrew has several shades of meaning:

	English	Hebrew	Hebrew Transliteration
20.	amen	אָמֵן	*amen*

"Amen" comes from a cluster of words that refers to what's true, trustworthy, reliable, and faithful. Here's the most popular of these words, which shows up over one hundred times in the Bible:

	English	Hebrew	Hebrew Transliteration
21.	truth, faithfulness	אֱמֶת	*emet*

Truth implies a commitment to reality, and faithfulness implies a commitment to others.

Words related to *amen* and *emet* describe not only God and people but also "solid," "secure" ground into which a tent peg can be hammered (Isa 22:23). In fact, they're also used to describe "reliable" sources of water. Because of how arid Israel could be, many springs and streams would run dry, placing people in life-threatening situations. The Bible uses words related to *amen* and *emet* to describe sources of water that were "trustworthy," no matter how bad the surrounding drought (Isa 33:16).

So, why do we say "amen" at the end of prayers? One way of seeing the word is as an affirmation that God is dependable, reliable, and faithful.[45] We end prayers with a vivid reminder that God is like an ever-flowing stream that provides life-giving water.

A more popular way of interpreting the word is that it reaffirms our agreement with the words of the prayer. As one scholar puts it, saying "amen" is like saying, "Precisely! I feel the same way about it, may God do it!"[46] When we say this word at the end of prayers, we're signaling not only that we agree with the prayer but also that we'll do what's needed on our part for the prayer to come true. We commit to living in a way that helps see the prayer reach fruition.[47]

Incidentally, *amen* is one of Jesus's favorite words. It shows up more than a hundred times in the Gospels.[48] (While the Gospels were written in Greek, they occasionally use a Hebrew or Aramaic word like *amen*.[49]) Jesus uses the word in a way that differs from its normal usage in the Old Testament and even today.[50] Instead of saying this word in response to something, Jesus usually says this word just *before* he's about to say something really important. Modern translations often translate Jesus's use of *amen* as "Truly I tell you" (see NIV and NRSV of Matt 6:16). Since few people speak like that today, a better translation of *amen* would be "Seriously!" "No joke!" "Listen up!" "For real!" or "Hey, I've got something important to tell you."

Hallelujah

"Hallelujah" is another worship word leaping the gap from Hebrew to English. Many people sing this word without knowing what it means. Churches use it just frequently enough that people are embarrassed to ask for a definition. Here it is:

	English	Hebrew	Hebrew Transliteration
22.	hallelujah	הַלְלוּ־יָהּ	*halelu-yah*

This word means simply "praise the Lord." It appears about twenty-five times in the Bible, exclusively in the book of Psalms. The "hallelu-" part is from a verb meaning "praise!" that shows up nearly 150 times in the Bible. Meanwhile, "-jah" is an abbreviated way of saying "the Lord" (similar to names ending "-iah").

Today, the word sometimes shows up as "alleluia." As noted above, "h" sounds don't always transfer from one language to another (especially when Greek exerts influence, as is the case here).

Like the word "bless" (see chapter 5), "praise" involves acknowledging how great someone is. In the Bible, humans are praised for similar reasons they're praised today, such as their attractiveness (Gen 12:15; 2 Sam 14:25) or insight (Prov 12:8). Meanwhile, God is praised for being, in the words of Psalm 145:8, "gracious and merciful, slow to anger and abounding in steadfast love" (NRSV, cf. 145:2). Showing praise can involve singing, dancing, speaking of God's goodness, and giving thanks. It's usually done with other people.[51] It leads to happiness: many verses that talk about praising also talk about rejoicing.[52] "Hallelujah" is a command we give one another in worship: a joyful call to remember and recount God's goodness.

Sabbath

Another English word used in faith communities is "Sabbath." It describes a day set aside from work for worship. It's been used to describe Saturdays for Jews, Sundays for Christians, and sometimes even Fridays for Muslims.[53]

Sabbath comes from this Hebrew word, which appears 120 times in the Bible:

	English	Hebrew	Hebrew Transliteration
23.	Sabbath	שַׁבָּת	*shabbat*

The Bible emphasizes that the Sabbath is a day for stopping all work. Like most nouns in biblical Hebrew, this one is related to a three-letter verb. In this case, the verb means "to stop."[54]

Healing Rest

"The proper amount of sleep heals wounds, helps with weight loss, maintains a healthy immune system, optimizes memory, and encourages emotional health. Few activities honor our bodies as richly as does sleep. Although sleep does not literally re-create our bodies, it does allow us to release our bodies into God's care. This too is part of what it means to live faithfully in and with the body God has provided each of us as tangible grace."[55]

—Evelyn L. Parker

In fact, this verb can be used for things completely unrelated to keeping the Sabbath day. Thus, Job and his three friends speak for many, many chapters. When they stop, the text reads, "Then these three men ceased [the verbal form of *shabbat*] answering Job" (Job 32:1 NASB). Two more times (32:3, 5), the text emphasizes that these friends gave no more answers to Job, leaving no doubt that the verbal form of *shabbat* means stopping and resting from previous activity.

To observe the Sabbath, then, is to stop. It's to stop one's work. It's to rest, even sleep. (See **Healing Rest**.) While some acts of worship can take place, the Bible emphasizes that all of creation rests on the seventh day: not just all types of people, but even God the Creator and the animals of the field (Exod 20:10-11; 31:16-17).[56] Some texts go so far as to talk of the land itself taking a sabbath rest (Lev 25:1-7).

A Most Important Commandment

The Sabbath commandment "is arguably the most important of the Ten Commandments: It is far longer than any of the others (it occupies about a third of the Decalogue), and it is the most frequently repeated of all 613 commandments in the Torah. Fittingly, then, this most important commandment looks back to the first story of the Bible and underscores its chief point: Creation achieves its culmination and crown, not with the appearance of *homo sapiens* on the sixth day, but with the Sabbath on the seventh."[57]

—*Ellen F. Davis*

The Bible knows that we are driven to work too much, whether because of an inner demand we place on ourselves or an external demand handed down on us by our bosses. However, the Bible requires—in the Ten Commandments, no less!—that God's people take a weekly day of rest (Exod 20:8-11; Deut 5:12-15). (See **A Most Important Commandment**.) Such a practice shows that the God in charge of our lives is drastically different from Pharaoh, who worked the Israelites to death. It's the antidote to the culture of "hurry" that haunts our lives. (See **Ruthlessly Eliminate Hurry**.)

Ruthlessly Eliminate Hurry

"'You must ruthlessly eliminate hurry from your life.'

"Imagine for a moment that someone gave you this prescription, with the warning that your life depends on it. Consider the possibility that perhaps your life *does* depend on it. Hurry is the great enemy of spiritual life in our day. Hurry can destroy our souls. Hurry can keep us from living well. As Carl Jung wrote, 'Hurry is not *of* the devil; hurry *is* the devil.'

"Again and again, as we pursue spiritual life, we must do battle with hurry. For many of us the great danger is not that we will renounce our faith. It is that we will become so distracted and rushed and preoccupied that we will settle for a mediocre version of it. We will just skim our lives instead of actually living them."[58]

—*John Ortberg*

Satan

Another English loanword from Hebrew is "Satan." However, this word is a bit complicated. That's because people today think of Satan as the head of all demons, the center of all evil, the supernatural being opposed to all that God is. For the most part, those ideas came *after* the Old Testament.

In the Old Testament, the word for "Satan" works differently. Here it is:

	English	Hebrew	Hebrew Transliteration
24.	Satan, enemy	שָׂטָן	*satan*

Although Satan plays a large role in many people's thinking about God, this word isn't very popular in the Bible. It shows up twenty-seven times. It basically means "enemy." It often describes human beings, including people who were enemies of:

- the Philistines (1 Sam 29:4)
- David (2 Sam 19:22 [23 Heb.])
- Solomon (1 Kgs 5:4 [18 Heb.]; 11:14, 23, 25)
- people praying in the Psalms (Ps 109:6; a closely related verbal form is found in Pss 38:20 [21 Heb.]; 71:13; 109:4, 20, 29)

When describing humans, the word is never translated as "Satan." Instead, English translations prefer words like "adversary" (or "accuser" in the Psalms).

In only four passages, this word describes a heavenly being:

- In Numbers 22:22, 32, God's angel functions as a threatening *satan* or "enemy" to a pagan magician trying to harm Israel. (See **What Were Angels Really Like?**)

What Were Angels Really Like?

Today, when people think of angels, they often envision creatures that look like babies or blonde women with wings and harps. The Bible never thinks of angels in this way. The Hebrew word translated "angel" means "messenger." In fact, it's used to describe several human beings who deliver messages (e.g., Gen 32:3 [4 Heb.]; Deut 2:26; 1 Sam 6:21).

When the word refers to one of God's messengers, this so-called angel is an immensely threatening creature. In several texts, God's messenger stands with sword drawn out (Num 22:22-23; 1 Chron 21:1-30). Other times, God's messenger kills people (2 Sam 24:16-17; 2 Kgs 19:35; Ps 78:49-50; Isa 37:36). As we read in Judges 13:6, "The woman went and told her husband, 'A man of God came to me; he looked like *an angel of God, very frightening*'" (NJPS, italics added).

- In 1 Chronicles 21:1, a *satan* causes David to take a census—something 2 Samuel 24:1 says the Lord causes.[59]
- In Job 1–2, "the *satan*" shows up among a group of heavenly beings, first questioning God and then harming Job once God gives permission.
- In Zechariah 3:1-2, "the *satan*" again makes an appearance, this time alongside the Lord's angel. God and "the *satan*" are opposed to each other.

A few things to note about these four passages. First, they don't speak about a capital-S "Satan" but rather about "a *satan*" or "the *satan*."[60] Second, this heavenly creature is associated with other heavenly beings (especially "the angel of the LORD"). It's even possible that the phrase "the *satan*" is a temporary title assigned to different heavenly beings at different times.[61] Third, in Job and Zechariah, the *satan* makes accusations. At the same time, aside from possibly Zechariah 3, the heavenly creature isn't opposed to God's will. In Job and Zechariah, the *satan* only does what God permits.

Satan and the New Testament

In the Old Testament, the word *satan* can refer to a being who shows up among God's angels in heaven. How did we move from this idea to the idea that this being utterly opposes God? The New Testament talks about this being falling from heaven around the time of Christ (Luke 10:18; Rev 12:1-12). One possible way of interpreting these New Testament texts is that having lost its power to make accusations before God in heaven, *satan* now promotes evil on earth.[63]

Because few details are given about the heavenly beings described with the word *satan*, it seems wise to be cautious in how we interpret these passages. Although the English word "Satan" can be traced back to the Hebrew word *satan*, the Hebrew had different associations than what the English word has picked up over the centuries.[62] Words can change meaning over time, especially when transferred from one language to another. The English word "Satan" carries with it ideas that come from places like the New Testament and John Milton's *Paradise Lost*. (See **Satan and the New Testament**.) We shouldn't assume all these later ideas are present in Old Testament passages. Instead, it's best to see the few supernatural references to *satan* in the Old Testament as references to a heavenly being that we don't fully understand: one that can be the angel of the Lord or even opposed to the angel of the Lord, depending on context. Sometimes, it's better for us as interpreters to say, "We don't fully understand this text," than to take modern assumptions and read them into the Bible.[64]

Conclusion

Hebrew is one of the countless languages from which modern English borrows. Hebrew sounds appear, at least in part, in many of the names found in the English Old Testament. However, even where audible connections can be made between modern English and biblical Hebrew, important differences exist. When English names echo Hebrew sounds, they unfortunately leave readers clueless about their rich meanings. When words like "hallelujah" persist in modern English, people don't always understand their meaning. Even words like "Satan" reflect a rather complicated history. All this to say, much is lost in Bible translation. By returning to the Hebrew, we arrive at a richer understanding of the Bible itself.

Chapter 3
Words We Lack in English

Cereal boxes, at least those marketed to children, often come with top-secret messages that can only be cracked by elite ten-year-olds. When I was a child, James Bond left a deep impression on me, and I seriously considered a career as a secret agent man. Unsurprisingly then, these cereal box codes beckoned to me. The secret message was written in gibberish, an odd collection of letters that made no sense. But, by using my prowess as a self-trained spy, I would slowly figure out that in a given code, the letter "T" really stood for the letter "A," the letter "Z" stood for "I," on and on. Eventually, I would emerge with the code cracked. With such knowledge in hand, the world was no doubt a safer place, even if the secret message had ever so subtly urged me to eat more of the same cereal.

As a child, I assumed that language translation wasn't too far removed from this type of code-cracking. Instead of substituting letters, you simply substituted words from one language with those of another. Then, it was just a matter of bringing everything together.

As I grew older and actually started working with languages, I learned that things aren't so simple. Sometimes, words in one language don't have precise equivalents in another.

I have a friend whose wife is from Korea. She told me about a Korean word that describes the general sense of sadness that people feel in autumn when days shorten and vegetation dies. She mentioned it, and I thought, "Yes! I've felt that, too, even though we don't have an English word to describe it." We might talk about "seasonal affective disorder," but that term implies a medical condition when autumn affects a person in such a way over the long term. The Korean language, however, implies such experiences are more widespread, a normal part of being human.

This chapter looks at Hebrew words that don't have precise equivalents in English:

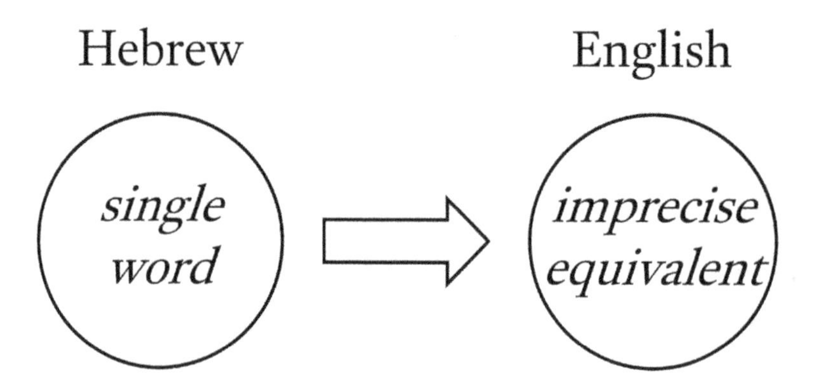

Figure 3

There are some ways to work around this problem in translation, like using multiple English words to get at the idea inherent in the Hebrew. However, such approaches come at a cost, giving up the speed and power with which the Hebrew can convey meaningful messages. (See **Translation Terms**.)

> **Translation Terms**
>
> Source Language: the language being translated. In this book, it's always Hebrew.
> Target Language: the language a translator is translating into. In this book, it's always English.
> Lexical Gap: what occurs when the target language (here, English) has no direct equivalent for a word present in the source language (here, Hebrew).
> Circumlocution: speaking about an idea in a roundabout way. When faced with a lexical gap in the target language, translators sometimes engage in circumlocution, using multiple words to communicate what the source language expresses with one or only a few words.

Create

The English word "create" often does a good job capturing the following Hebrew word[65]:

	English	Hebrew	Hebrew Transliteration
25.	create	בָּרָא	*bara*

However, there are two unique features to the Hebrew word, things that English translations cannot capture. First, the objects of this verb—that is, the things created—are remarkable. One scholar calls them "special, extraordinary, new," noting they include the heavens, the earth, people, and wonders.[66]

Second, only God can serve as the subject of *bara*. That is to say, in the Bible, humans don't create. There are close synonyms that can have humans as subjects, such as the Hebrew verbs for "make" (*asah*, עָשָׂה) and "form" (*yatsar*, יָצַר). But "create" in the sense of *bara* (בָּרָא) is reserved for God alone.[67] That's quite different from English. I have a t-shirt that says, "All I want to do is drink coffee, create stuff, and sleep." In biblical Israel, it would be blasphemous to wear such a shirt. Only God creates stuff. (See **Another Example**.)

Another Example

Hebrew has several verbs that mean "forgive." However, one of them is *salakh* (סָלַח). Only God can *salakh*. When this word is in play in the Bible, it suggests that we are dealing with a special type of forgiveness, one that only God can accomplish—something different from what humans do when they try to forgive.[68]

That's something difficult to communicate in translation. Obviously, it would be awkward if our Bibles began (to amend the NIV), "In the beginning God created—oh, and by the way, only God is the subject of this verb in the Old Testament—the heavens and the earth."

Definitions Versus Glosses

"In a case like ancient Hebrew the dictionary provides not definitions...but glosses, that is, English words that sufficiently indicate the sort of area in which the Hebrew meaning must lie. The meaning itself, for the user of the dictionary, must remain within the Hebrew."[70]

—*James Barr*

At least in terms of word counts, English translations tend to be much longer than the original Hebrew and Greek texts.[69] Adding more words of explanation may give readers a better idea of the biblical text, but they also make it bloated and clunky. (See **Definitions Versus Glosses**.)

Nevertheless, there are times when there's no better word than this one whose subject can only be God. For example, Isaiah 44–45 addresses a group of Jewish refugees in the sixth century BCE. Decades earlier, Babylonians destroyed their homeland and brought them into captivity. These refugees were told they backed the wrong horse: "Babylon's god Marduk is the supreme warrior! There's no reason to hope in your God any longer. Marduk defeated your God. That's why Jerusalem fell."[71]

With such messages ringing in their heads, these refugees heard the words of Isaiah 44–45. The prophet launched a full, frontal assault on everyone daring to collect idols symbolizing their allegiance to Marduk. In 44:9, idol-makers are equated with nothingness. Notably, the blacksmith can't make idols without growing hungry and thirsty (44:12). Meanwhile, the carpenter uses part of a tree for firewood, part for sitting, and absurdly, part for a god to worship (44:13-20). The idol that emerges can neither see nor think (44:18). Its maker has fabricated a lie, an object of disgust (44:19-20).

In sharp contrast, the God of Israel stretches out the heavens and hammers out the earth (44:24). This Creator stands alone over everything (45:5-6). The people of Israel—who have long tasted the bitter bread of disgrace while drinking salty tears of shame—will know humiliation no longer! Instead, idol-makers will find themselves exposed and red-faced as the frauds that they are (45:16). Isaiah 45:18:

> For this is what the LORD said, who created [*bara*] the heavens,
> who is God,
> who formed the earth and made it,
> who established it,
> who didn't create it a wasteland but formed it as a habitation:
> I, the LORD, and none other! (CEB)

This passage contrasts Israel's God and foolish idol-makers. In this context, what could be more appropriate than this verb for "create" that can only take God as its subject? Defeated refugees receive strength and hope—the conviction that they have *not* pledged allegiance to the wrong god, but instead still have a God who is with them, despite all that has transpired. Who alone can create? No human. No idol. No idol-maker. Only the Lord, the God of Israel. Such a message is reinforced by the unique nature of the Hebrew verb *bara*.

Heart

In English, we associate different body parts with different functions. We see the brain as the center of our thinking. The heart, meanwhile, is on a scientific level the blood-pump, but on an everyday level the home to our feelings and emotions.[72]

In the Old Testament, body parts have different associations. Heads were important. In fact, things that were first or at the beginning were described with words closely related to the word for "head." Most likely, the birthing process gave rise to such features of the Hebrew language. While the head has connections with things that were first, however, it wasn't closely related with thinking.

In biblical Hebrew, the heart was seen as the center of thinking.[73] In Genesis 6:5, for example, we read about the "thoughts" of the human heart. In the Old Testament, the heart was also the center of emotion, identity, belief, ethics, and conviction.[74] That may seem odd to us today. Science has made clear that our minds drive us. So, what do we make of the Bible's assumptions about the heart?

Obviously, the Bible's main point isn't to give us an anatomy lesson. Biblical Hebrew was spoken long before science revealed the functions of internal organs. Furthermore, a metaphor may have provided the ground for this way of speaking. (See **Cognitive Linguistics and Conceptual Metaphor**.)

Cognitive Linguistics and Conceptual Metaphor

Cognitive linguistics is, as its name suggests, a field that brings together brain science with the study of language.

Conceptual metaphor is one of the chief subfields within cognitive linguistics. It examines how metaphors inform our ways of speaking. Here, I suggest that a conceptual metaphor may be at play within biblical Hebrew when it comes to the heart/chest/*lev*(*av*): the literal center provides a way of talking about the figurative center that lies behind human action.[75]

Humans can intuitively sense that our thoughts, emotions, convictions, character, and sense of identity flow out from someplace within, guiding what we do and who we are. How do we describe our inner drivers? Biblical writers spoke about the physical center of our bodies. Our heads, arms, legs, and blood literally come out from this center, while our actions, behaviors, and deeds figuratively come out from here.[76] So, to describe this center, biblical authors used their word for "heart." It can also be translated "chest."[77] It's spelled with one or two syllables in Hebrew:

	English	Hebrew	Hebrew Transliteration
26.	heart	לֵב	*lev*
	heart	לֵבָב	*levav*

These words appear over 850 times in the Bible. We see *lev* as a person's driving core in a text like Proverbs 4:23: "More than anything you guard, protect your *lev*, for life flows from it" (CEB, alt.).

The Center

"The *lev* functions in all dimensions of human existence and is used as a term for all the aspects of a person: vital, affective, noetic, and voluntative."

—*H.-J. Fabry*

"The heart (לב) is the locus of the person's moral will, and it is this organ that is responsible for a person's words and actions. It is, as Thomas Krüger puts it, the 'moral control and guidance center' of the person. It is the executive self."[78]

—*Carol Newsom*

In the Bible, God wants nothing less than people's hearts. That is to say, the inner drivers of our outward actions should align with God. (See **The Center**.) We see this idea expressed repeatedly in the book of Deuteronomy. For example, in 6:6, just after Moses tells the people to love God with all they are, he preaches: "These commandments that I give you today are to be on your hearts [*levav*]" (NIV). It's possible to read this verse on a superficial level, assuming that it has to do with our emotions. Such an interpretation fits perfectly with English assumptions about the word "heart." However, this assumption reinforces sentimental forms of Christianity, reducing faith to a realm of our lives having to do with positive feelings. It's also far removed from what the Hebrew actually describes.[79] This verse says that God's commandments should be all over the very things that drive us: not only our emotions, but also our thinking, our identity, and our convictions. In Hebrew, this verse doesn't lead people into sentimentalized spirituality. It causes people to integrate God's words with every aspect of their lives, including all their thinking.[80]

It's difficult to convey in the middle of a verse that the word *levav* has much broader associations than the English "heart." It involves not only feelings but also thoughts: it's the core driver of who we are. Again, much is lost in translation.

Soul

The following word is closely related to *levav*. It appears approximately 750 times in the Bible:

	English	Hebrew	Hebrew Transliteration
27.	soul, throat, self, life	נֶפֶשׁ	*nephesh*

A number of texts, especially in Deuteronomy, talk about loving God "with all your heart and with all your soul" (Deut 6:5; 11:13 NASB). The word for "heart" there is *levav*, while the word for "soul" is *nephesh*.

What exactly is a soul? It depends on whom you ask. For some people, a "soul" is the eternal part of human beings. It differs from our bodies, which rot away. They would say that after we die, our souls go to heaven or hell.

While that's a commonly held belief, the Bible doesn't tend to talk about souls in this way.[81] It talks about the bodily resurrection in the New Testament, and in the Old Testament it talks about a place called *sheol*, which we will discuss in a moment.

When the Old Testament uses the word *nephesh*, it's discussing what makes us alive, what constitutes our very selves, what makes us who we are.[82] It's connected with the life that resides in our blood (Gen 9:4-5; 37:21-22; Lev 17:11, 14; Deut 12:23). In fact, translations have gradually moved away from translating the word *nephesh* as "soul":

- The King James Bible (early 1600s) contains the word "soul" over five hundred times.
- The New Revised Standard Version (1989) mentions "soul" almost two hundred times.
- The New International Version (1973–2011) mentions "soul" almost one hundred times.
- The Common English Bible (2011) mentions "soul" just nine times.

I applaud this movement away from using the word "soul." The word suggests that one component of ourselves is soulful or spiritual, while the rest is physical and fleshly. The Old Testament doesn't make this sort of distinction. When it talks of the *nephesh*, it usually envisions what makes us alive.[83]

In fact, my favorite way to translate *nephesh* is "life." This translation not only tends to match the Hebrew meaning and biblical context. It also allows readers to see familiar passages in fresh ways. Below, I list important verses containing *nephesh*, first using a more familiar translation and then using a fresh translation:

> He restores my soul [*nephesh*]. (Ps 23:3 NASB)
> He renews my life [*nephesh*]. (Ps 23:3 NJPS)
>
> You shall love the LORD your God with all your heart [*levav*], and with all your soul [*nephesh*], and with all your might. (Deut 6:5 NRSV)
> "You *will* love the LORD your God with all your core [*levav*], with all your life [*nephesh*], and with all your *umph*!"[84] (Deut 6:5, translation mine)
>
> To you, O LORD, I lift up my soul [*nephesh*]. (Ps 25:1 NRSV)
> I offer my life [*nephesh*] to you, LORD. (Ps 25:1 CEB)

The word "life" doesn't always work as a translation for *nephesh*.[85] In some contexts, it makes sense to translate the word as "throat" or "neck" (Ps 105:18; Isa 5:14; Hab 2:5). Other times, translations render the word "breath" (e.g., Gen 1:30 NRSV, NIV; Job 41:13). *Nephesh* is often connected with one's appetites and desires (e.g., Deut 23:24 [25 Heb.]; Ps 78:18).[86] Still other times, it's clear that *nephesh* is used simply to talk about oneself.[87]

All in all, *nephesh* is a rich and multivalent word. There's more going on with it than modern translations typically suggest.

Name above All Names

I'm a human, and my name is Matt.

Hebrew has both a general word for "God" and a name for God. The general word for "God" is extremely common, appearing 2,600 times in the Bible. Here it is[88]:

	English	Hebrew	Hebrew Transliteration
28.	God	אֱלֹהִים	*elohim*

If *elohim* is the general word for "God," then God's name is found here[89]:

	English	Hebrew	Hebrew Transliteration
29.	the LORD, YHWH	יהוה	*yhwh*

It's likely that this name should be pronounced "Yahweh." It's even more popular than *elohim*, showing up over 6,800 times in the Old Testament. With so many appearances, presumably we'd know exactly how to pronounce it. But that's not the case. Here's why:

1. The Old Testament was originally written with only consonants. Scribes were trained to read words and supply vowels themselves.
2. By the third century BCE, people had stopped saying *yhwh* aloud. Why? The third commandment says that God would not acquit anyone who misuses this name (Exod 20:7). So, out of reverence and respect, people avoided saying it altogether.
3. With no one saying the name aloud and no textual record of what vowels to add to the Hebrew, the exact pronunciation became lost over time.
4. Translations today usually render *yhwh* as "the LORD." This practice reflects how ancient translations treated God's name, as well as notations medieval scribes put in their manuscripts. (See **God's Name**.)

God's Name

Tetragrammaton: This is how scholars sometimes talk about God's name *yhwh*. It literally means "four letters."

Kurios: The Greek word meaning "Lord." When the Old Testament was translated into Greek about 250 years before Jesus, *yhwh* was usually translated with *kurios*, the same word found in *Kyrie eleison*, the liturgical phrase meaning, "Lord, have mercy." The New Testament often uses *Kurios* to talk about Jesus.

Adonay: The Hebrew word אֲדֹנָי meaning "the LORD." It's also spelled *adonai*. Many medieval scribes wanted readers to say *adonay* rather than trying to pronounce *yhwh*.

Hashem: The Hebrew word הַשֵּׁם meaning "the name." Sometimes, communities say *hashem* instead of *yhwh* or *adonay*. In fact, the oldest complete manuscript of the Hebrew Bible is called the Leningrad Codex, and it usually tells readers to say the Aramaic equivalent of *hashem* (*shema*, שְׁמָא).

Jehovah: This also refers to God's holy name. It's basically a combination of the vowels from *adonay* and the consonants *yhwh*. Although some medieval scribes wrote God's name in a similar way, they never intended people to utter those consonants and vowels together. They intended for people to see the vowels and say *adonay*, meaning "the LORD." "Jehovah" was first used in 1520.[90]

God's name *yhwh* is mysterious—not only in terms of pronunciation, but also in terms of meaning. The name likely comes from the Hebrew verb meaning "to be" (cf. Exod 3:12-15). One theory is that the name means "He causes to be." This definition fits with the idea of God as creator.[91] Another possibility is that it means simply "He is" or "He will be." These meanings point to God being nearby, unchanging, and eternal.[92]

I sometimes hear Christians use the name "Yahweh." There's even a movement underway to translate the Bible in a way that renders God's name as "Yahweh" rather than "the LORD."[93] Is such a practice wise?

On the one hand, the Bible's revelation of God's name is important for several reasons, as biblical scholar Terence Fretheim notes. God's name distinguishes God from other gods. Furthermore, when we don't know a person's name, there's a distance from that person. Names make people more accessible. A closeness can be enjoyed. The Bible suggests God is nearby, able to be called by name.[94]

On the other hand, there are also reasons to avoid saying God's name. Large segments of the church today have lost a sense of God's holiness. One way to re-glimpse God's transcendence and mystery is by not saying this name aloud. It's good to keep in mind the following words, written by a famous Jewish philosopher and interpreter:

> There is hardly a symbol which, when used, would not impair or even undo the grasp or remembrance of the incomparable. Opinions confuse and stand in the way of intuitions; surveys, definitions take the name of God in vain. We have neither an image nor a definition of God. We have only His name. And the name is ineffable. . . .
>
> God begins where words end.[95]

God's Hebrew name remains clouded in mystery; we can't be absolutely certain how it sounds or even what it means. Yet, such mystery can serve as a reminder of God's mysterious ways. While the Bible reveals much about God, we shouldn't forget that God's fullness is beyond what our minds can comprehend and what our words can express.[96]

Though our English Bibles contain thousands of references to "the LORD," the underlying Hebrew has far more taking place than can be conveyed in translation.

Sheol

Our next word has to do with where people go after they die:

	English	Hebrew	Hebrew Transliteration
30.	Sheol, grave	שְׁאוֹל	*sheol*

There isn't a perfect English equivalent for this word. Centuries ago, the King James Version would often translate the word "hell."[97] However, the Bible's concept of *sheol* has no connection with a place of fire or the devil.

The NASB, NRSV, and NJPS translate the Hebrew using the word "Sheol," replacing the Hebrew letters with their closest English equivalents. Although "Sheol" sometimes appears in English, it's not especially well known (which is why I'm treating it here and not in chapter 2). Translations such as the NRSV assume that there's no English word that can perfectly replace the Hebrew. Readers need to learn "Sheol" if they are to make sense of the texts containing this word.

Meanwhile, the NIV and CEB go with a variety of words, including (in descending order of popularity):

- grave
- the realm of the dead
- the underworld
- death

Translating the word as "grave" isn't a bad choice.[98] However, it's important to keep in mind that the noun "grave" in English has two basic meanings. First, it can refer to the literal physical space where a person is buried (like a "burial plot"). When we talk about a "graveyard," we use "grave" in this sense. Hebrew has another word besides *sheol* to talk about this literal sort of a grave (קֶבֶר, *qever*). Second, the English word "grave" can mean, to use the *Oxford English Dictionary*'s wording, "the natural destination or final resting-place of every one. Hence ['grave' is] sometimes put for: The condition or state of being dead, death."[99] This meaning fits rather nicely with the Hebrew term *sheol*. Just as we acknowledge that everyone goes to the grave, so the Old Testament spoke of everyone going to *sheol* (Ps 89:48 [49 Heb.]).[100]

Even with this understanding of the grave, we need to keep some points in mind. First, the Old Testament doesn't see people doing much in *sheol*. As Ecclesiastes 9:10 puts it: "Whatever your hand finds to do, do with your might;

for there is no work or thought or knowledge or wisdom in Sheol, to which you are going" (NRSV). In fact, the Old Testament says that in *sheol*, people don't even speak about or praise God: "For in death there is no remembrance of you; in Sheol who can give you praise?" (Ps 6:5 [6 Heb.] NRSV; cf. Isa 38:18). Just as we don't see corpses doing things in the grave, so biblical authors didn't see people doing things in *sheol*. Several texts even talk about the dead as those who sleep with their ancestors (e.g., 1 Kgs 2:10).

A second point to remember: the Old Testament is brutally realistic about the reality of death. It doesn't try to sugarcoat our fragile existence or pretend things are better than they really are. From what we can tell, the average adult Israelite lived to be less than forty years old. Infant mortality rates were very high.[101] Unsurprisingly, then, the Old Testament speaks about the ravenous appetite of the grave: "Therefore, *sheol* opens wide its jaws, opens its mouth beyond all bounds, and the splendid multitudes will go down, with all their uproar and cheering" (Isa 5:14 CEB, alt.).[102] In ancient Israel, death stole people's lives much earlier than is commonly the case today.

Third, the God of the Old Testament is first and foremost the God of life. Unlike other ancient religions that had a separate deity to reign over the underworld, the Bible emphasizes one God, and this God rules over heaven and earth. So, biblical prayers frequently include thanksgiving that God has kept people in the realm of the living, reviving their lives and rescuing from the grave's power: "O Lord my God, I cried to You for help, and You healed me. O Lord, You have brought up my soul [*nephesh*] from Sheol; You have kept me alive, that I would not go down to the pit" (Ps 30:2-3 [3-4 Heb.] NASB; cf. 1 Sam 2:6; Jonah 2:2 [3 Heb.]). In the short term, these prayers were understood as thank-yous that God didn't allow people to die early, that they could instead hopefully reach a ripe old age.

However, as the biblical narrative progresses, *sheol* is no longer seen as a place where people are removed from God: "If I ascend to heaven, you are there; if I make my bed in Sheol, you are there" (Ps 139:8 NRSV; cf. Job 26:6; Prov 15:11; Amos 9:2). In fact, before the Old Testament ends, readers gain glimpses that death itself will be destroyed for all time. Instead of *sheol* swallowing humanity, it's God who will devour death: "He will swallow up death forever. The Lord God will wipe tears from every face; he will remove his people's disgrace from off the whole earth, for the Lord has spoken" (Isa 25:8 CEB; cf. Dan 12:2-3; 1 Cor 15:54). We'll return to this verse in our next chapter.

To summarize our discussion of *sheol*, Old Testament writers didn't emphasize people going to heaven or hell after they died. They instead spoke about *sheol*, the place of the dead, the grave. That in itself is quite remarkable: most Old Testament texts presuppose that even if all we have is this life, our best bet is to live faithfully to God. Rather than trying to seek pleasure relentlessly, Old Testament writers thought that the best possible life now was one in accord with God's instruction. At the same time, in part because life isn't always fair, a handful of texts dare to break out even beyond the emphasis on rewards in this lifetime, envisioning a future beyond death. For Christians, these texts ultimately point to Easter. The God of life makes a way beyond the grave.

Ban

The last word of this chapter is perhaps the most disturbing word in the entire Bible. It's used to say that the Israelites should kill every inhabitant of Canaan. Here it is:

	English	Hebrew	Hebrew Transliteration
31.	what is banned, what should be destroyed, or what belongs to God	חֵרֶם	*kherem*

This word, along with its closely related verbal form (meaning "ban," "destroy," or "devote"), shows up about a hundred times in the Bible.

Usually, God uses the word to say that the Israelites should kill every last Canaanite:

> When the LORD your God brings you into the land that you are about to enter and occupy, and he clears away many nations before you—the Hittites, the Girgashites, the Amorites, the Canaanites, the Perizzites, the Hivites, and the Jebusites, seven nations mightier and more numerous than you—and when the LORD your God gives them over to you and you defeat them, then you must utterly destroy [verbal form of *kherem*] them. Make no covenant with them and show them no mercy. (Deut 7:1-2 NRSV)

Verses like these are inherently disturbing. In a moment, I'll make some remarks about what to do with the fact that such verses are in the Bible of all places. But first, it's important to understand what *kherem* means.

Some Bible translations render *kherem* with such a word as "destruction" or "annihilation" as seen above. Other times, they'll talk about things being "devoted to the LORD" (e.g., Num 18:14 CEB). Meanwhile, other translations talk instead about "that which is put under the ban" (Deut 13:17 [18 Heb.] NASB). What's taking place here? How could the same word relate to destruction, devotion, and some sort of ban?

The word *kherem*, as it's typically used in the Bible, pertains to what happens to a defeated people after a war has ended. In particular, it relates to the survivors and personal property of the side that lost. Throughout history, victors have claimed such spoils, often making the conquered people slaves while possessing their valuables.

However, a dominant note of the Bible is that Israel doesn't win military battles by its own strength. The text makes clear that left to their own devices, the Israelites would be defeated and thus either dead or homeless. It's only by the supernatural intervention of God that Israel walks away with military victories. The ultimate victor is God—not the Israelites.[103] So, some of these texts say, all the spoils of war belong to Israel's God. The Israelites cannot take them for themselves. A fear is that if the Israelites took spoils for themselves, the conquered people would steal Israel's heart away from the very God who brought them victory (Deut 20:17-18). So, the text says that every spoil of war—man, woman, child, animal, property—belongs to God (e.g., Deut 13:15 [16 Heb.]). Shockingly and disturbingly, the texts say that everything needs to be sacrificed to God. All that breathes should die, and all personal property should go up in smoke.

The Ritual of Kherem

"The background and motivation of these practices are very different from what the general lay public, seeing the matter from outside, might imagine. Thus, for example, it can be pointed out that consecration to destruction is not a sanction for hatred and vengefulness. On the contrary, it is something more like a ritual, a sort of sacrifice, whereby the population of captured cities, including even the domestic animals, are destroyed; notice in particular that, by the same rule, indestructible assets, objects of gold and silver, are not plunder to be kept by anyone but are to be taken and donated as offerings to the God of Israel. To the non-Hebraist it is not visible that the root [of *kherem*] belongs to the semantic field of 'sacred, holy', which fact justifies our rendering as 'consecration to destruction' or the like."[104]

—*James Barr*

Kherem is the word used to describe this practice. It's more than simple destruction or annihilation, although it certainly entails that. It's the practice of setting the spoils from war aside for God who brought the victory. In recognition that there's a logic behind this destruction, translations sometimes prefer "devote to God" or "place under a ban." (See ***The Ritual of Kherem***.)

Obviously, it's not possible to translate a single verse of the Bible and launch into this lengthy explanation of what *kherem* is, how it relates to spoils of war, and how it reinforced the Bible's ideology that God rather than human strength brings about military victories.[105] So, translators make choices. Sometimes, they talk about *kherem* in terms of straight-up destruction, which may imply senseless killing. Or, they talk ambiguously about things being devoted or somehow banned. The truth is that the word reflects an ancient practice that is no longer around today, and contemporary English lacks adequate terms to reflect what's actually taking place with the ancient Hebrew.

I should add that even when we understand what's going on with the Hebrew, these parts of the Bible remain disturbing. As I describe in my book *This Strange and Sacred Scripture*, some parts of the Bible simply don't make sense to us.[106] It's okay to admit that fact and be honest about it. We're humans reading a book that's thousands of years old. Some questions about the Bible are unanswerable. That's okay. We can ask God for illumination. We can even ask God why certain things appear in the Bible. We don't need to act as though we have every answer.

We should also recognize that this practice of *kherem* is presented in the Bible as a one-time event, not something to be repeated in subsequent ages.[107] Instead, the Bible envisions *shalom* as the goal for which creation yearns (see chapter 8).

Conclusion

I have three children, one of whom is a two-year-old. Her name is Anna, and she loves doing puzzles, especially those with fifteen to twenty-five pieces. She sits there and tries to get each piece to fit, then claps when the whole thing is finished. Sometimes, however, she says, "Uh oh! A piece is missing!" Amid the craziness of raising three kids while my wife and I work full-time jobs, puzzle pieces end up under the couch, under rugs, and wherever else puzzle pieces go to die. (It's probably near a bunch of missing socks.)

When translators move from Hebrew to English, they often feel like English is missing some pieces. We don't have words that perfectly capture the unique features of Hebrew words for "create," "heart," and others. English translations can come close. But for those wanting to dig deeper into the Bible, it's enormously helpful to know at least parts of Hebrew. By better understanding the Bible's first language, we can better understand God's word across the centuries.

Chapter 4

Missing Multiple Meanings

Look up a word in an English dictionary. You'll often find more than one definition listed. The same is true of Hebrew words. They often have many meanings. The trouble is that English translators need to pick one English word corresponding to the Hebrew word. Sometimes, more than one definition is relevant to the text at hand. (See **Polysemy**.)

Polysemy

A word is polysemous when it has multiple definitions. Polysemy creates special challenges for translators, especially when the source text uses a polysemous word and evokes more than one definition. That's because there rarely if ever is a single word in the target language that functions similarly.

As we'll see in this chapter, particular Hebrew words can mean not only "hear" but also "obey," not only "wind" and "breath" but also "spirit," not only "hope" but also "wait." The problem is that we have English words that correspond to one of the Hebrew definitions, but not all of them. Sometimes, it's okay to go with an English word that just corresponds to one Hebrew definition. However, other times, we lose the depth of meaning present in the biblical text:

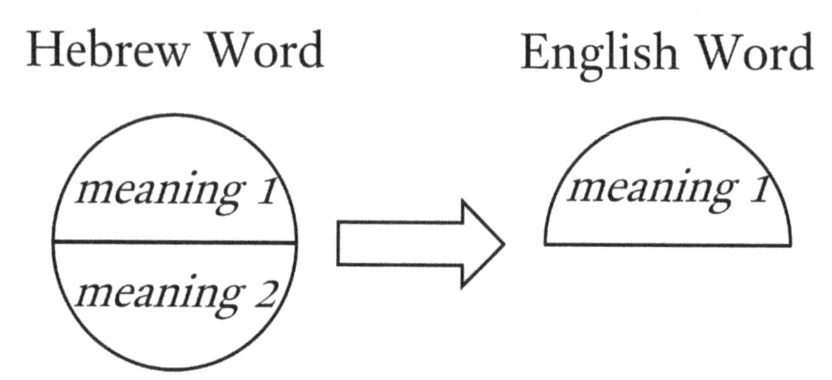

Figure 4

Hear and Obey

In English, hearing and listening involve using our ears. Centuries ago, "to hear" could also mean "to obey." However, that meaning is now obsolete.[108] In certain circumstances, we might say, "Listen up!" or "Listen to me!" Those phrases could carry overtones of "Obey!" if a command came next. Generally, however, we see listening as using our ears and obeying as submitting our will.

In Hebrew, however, things are different. The word translated "obey" is also its word for "hear":

	English	Hebrew	Hebrew Transliteration
32.	hear, pay attention, obey	שָׁמַע	*shama*

This word shows up over one thousand times in the Bible. Roughly 10 percent of those appearances are translated as "obey" rather than "hear" or "listen."[109]

Sometimes, it's obvious whether to translate *shama* as "hear" or "obey."[110] In Ecclesiastes 1:8, for example, it obviously means "hear": "All words are tiring; no one is able to speak. The eye isn't satisfied with seeing, neither is the ear filled up by hearing [*shama*]" (CEB). It makes no sense to translate *shama* as "obeying" in the above verse. However, it makes perfect sense in Exodus 24:7: "We will do everything the Lord has said; we will obey [*shama*]" (NIV). Clearly, when *shama* is used after "doing everything" God has said, the idea isn't just that the people will hear God. It's that they will obey what they've heard.

Sometimes, it's unclear whether to translate *shama* as "hear" or "obey." For many Jews and Christians, the most important verse of the Hebrew Bible is Deuteronomy 6:4. Just before the Bible talks about loving God with all we are, it says: "Hear, O Israel: The Lord is our God, the Lord alone" (NRSV). At first glance, a command to hear seems to be a way of emphasizing the rest of the verse, as though Moses is saying, "Pay attention!"

However, this statement occurs in Deuteronomy, a book filled with God's laws. In fact, Deuteronomy even means "Second Law." The idea is that God gave the first law at Mt. Sinai, and here, just before the people cross the Jordan River to the promised land, Moses gives the law a second time.

Furthermore, the immediate context of Deuteronomy 6:4 overflows with references to obeying God's commands. The previous chapter reiterated the Ten Commandments. Then we read, starting with 6:1:

> Now this is the commandment—the statutes and the ordinances—that the Lord your God charged me to teach you to observe in the land that you are about to cross into and occupy, so that you and your children and your children's children may fear the Lord your God all the days of your life, and keep all his decrees and his commandments that I am commanding you, so that your days may be long. Hear therefore, O Israel, and observe them diligently, so that it may go well with you, and so that you may multiply greatly in a land flowing with milk and honey, as the Lord, the God of your ancestors, has promised you.
>
> *Hear, O Israel: The Lord is our God, the Lord alone.* You shall love the Lord your God with all your heart, and with all your soul, and with all your might. Keep these words that I am commanding you today in your heart. Recite them to your children and talk about them when you are at home and when you are away, when you lie down and when you rise. Bind them as a sign on your hand, fix them as an emblem on your forehead, and write them on the doorposts of your house and on your gates. (Deut 6:1-9 NRSV)

As the above underlining suggests, there's a great emphasis on obedience and God's commands throughout this passage. The end even talks about God's law being bound to foreheads, forearms, and doorposts. Some Jews observe this practice literally while others believe the text is talking about God's commandments becoming thoroughly incorporated into everything we think and do.

Near the center of this text emphasizing obedience, we find the commandment to hear. However, given the emphasis on obedience all around, surely readers of the Hebrew text were expected to see this verse as referring not only to hearing what comes next, but also to obeying the Lord their God. (See **Shema**.)

The double meaning "hear-obey" can also help us understand otherwise confusing passages. For example, slavery in biblical Israel differed in significant ways

Shema

In Hebrew, the command "Hear!" is pronounced *shema*. (The imperative *shema* has slightly different vowels than the dictionary form *shama*.) So Deuteronomy 6:4 and sometimes the verses that follow (Deut 6:4-9) are called "The Shema."

from slavery in the United States. In biblical Israel, domestic slaves were set free after a period of time. Additionally, they could choose to stay as slaves if they wanted to. Some of them were treated well. A slave choosing to stay in slavery would go to a doorpost (either at a sanctuary or at the owner's house). There, according to Exodus 21:6 and Deuteronomy 15:17, the owner of the slave would thrust an awl through the slave's earlobe. It was a sign that the slave chose to stay in slavery.

What could possibly be going on with such a strange practice? First, it's important to keep in mind that even modern cultures practice things like ear piercings. Second, slaves were often physically marked in the ancient world through means such as branding or unique haircuts.[111] Third, the ear may have been chosen in biblical Israel because of the close connection between hearing—which involves the ear—and obedience.[112] This ceremony, though obviously odd and problematic for modern readers, may have made a fair amount of sense within the biblical world.

A final example: many biblical texts say that disobedient people have "ears but don't hear" (Jer 5:21 CEB).[113] The connection between not hearing and disobedience makes much more sense when one realizes that the Hebrew word *shama* carries with it ideas of obeying.

So, when the Old Testament talks about hearing and ears, it can be helpful to see if the text also evokes the idea of obedience. Such connections would have been easily grasped by the earliest readers of the Bible.

Evil and Disaster

We've all heard the expression, "You reap what you sow." The idea is that if you do good things now, you'll later experience the rewards of it. However, if you do bad things now, they'll come back to bite you. Many biblical writers would affirm such ideas. In fact, in biblical Hebrew, the same word can mean "evil" and "disaster."[114] Here it is:

	English	Hebrew	Hebrew Transliteration
33.	evil (*noun*), disaster	רָעָה	*raah*

This noun is related to a verb and adjective that similarly can convey both evil and disaster:

	English	Hebrew	Hebrew
34.	be bad, be evil, make disaster	רָעַע	*raa*
35.	evil (*adjective*), disastrous	רַע	*ra*

These three words show up about 750 times in the Bible. Many verses play on the two meanings, saying that the people's evil deeds (*raah*) will lead to disaster (*raah*). For example, we have this verse in Deuteronomy: "Terrible things [*raah*] will happen to you in the future because you will do evil [*ra*] in the LORD's eyes" (Deut 31:29 CEB). Few English readers know that the Hebrew word for "terrible things" early on in the verse is almost the exact same word as the word for "evil" later on. *Raah* leads to *raah*. Evil is fundamentally harmful. Or, as Jeremiah 2:19 puts it, "Your wickedness [*raah*] will punish you" (NRSV and NIV).[115]

At one point, King Solomon uses this word, talking to one of his father's enemies. He says: "You know quite well all the evil [*raah*] that you did to my father David. May the LORD return your evil [*raah*] on your own head" (1 Kgs 2:44 CEB; see also 1 Kgs 21:20-21). The idea is that we live in a moral universe. In this space, our actions set forces in motion that later may come down upon us. While good actions result in beauty and blessings, evil actions result in disaster.

The great temptation is that we see evil as something other than evil. People think there is something good about things that lead only to destruction. We fail to trust that the things God calls evil actually are evil. As noted above when discussing "Sheol," the Israelites didn't place great faith in an afterlife of rewards and punishments. They believed that here and now, goodness gives birth to goodness, whereas evil yields disaster.

Yet, even with this idea of evil leading to calamity, sinners have hope. So, in Jeremiah 18:8, God says the following: "If that nation, concerning which I have spoken, turns from its evil [*raah*], I will change my mind about the disaster [*raah*] that I intended to bring on it" (NRSV). In Jonah, things work out just the way Jeremiah describes: "When God saw what [the Assyrians] did, how they turned from their evil [*ra*] ways, God changed his mind about the calamity [*raah*] that he had said he would bring upon them; and he did not do it" (Jonah 3:10 NRSV). We don't always think about God changing God's mind. However, God is so wrapped up in a relationship with human beings that when they change, God's plan of action changes too.

So, it's important to keep in mind that biblical writers didn't just think that evil acts led to disastrous consequences. Their very language pointed in this direction.

Justice and Judgment

The antidote for evil is justice. While talking about the parable of the vineyard above, we briefly discussed the Hebrew word for "justice." It deserves a closer look:

	English	Hebrew	Hebrew Transliteration
5. (see above)	justice, judgment	מִשְׁפָּט	*mishpat*

This word shows up about four hundred times in the Hebrew Bible.

At times, the Bible draws a sharp contrast between *raah* and *mishpat*. Here are some examples from the prophets:

> Truth [*emet*] is missing;
> anyone turning from evil [*ra*] is plundered.
> The Lord looked and was upset at the absence of justice [*mishpat*].
> (Isa 59:15 CEB)

> [The wicked] are fat and sleek,
> and there is no limit to their wicked [*ra*] deeds.
> They refuse to provide justice [*mishpat*] to orphans
> and deny the rights of the poor. (Jer 5:28 NLT)

> House of David! The Lord proclaims:
> Begin each morning by administering justice [*mishpat*],
> rescue from their oppressor
> those who have been robbed,
> or else my anger will spread like a wildfire,
> with no one to put it out,
> because of your evil [*ra*] deeds. (Jer 21:12 CEB)

Hate evil [*ra*], love good;
maintain justice [*mishpat*] in the courts. (Amos 5:15a NIV)

This word *mishpat* can mean both "justice" and "judgment."[116] On at least a theoretical level, most of us know that these words are related. There can't be justice in this world without judges making fair judgments, and judgment should be the execution of justice. Yet, we often perceive justice as a good thing and judgment as a negative thing. In fact, one of my former students talked about this Hebrew word with her youth group. The kids responded with enthusiasm about justice, but they didn't like the idea of being judged.[117]

Sometimes, it isn't clear whether *mishpat* is best translated "justice" or "judgment." Consider Psalm 9:7 [8 Heb.] in two different translations:

But the LORD rules forever!
He assumes his throne
for the sake of justice [*mishpat*]. (CEB)

The LORD reigns forever;
he has established his throne for judgment [*mishpat*]. (NIV)

Each translation works from the same Hebrew text, and each can be defended as an accurate translation. The CEB translation, however, is probably more appealing to more people. Most of us want God to be good, fair, and just. The thought that God might actually judge us, however, is frightening. It's bad enough when another person judges what we do. Even worse, it seems, would be an all-knowing, all-powerful God finding fault with us. Given that God loves us, is it safe to assume that "justice" is a better translation than "judgment" in this verse?

To answer this question, we shouldn't rely on personal preference. Instead, we need to ask, which definition best fits with the surrounding verses? In Psalm 9 the surrounding text does describe significant punishments coming from God (9:3, 5-6 [4, 6-7 Heb.]), which suggests that "judgment" is the best choice. However, it then talks of God acting with equity and fairness (9:8 [9 Heb.]), reinforcing the idea that God exercises justice. So, both the concepts of judgment and justice are present. Unfortunately, English translators need to pick which word to put on paper, whereas the Hebrew word here refers to both concepts.

That's not to say that the Hebrew word always refers to both ideas, however. As is the case with other words in this chapter, there are instances in which just one meaning is present in the Hebrew text. (See **Multiple Meanings**.) To give an obvious example, Zephaniah 3:15 reads, "The LORD has taken away the judgments [*mishpat*] against you, he has turned away your enemies. The king of Israel, the LORD, is in your midst; you shall fear disaster [*ra*] no more" (NRSV). In this verse, it would make no sense to translate *mishpat* as "justice."[119] The text is saying that Israel's time of judgment has ended. It's *not* saying that justice has no more role in Israel.

> **Multiple Meanings**
>
> As this chapter describes, it's helpful to know the various things Hebrew words can mean. When context indicates it, more than one meaning can be present in the Hebrew text. However, we shouldn't assume that every meaning is always present. We would end up with nonsensical interpretations, as with Zephaniah 3:15. This mistake of taking everything a word *can* mean and assuming all those definitions are at work, even when context doesn't warrant it, is sometimes called the illegitimate totalitarian transfer.[118]

About one-fourth of the verses containing *mishpat* also include a word we saw earlier with the parable of the vineyard:

	English	Hebrew	Hebrew Transliteration
6. (see above)	righteousness	צְדָקָה	*tsedaqah*

Isaiah 33:5 is typical: "The Lord is exalted; he lives on high, filling Zion with justice [*mishpat*] and righteousness [*tsedaqah*]" (CEB). Another example is Amos 5:24, whose words were paraphrased by Martin Luther King Jr. and now adorn the Civil Rights Memorial in Montgomery, Alabama[120]: "But let justice [*mishpat*] roll down like waters, and righteousness [*tsedaqah*] like an ever-flowing stream" (CEB).

Figure 5

Today, people often see justice as a social issue, related to more liberal priorities like fighting poverty. Meanwhile, righteousness is seen as a personal issue, related to more conservative emphases like sexual fidelity. The Bible, however, doesn't usually classify human behavior the way people do today. The words *mishpat* and *tsedaqah* can refer to both personal and societal issues.[121]

In other words, the God of the Bible is concerned with both social justice and personal righteousness. We mute huge segments of the Bible whenever we overlook either one.

Breath, Wind, Spirit

In English, we know that the words "breath" and "wind" refer to moving air. However, each has its own set of associations. "Breath" is linked to human beings and "wind" to the outdoors.

A Hebrew word appearing nearly four hundred times in the Bible can refer to both "breath" and "wind":

	English	Hebrew	Hebrew Transliteration
36.	breath, wind, spirit	רוּחַ	*ruakh*

So, we have texts like Ecclesiastes 3:19 that use *ruakh* to talk about breath in humans and animals: "Surely the fate of human beings is like that of the animals; the same fate awaits them both: As one dies, so dies the other. All have the same breath [*ruakh*]" (NIV). We also have texts using the same word to talk about wind. Ezekiel 17:10 reads: "Will [the vine] not wither completely when the east wind [*ruakh*] strikes it—wither away in the plot where it grew?" (NIV). For biblical people, the east wind came from the scorching desert, unlike the cooler western wind, which came from the Mediterranean Sea.

When God is in view, the word *ruakh* can refer to both breath and wind: "The grass withers and the flowers fall, because the breath [*ruakh*] of the Lord blows on them" (Isa 40:7 NIV). Most translators go with "breath" here. However, it's clear that the idea of wind is also present. At least on a figurative level, God's breath is the wind, and this wind causes the grass and flowers to wither.

Because breath plays such a vital part of our lives, the word *ruakh* took on additional meanings. Speakers of biblical Hebrew recognized that without the breath of life, we die. It's an essential part of who we are (e.g., Pss 32:2; 104:29; Isa 26:9).

Additionally, our breath is closely linked to various emotional states. We breathe differently when we're engaged in ruthless passion than when we're acting with steady and skillful wisdom.

So, the Hebrew Bible connects the *ruakh* with both the core of who we are and different emotional states. Thus, when God describes how courageous Caleb differs from the other Israelite spies too afraid to enter Canaan, God says: "But I'll bring my servant Caleb into the land that he explored, and his descendants will possess it because he has a different spirit [*ruakh*], and he has remained true to me" (Num 14:24 CEB). Literally, God's saying that Caleb has a different breath than the other spies, but the idea is that his inner disposition is different.

Courage isn't the only emotion described with *ruakh*. Proverbs 14:29 talks about anger: "Whoever is slow to anger [literally "long of nostrils"] has great understanding, but one who has a hasty temper [literally "is short of *ruakh*"] exalts folly" (Prov 14:29 NRSV). Meanwhile, Psalm 51:17 [19 Heb.] uses *ruakh* to talk about humility. The NRSV reads: "The sacrifice acceptable to God is a broken spirit [*ruakh*]." Here, the text literally says that the acceptable sacrifice is a shattered breath (*ruakh*).

At times, the Bible talks about humans sharing in God's breath. Using a synonym for *ruakh*, Genesis 2:7 says that God created the first human by blowing the breath of life into the creature formed from the dust of the ground. Meanwhile, when Exodus describes Bezalel, the artist who will create key parts of the tabernacle (God's mobile tent-like sanctuary), God says: "I have filled him with the divine spirit [*ruakh*], with skill, ability, and knowledge for every kind of work. He will be able to create designs; do metalwork in gold, silver, and copper; cut stones for setting; carve wood; and do every kind of work" (Exod 31:3-5 CEB). Bezalel's work is divinely inspired. Similarly, some prophets encounter God's *ruakh*, allowing them to communicate God's messages (Ezek 2:2; Mic 3:8; Zech 7:12). Other leaders similarly accomplish extraordinary feats because of God's *ruakh* being with them (e.g., leaders in Judges).

The Bible presents breath (*ruakh*) as a central component of who we are. It shortens when people are angry and shatters when people feel deep remorse. When alive or under God's inspiration, a person essentially breathes God's own breath (*ruakh*).[122]

As seen above, translators often translate *ruakh* as "spirit." However, that can be confusing. Although there are some similarities between "spirit" and *ruakh*, there are also important differences.[123] "Spirit" can mean "ghost," which the Bible doesn't have in mind. Other times, what's "spirit" is connected with a non-physical realm, not of this earth. In the Hebrew Bible, however, *ruakh* isn't used in this way. You can feel your own *ruakh* just as you can sense your own breath.

The Bible often portrays God in human terms. Psalm 34 talks about God having eyes and a face and being able to hear (34:15-17 [16-18 Heb.]), while a variety of other psalms talk about God's hand (e.g., 10:12, 14). Still other texts talk about God's emotions, including anger (Jer 4:4), love (Deut 5:10), and compassion (Ps 103:13). Given that the Bible uses these human images to talk about God, it isn't too surprising that the Bible also talks about God's breath (*ruakh*), which, as already noted, can be visualized as wind.

However, talk of God's *ruakh* raises questions. Can it also mean God's "spirit"? If so, does the Old Testament talk about the Holy Spirit, or is that more of a New Testament concept?

On the one hand, in the New Testament, Jesus talks about the Holy Spirit coming and residing with believers in a new way not previously experienced (John 14:16-17; 15:26; 16:7-14). The church affirms that this coming of the Holy Spirit happened during the feast of Pentecost, described in Acts 2. So, there would be problems with saying that the Holy Spirit was fully revealed prior to the New Testament. Therefore, many of the Old Testament references to God's spirit are probably talking about the wind, God's breath, or God's core qualities.[124]

On the other hand, the Christian doctrine of the Trinity, as hammered out by the early church, states that the three persons of the Trinity exist in

Perichoresis and Anachronism

Eugene Peterson talks about

> ...*perichoresis*, the Greek word for dance. The term was used by our Greek theologian ancestors as a metaphor to refer to the Trinity.... Imagine a folk dance, a round dance, with three partners in each set. The music starts up and the partners holding hands begin moving in a circle. On signal from the caller, they release hands, change partners, and weave in and out, swinging first one and then another. The tempo increases, the partners move more swiftly with and between and among one another, swinging and twirling, embracing and releasing, holding on and letting go. But there is no confusion, every movement is cleanly coordinated in precise rhythms (these are practiced and skilled dancers!), as each person maintains his or her own identity. To the onlooker, the movements are so swift it is impossible at times to distinguish one person from another; the steps are so intricate that it is difficult to anticipate the actual configuration as they appear: *Perichoresis* (*peri* = around; *choresis* = dance).[125]

The *ruakh* of God is like one of these dance partners, moving in and out and around and about God the Father and God the Son.

Anachronism: a technical term for things that are out of order. The doctrine of the Trinity wasn't truly formulated until the fourth century CE. Prior to that, the New Testament pointed in its direction, while the Old Testament contained clues that could be interpreted in a trinitarian framework. It's an anachronism to say the Old Testament articulates a doctrine of the Trinity.

the closest possible unity. It's hard to say where one ends and the other begins. Interestingly, then, we have this talk in the Old Testament about God's breath, which from the Old Testament's vantage point appeared very much to be part and parcel of God's own being. From a Christian perspective, however, we could say that we see this breath or wind of God in the New Testament in new ways. There, it appears to be not just something operating in, with, and of God but a person of God coexisting with God the Father and God the Son. In other words, the New Testament reveals the Holy Spirit in ways not previously imagined.

We wouldn't want to assume that Old Testament writers already had a fully developed idea of the Trinity. That'd be getting things out of sequence. However, we could say that we catch a glimpse of something in the Old Testament that, upon further inspection in light of the New Testament, led the early church to talk about the Trinity. (See **Perichoresis and Anachronism**.)

In fact, when Peter talks about the coming of the Holy Spirit in Acts 2:17-18, he quotes Joel 2:28-29 [3:1-2 Heb.], which talks of God's *ruakh* being poured out on everyone. In Old Testament times, Joel 2 would be interpreted as simply saying that people would be inspired by God the same way various prophets were inspired.[126] In Acts 2, however, these words take on new meaning as the promised Holy Spirit is manifest in new ways.

This talk of the Trinity has interesting bearings on the Bible's second verse. In translations like the NIV, we read this in Genesis 1:2: "Now the earth was formless and empty, darkness was over the surface of the deep, and the Spirit [*ruakh*] of God was hovering over the waters." I'm reluctant to translate *ruakh* as "Spirit" with a capital "S" right there. The Old Testament never pretends to offer a straightforward doctrine of the Trinity. More at home with Hebrew thinking is a translation like the Common English Bible (cf. NRSV): "the earth was without shape or form, it was dark over the deep sea, and God's wind [*ruakh*] swept over the waters." The earliest readers of this text probably visualized the wind when reading this verse.[127] Furthermore, preferring the CEB doesn't mean we disavow the doctrine of the Trinity. Instead, it's a recognition that we don't get the highly complicated doctrine of the Trinity already in the Bible's second verse. Sometimes, God reveals things in bits and pieces. Our tiny brains need time to process the infinite.

To summarize: the Old Testament may hint at things later developed into the doctrine of the Trinity. However, in the Old Testament, God's *ruakh* appears first and foremost as the wind, God's breath, and God's core qualities. When the word *ruakh* is used to talk about humans, it describes their breath and core qualities.

Hoping and Waiting

If there's one thing the modern world hates, it's waiting. To get rich today, people simply need to invent something that reduces wait time. Companies vie for ever-quicker delivery systems. Businesses and individuals strive to squeeze every last drop of usefulness out of every last second. We carry around tiny computers called smartphones that occupy us each moment we're waiting for something. Our society conditions people to expect instant results. When something like traffic interferes with plans, people grow incredibly frustrated. Busy intersections have "fast" food restaurants on their corners.

But what if there's something redemptive about waiting? What if good could come out of it? What if we accepted the basic truth that *everyone on earth waits for things*? What if we focused less on *reducing wait times* and more on *what we're waiting for*?

In the Bible, *waiting* has less to do with *wasting time* and more to do with *hope*. In fact, the Hebrew word for "hope" is *tiqvah*, and its root (*qavah*) means "wait."

	English	Hebrew	Hebrew Transliteration
37.	hope	תִּקְוָה	*tiqvah*
38.	wait	קָוָה	*qavah*

To hope for something, then, is closely related *to waiting for it to happen*. Consider Genesis 49:18: "I wait [*qavah*] for your salvation, O Lord" (NRSV).[128] The NRSV correctly translates the verb as "wait." Yet, we can see how it communicates something closely related to hoping in God's salvation. We see a similar idea in Psalm 62:5 [6 Heb.]: "For God alone my soul [*nephesh*] waits in silence, for my *hope* [*tiqvah*] is from him" (NRSV). Hebrew sheds additional light on the relationship between waiting and hoping.

As we'll see in greater depth in our next chapter, many Hebrew words have a concrete image at their heart. These words for "hope" and "wait" have connections with the Hebrew word for "cord." We see this in Joshua 2, when Israelite spies scope out the city of Jericho. They spend the night with a woman named Rahab. The spies promise her that no harm will come during their invasion if she ties a red cord (*tiqvah*) in her window. When Jericho falls, the house with the red *tiqvah* stands alone.

What exactly is the connection between hope and a cord? The basic idea seems to be that Hope is a cord attached to something bigger in the

FUTURE.[129] Rahab's cord came out of her window on the city wall, dangling out to the Israelites, a sign of her allegiance with them, a symbol that her hope is attached to their God. (See **Figure 6**.[130])

Proverbs 10:28 is helpful when thinking about hope in terms of a cord: "The expectations of the righteous result in joy, but the hopes [*tiqvah*] of the wicked will perish" (CEB). In other words, the wicked hold to a cord that leads nowhere good. The righteous, meanwhile, find their way to gladness. They are attached to something bigger and better than they are, something that will endure.

Figure 6

One point of this proverb is that both the good and the wicked have hopes and dreams. Those who align their future with God will ultimately experience joy. Those who place their faith in money or material goods will be sorely disappointed: "When the wicked die, their hope [*tiqvah*] perishes, and the expectation of the godless comes to nothing" (Prov 11:7 NRSV). Jesus joins Proverbs in describing the foolishness of hoping in material goods. Moths eat away at fine clothes, rust eats away at metal, thieves rob people of property, and people die before enjoying their riches (Luke 12:13-34). Today, we might add that as the stock market plunges, people watch a lifetime of savings vanish.

Waiting for God

"Above all, trust in the slow work of God."

—*Pierre Teilhard de Chardin*

A Prayer: "As we are able, we submit our hopes to you. We know about self-focused fantasy and notions of control. But we also know that our futures are out beyond us, held in your good hand. Our hopes are filled with promises of well-being, justice, and mercy. Move us this day beyond our fears and anxieties into your land of goodness. We wait for your coming. We pray for your kingdom."[132]

—*Walter Brueggemann*

The Bible's heroes are far from perfect, but they do place their hope in God to do concrete things in their lives. The elderly Abraham and Sarah wait for God to give them children. The slaves in Egypt wait for freedom. The desert wanderers wait for entry to the promised land. The besieged city waits for miraculous rescue. The refugees in Babylon wait for God to bring them home. Christians wait for Jesus's return.[131] (See **Waiting for God**.)

According to some sources, the most popular verse of the Old Testament is Jeremiah 29:11, second only to John 3:16 in terms of being the most popular from the Christian Bible as a whole.[133] It reads: "I know the plans I have in mind for you, declares the LORD; they are plans for peace, not disaster, to give you a future filled with hope [*tiqvah*]" (CEB). By itself, this verse has brought comfort to many Christians. However, in context it becomes particularly significant. These words are not uttered to individuals trying to achieve success by the world's standards. They're told to a group of refugees in Babylon (modern-day Iraq) who lost their homes and loved ones. There, in a foreign land that knew its share of disappointment, people received a hope-filled letter from Jeremiah containing these words.[134] God wasn't done with these people—even when they felt the harsh brunt of their own sins. God still had a good future in store for them.

Things don't always go well for people who hope in God. The ever-realistic Bible deals extensively with unfulfilled hope. In fact, the book of Job uses the word *tiqvah* more than any other book of the Bible. Even though Job has a reputation for being patient, readers of the book know that he rarely lives up to his name. He rages, he laments, and he shakes his fist at God for all the suffering he receives. At one point, he shouts out: "Where then is my hope [*tiqvah*]? My hope [*tiqvah*]—who can see it?... Will we descend together to the dust?" (Job 17:15-16 CEB). While Job's friends try to console him with platitudes, Job expresses profound hopelessness.

Biblical hope isn't simple optimism. The Bible's too realistic about life's frailty to suggest things will automatically turn out okay in the future. Biblical hope is less about blind faith in what's to come and more about trusting God. It's attaching our cords to God—the only one who will still be around in the future—aligning ourselves with what God wants and having faith in God to set things right.

At my grandmother's funeral, my family asked me to read Isaiah 25:6-9. Although I've quoted one of these verses in our last chapter, it's worth repeating:

On this mountain,
the LORD of heavenly forces will prepare for all peoples
a rich feast, a feast of choice wines,
of select foods rich in flavor,
of choice wines well refined.

He will swallow up on this mountain the veil that is veiling all peoples,
the shroud enshrouding all nations.
He will swallow up death forever.
The LORD God will wipe tears from every face;
he will remove his people's disgrace from off the whole earth,
for the LORD has spoken.
They will say on that day,
"Look! This is our God,
for whom we have *waited* [*qavah*]—
and he has saved us!
This is the LORD, for whom we have *waited* [*qavah*];
let's be glad and rejoice in his salvation!" (CEB)

The Hebrew words for "waited" in the last verse could also be translated as "hoped." And that's the incredible beauty of this passage: it articulates our deepest hopes. It describes what we've all been waiting for all along. It's about all our hoping and waiting coming to an end as God shows up and destroys death itself so that we can all celebrate in a party that doesn't end.[135]

The native tongue of biblical writers connected waiting, hoping, and cords. For us today, the words *tiqvah* and *qavah* can alter how we think about delays and expectations. God has much in store for us.

Law and Instruction

"Law" is a word that seems to take the fun out of everything. We contrast it with freedom and liberty. As a society, we disdain lawyers, making them the target of a whole class of jokes. People overly attentive to the law and rules are quickly dismissed as "prudes."

Several rock and roll songs celebrate violating the law. Judas Priest's album featuring the song "Breaking the Law" has gone platinum. Sammy Hagar's "I Can't Drive 55" lifted him to stardom and became a standard part of Van Halen's repertoire after Hagar became the band's front man. That song was named one of VH1's top 100 heavy rock songs, along with other tracks that pointed to the difficulty of obeying the law, like Steppenwolf's classic "Born to Be Wild." Meanwhile, the song "I Fought the Law" has made it onto several charts over the decades while being performed by such diverse artists as Bobby Fuller, the Clash, and Hank Williams Jr.

We dismiss forms of religion that focus too much on the law, calling it legalism. We're also aware that Christians don't obey all of the Old Testament laws, as any bacon-loving believer could tell you.

So, what do we make of Old Testament laws? How do we understand them? How do we respect them as part of our Bibles while at the same time avoiding a religion of legalism?

The Hebrew word traditionally translated "law" holds some important answers. Here's how it looks:

	English	Hebrew	Hebrew Transliteration
39.	law, teaching, instruction	תּוֹרָה	*torah*

This word shows up over two hundred times in the Bible. You may have heard the Hebrew before. Today, when "Torah" is capitalized, it's often associated with the first five books of the Bible. In biblical times, however, the word usually referred less to those fixed books and more generally to God's instruction.[136]

It's easy to see why this word has traditionally been translated "law." For example, in Deuteronomy 4:44-45, we have an introduction to a major section of the book. Here's what those verses say: "This is the law [*torah*] that Moses set before the Israelites. These are the decrees and the statutes and ordinances that Moses spoke to the Israelites when they had come out of Egypt" (NRSV). In what follows, we find the Ten Commandments (Deut 5), the Shema (Deut 6), and a long set of regulations and laws dealing with topics like worship, uncleanliness, leaders, violence, honesty, and property (Deut 7–26). At least at first glance, all of these chapters sound like legal material. God gives commandments that fit into the broad category of requirements, laws, and rules.

However, a closer look shows that "instruction" or "teaching" is just as good a translation as "law." Many scholars believe the word is closely related to the Hebrew verb meaning "teach."[137]

On several occasions, the Bible talks about God as our teacher. Thus, the psalmist prays, using the same verb: "<u>Teach</u> me your way, O LORD" (Ps 27:11a NRSV). In fact, one interesting thing about Old Testament religion is that the priests bore primary responsibility for teaching the people the ways of God (e.g., Lev 10:11; Deut 33:10; Ezek 44:23).

Another reason for translating *torah* as "teaching" instead of "law" is that laws typically involve criminal actions. Yet, books like Deuteronomy contain many things that don't fit this definition. Some texts focus on inward attitudes, not outward actions. So, the last of the Ten Commandments forbids people from coveting: "You shall not covet your neighbor's wife. You shall not set your desire on your neighbor's house or land, his male or female servant, his ox or donkey, or anything that belongs to your neighbor" (Deut 5:21 NIV). Naturally, people who obey this commandment will have a much easier time with commandments forbidding adultery or theft. However, it would be difficult for ancient Israelites to face punishment based on whether or not they were coveting. How could anyone tell? Here we have more a teaching than a straightforward law. God doesn't just tell people not to steal or sleep around. God teaches what else needs to happen so they don't end up making horrible choices. God instructs people how to be faithful.

We also see a focus on inner attitude when Deuteronomy gives what Jesus calls the most important commandment of all: "Love the LORD your God with all your heart [*levav*] and with all your soul [*nephesh*] and with all your strength" (Deut 6:5 NIV). Again, this commandment is less about legalities and more about faithfulness. It's a teaching about how to get your life right, not a law linking a forbidden action to a specific punishment.

Among God's *torah*, we find other things that aren't really laws. Frequently, the Bible will motivate people to obey commandments. For example, several times, the book of Deuteronomy calls on people to remember that they were slaves in Egypt and rescued by God.[138] Because they were slaves, they should observe a day of rest—something Pharaoh would never command (5:15). Because they were slaves, they should treat their own slaves far differently than they were treated in Egypt (15:15). Because they were slaves, they should care for the most vulnerable in society (24:18, 22).[139] God educates people in both what they should do and why they should do it.

Even in the Old Testament, God doesn't look like a judge who impartially doles out punishments. God is more like a teacher lovingly committed to students. Sometimes, God even finds reasons for exceptions to earlier instructions.[140] For example, Rahab—a Canaanite prostitute—ends up becoming part of God's people, even though earlier instruction about warfare never talked about such a possibility (see Deut 7:1-5; 20:16-18; Josh 2:1-22, 6:17-25).

Deuteronomy 4 provides another example of God's leniency with the *torah*. There, God says that if the people make idols in Canaan, then they will cease being a nation and instead be scattered among the nations (4:25-27). Sadly, the people waste little time violating God's word. In Judges, people repeatedly go after other gods (2:17). While King David offers a reprieve from apostasy, once Solomon takes the reins of power in the middle of the tenth century BCE, God's people again turn to other gods and idols.

Yet, they don't die immediately. They aren't immediately forced off the land. It's only after many generations of faithlessness that this punishment finally comes to Jerusalem in the sixth century BCE. God's instruction correctly warns of dangerous consequences. But punishments don't materialize the moment the student Israel stumbles. *Torah* is more flexible than a rigid law.

A couple of final examples from the Psalms: Psalm 119 is the longest chapter of the Bible. It's about one thing: how wonderful God's *torah* is. If we translate *torah* as "law," then it can be difficult to relate to this psalm. The writers sound like they've got a bad case of legalism and are proud of it: "Open my eyes that I may see wonderful things in your law [*torah*]" (Ps 119:18 NIV). However, when we translate *torah* as "instruction," then it all makes sense. We can now see why the psalmists would say: "Open my eyes so I can examine the wonders of your Instruction [*torah*]!" (CEB). God isn't a police officer out to write tickets for spiritual missteps. God's a teacher out to instruct us in how to care for ourselves and all of creation.

So, although the word *torah* can relate to legal material, the translation "law" doesn't fit with all that the word means in the Hebrew. This basic point has huge consequences for how people think about God. Seeing chunks of the Bible as "law" leads to seeing God as less compassionate than God actually is. God becomes demanding, fierce, and compassionless. People end up with a natural aversion to the Old Testament. In contrast, if we recognize that *torah* really means "teaching," then we discover that the God of the Old Testament is actually the same God of the New Testament: patient, full of mercy, and abounding in compassion and loyalty—an educator who teaches us faithfulness and goodness.

Conclusion

In English Bibles, it's easy to miss key relationships between biblical words:

- "hear" and "obey"
- "evil" and "disaster"
- "justice" and "judgment"
- "breath," "wind," and "spirit"
- "hoping" and "waiting"
- "law" and "instruction"[141]

Translators naturally need to decide which English word to use when replacing a Hebrew word. So, they make educated choices. But there are various meanings inherent in Hebrew that become lost in such a process. Certainly, we can understand the basics of the Bible without Hebrew. But paying attention to these meanings reveals new dimensions of scripture.

Chapter 5

Visualizing the Abstract

Biblical Hebrew is a language close to the body. It's tactile. More often than not, its words can be seen, touched, felt, tasted, smelled, and experienced. This observation applies as much to theological words as anything else. We've already discussed how a word like "hope" can also mean "cord" and how the word for "spirit" more literally means "wind" or "breath." Many other religious words have close connections with concrete meanings. Unfortunately, these concrete meanings are often lost in translation:

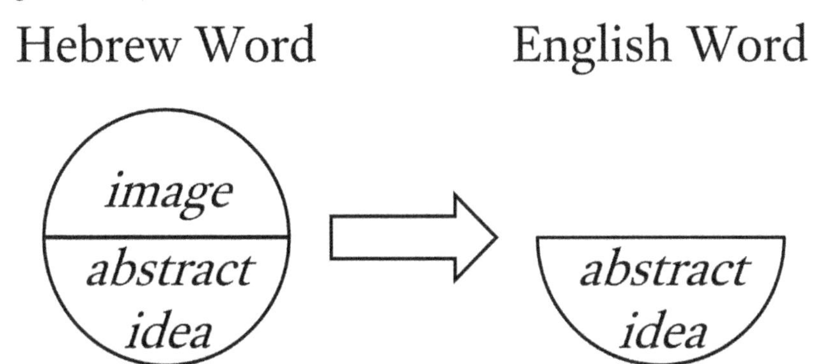

Figure 7

This chapter looks at a variety of words that seem, at first glance, to have an abstract meaning:

- vanity
- transgression
- keeping
- sin and forgiveness
- repentance
- blessing

This chapter then shows connections between these words and concrete images.[142] It ends by reflecting on the significance of vivid language for the church today.

Vanity

"Vanity of vanities, says the Teacher, vanity of vanities!" So begins the book of Ecclesiastes (at least in the NRSV, 1:2). If the speaker wasn't identified as "the Teacher," we might think we were hearing a sales rep boast about bathroom cabinets for sale. Or, if we thought more abstractly, we might still be confused. "Vanity" can refer to the state of being vain in the sense of overestimating one's self-importance. However, it can also refer to worthlessness, futileness, and unprofitability. What's actually in view, and why is this word uttered so frequently in Ecclesiastes?

The Hebrew word here is the same one mentioned in chapter 2 to translate "Abel," Adam and Eve's second son, in Genesis 4. Here's how it looks:

	English	Hebrew	Hebrew Transliteration
14. (see above)	Abel, puff of air	הֶבֶל	*hevel*

The word literally refers to a fleeting breath, a puff of air. It's here one moment and gone the next. One of my college professors suggested that the word functions much like a bubble: it exists shortly before disappearing.[143] Whereas the word *ruakh* tends to carry positive associations having to do with life-giving breath, the word *hevel* carries negative associations relating to what vanishes.[144]

Ecclesiastes talks repeatedly about everything being *hevel*. In making this statement, the text evokes a concrete image that readers can immediately relate to. It says that life is filled with things that vanish as quickly as a breath of air. We seek pleasure, laughter, enjoyment, and youthfulness, but they vanish quickly. These things are *hevel*, a puff of air (2:1; 7:6; 9:9; 11:10). We try to become wise, but we suffer the fate of the fool (2:15-17, 26; 7:15; 8:10, 14). Our insights are *hevel*, a puff of air. People all around us—and even we ourselves—move ever closer to death no matter how much we wish things were otherwise (3:19; 6:11-12). Our lives are *hevel*, a puff of air. We have dreams, but they come to nothing (5:7 [6 Heb.]; 6:9). They are *hevel*, a puff of air. We work hard but have so little to show for it in the end (2:19, 21, 23; 4:4, 7-8; 5:10 [9 Heb.]). Our accomplishments are *hevel*, a puff of air. Ecclesiastes 2:11 reflects the book's overall message: "But when I surveyed all that my hands had done, and what I had worked so hard to achieve, I realized that it was pointless [*hevel*]—a chasing after wind [*ruakh*]. Nothing is to be gained under the sun" (CEB).

The Teacher's word still holds true today. Doctors and nurses tend to the sick, but in the end, the sick die anyway. Construction workers erect buildings that one day will fall down or be torn down. Teachers say things that are quickly forgotten. Sales reps sell things that end up in garbage dumps. Workers store up a lifetime of savings, but they still want more. We wash dishes, but the next day they're dirty again. We work hard, but our fruits often vanish like our breath on a cold morning. We see it, and then it's gone. (See **Total Untrustworthiness**.)

Total Untrustworthiness

Hevel is used "in Prov 31:30 to indicate the deceitfulness of youth and beauty. The word indicates the total untrustworthiness of that to which it is an attribute. One cannot place much stock in youth or beauty; they vanish like the wind."[145]

—*Milton P. Horne*

Because *hevel* refers to things that pass away, it's used to talk about idols. Wood eventually rots. Stone eventually crumbles. What we make with our hands eventually gives way over time.

In Deuteronomy 32:21, God grows upset that people have run after fleeting idols while ignoring what truly lasts: "They have made Me jealous with what is not God; They have provoked Me to anger with their idols [*hevel*]" (NASB). Given that the word there for "idols" refers to what's passing away, the Common English Bible takes a more vivid approach to translating the word: "They provoked me with 'no-gods,' aggravated me with their pieces of junk [*hevel*]." The things that charm us away from God are as disposable as a dirty paper plate. They're as fleeting as a puff of air, as enduring as a bubble.

Philosophers have pointed out that how we talk about things determines what we do with them. "Climate change" feels less threatening than "global warming." "Fruit snacks" sound healthier than "congealed sugar gummies with a fruitlike flavor." "Blacks" and "whites" sound like they have nothing in common, unlike "African Americans" and "European Americans." (See **Talk and Action**.)

Talk and Action

"How we talk about sin, philosophers would argue, influences what we will *do* about it."[146]

—*Gary A. Anderson*

The point: when idols are reduced to puffs of air, they lose their power. Or when Ecclesiastes reminds us that work amounts to a vanishing breath, then workaholics like me need to reevaluate our lives. The Hebrew word *hevel*, as used in the Bible, calls readers to new ways of thinking and acting in the world. It refers to something we all can feel: a momentary breath. The Bible uses this sensory word to make us rethink our priorities.

Transgress

Hebrew uses concrete images not only for specific sins like idolatry but also for general expressions about sin. On several occasions, it uses a verb that often means "to pass through" something. Here it is:

	English	Hebrew	Hebrew Transliteration
40.	transgress, pass through	עָבַר	*avar*

This word appears over six hundred times in the Bible. Normally, it's used to talk about people moving from one location to another. Along the way, they temporarily *pass through* something:

- In Genesis, Jacob *passes through* different rivers (31:21; 32:10, 22-23 [11, 23-24 Heb.]).
- In Numbers, twelve spies *pass through* the promised land, scouting it out (14:7).
- In Joshua, the people *pass through* the Jordan River (3:14-17).
- The book of Psalms describes how the wind *passes over* the flower (103:16).
- Proverbs talks about *passing through* a lazy person's field, which is covered with thorns and weeds (24:30-31).
- The book of Isaiah describes how God will be with those who *pass through* the waters (43:2).
- Jeremiah talks about how the time of harvest has *passed by* (8:20).

In all of these cases, what's passing is on the move. The subjects don't set down roots. They move on their way to something else. Sometimes, the verb is translated "transgress." Although that translation sometimes works, the primary emphasis with the verses above isn't simply crossing a boundary. It's quickly moving through a piece of land or a body of water with little attention to what's there.[147]

On several occasions, this image is used to speak about disobeying God.[148] The idea is that people hear God's command but pass through it. They don't dwell in or with God's instruction. They are quick to move on to other things. Distraction takes them away from what God has said.

So, in Numbers 14:40, the people insist on going directly to the promised land, even though God has made it clear that they will instead wander in the desert due to their sins. In response, Moses says to the people: "Why are you disobeying [*avar*] the LORD's command? This will not succeed!" (14:41 NIV). This translation gets at the basic idea present in the Hebrew. However, the Hebrew uses the verb *avar*, invoking the image that the people wanted to *walk past* God's word as though it didn't exist. Moses's question could be translated more literally, "Why are you passing through [*avar*] the LORD's command?" The idea is that people aren't willing to live within what God ordered. They want to move on to something else.

Repeatedly, the Old Testament talks about people passing through their covenant with God, as though it somehow weren't binding any longer. In fact, here's how the Bible explains the fall of the northern kingdom of Israel to the Assyrians[149]: "The king of Assyria deported Israel to Assyria. . . . This happened because they had not obeyed [*shama*] the LORD their God, but had violated [*avar*] his covenant—all that Moses the servant of the LORD commanded. They neither listened [*shama*] to the commands nor carried them out" (2 Kgs 18:11-12 NIV). The NIV could have better conveyed the metaphor present in the original Hebrew concerning what happened with God's covenant. Surely, the people "violated" the covenant, as this translation puts it. But more specifically, the text is saying that the people temporarily walked through the covenant instead of dwelling within it.[150]

The force of the verb *avar* is especially apparent in Isaiah 24:5, where it appears beside another verb that similarly means "move through":

> The land reeks under its inhabitants, for they passed over [*avar*] instructions [*torah*], moved through law, and shattered the ancient covenant. (translation mine)

The interesting thing about this metaphor is that it suggests people actually know God's instructions. They simply refuse to do what God expects. They keep moving as though they never heard God's voice. As with the Hebrew word *hevel*, the word *avar* can exert powerful influence over how we think about obedience.

Keeping the Law

Conceptually, the opposite of moving past God's instruction is sticking with it. To get at this idea, the Old Testament uses this verb, which appears over four hundred times in the Bible:

	English	Hebrew	Hebrew Transliteration
41.	keep, protect	שָׁמַר	*shamar*

This word is easily confused with *shama*, meaning "hear" or "obey." However, it has an "R" sound at the end. It's often translated "keep." However, "keep" isn't the best translation imaginable. The idea certainly isn't that you're holding onto something the way that, say, some of us "keep" old pens in a junk drawer or magazines atop the toilet. The force of the verb in Hebrew is much stronger. It has to do with protection: staying with something, making sure it remains safe, and seeing that it flourishes. This idea of protection is certainly present in some definitions of "keep," but many of these definitions are now obsolete. Furthermore, the word "keep" itself has so many definitions—the *Oxford English Dictionary* lists forty-one!—that it's easy to miss the emphasis in the Hebrew Bible on protection.[151] *Shamar* even has connections with loyalty and devotion.[152]

We find this word in Genesis 2, where we read, "The LORD God took the human [*adam*] and settled him in the garden of Eden [literally, 'of delight'] to farm [literally, 'to serve'] it and to take care [*shamar*] of it" (Gen 2:15 CEB). In other words, the first human is to stay inside the garden, tending to it, protecting it, and ensuring it grows.

Shamar also appears two chapters later in Genesis 4. God asks Cain where his brother is. In most translations, Cain replies, "Am I my brother's keeper [*shamar*]?" (4:9). That's an unfortunate translation because people today are hardly ever described as another person's keeper. A much better translation is, "Am I my brother's bodyguard?" As we all know, bodyguards stay with persons, looking after them and making sure no harm comes. Cain claims he doesn't know where Abel is, asking if he's supposed to serve this role. Certainly, he's not supposed to be his bodyguard, but as we know from earlier in the story, Cain has gone to the opposite extreme, killing Abel.

This same word is used at the end of Joshua. Looking back at what's happened since the book of Exodus, the people say: "It is the LORD our God who brought us and our ancestors up from the land of Egypt, out of the house of slavery, and who did those great signs in our sight. He protected [*shamar*] us along all the way that we went, and among all the peoples through whom we passed [*avar*]" (Josh 24:17 NRSV). God has guarded and protected Israel throughout the wilderness period.

The word *shamar* is also used in the famous benediction mentioned in chapter 1. Numbers 6:24 reads, "The LORD bless you and keep [*shamar*] you" (NASB, NRSV, NIV). The core idea of God's keeping people is protection, which is a key theme of the Psalms. Here's Psalm 121:7 (see also 16:1; 25:20; 37:28; 91:11)[153]: "The LORD will keep [*shamar*] you from all evil [*ra*]; he will keep [*shamar*] your life [*nephesh*]" (NRSV). God protects people from evil and disaster (*ra*). Additionally, God protects people's lives.

Any healthy relationship with God is a two-way street. God protects people. In return, God's people aren't asked to protect God—who obviously can handle things just fine. Instead, God's people are asked to protect God's instruction, covenant, and laws. In fact, roughly half of the time the word *shamar* appears, it shows up in verses that talk about people following God's instructions. Deuteronomy 11:1 is one of over a hundred possible examples: "You shall therefore love the LORD your God, and always keep [*shamar*] His charge, His statutes, His ordinances, and His commandments" (Deut 11:1 NASB). When this verse talks about keeping God's decrees, it's saying that we should stick close to God's word, protecting it and seeing it to fruition—just like the first human was instructed to keep the garden in Eden. Like a bodyguard, we're to dwell alongside God's word, looking after it, going where it takes us—making sure it doesn't become broken.

In this sense, protecting God's instruction is the polar opposite of passing through (*avar*) God's instruction. When we tend to and protect God's commands, we experience the type of spiritual growth that the Bible envisions.

Sin and Forgiveness

Many people have pointed out that "to sin" means "to miss the target." The Bible reflects this meaning. Judges 20:16 talks of extremely skilled warriors who could shoot slingshots within a hair of their targets "and not miss" (NASB, NIV, CEB). The word for "miss" in that verse is the same word that ordinarily means "to sin" (חָטָא, *khata*). Applied metaphorically, sinning means we miss the target of obeying God.

However, the most significant imagery evoked by the Hebrew word "sin" does not relate to missing targets. Throughout much of the Old Testament, sin creates and even is a burden. That burden is initially borne by the person who sinned. When people ask God for forgiveness, they literally ask God to bear their sin instead of them. (See **Sin as a Burden**.)

Sin as a Burden
"Most readers of the Bible have not realized how important the metaphor of sin as a burden is in the Old Testament. . . . This is because translators have almost never rendered the idiom literally. Whereas other verbal metaphors are rendered transparently—to wash away, cover over, or wipe away a sin—the idiom 'bearing a sin' has almost always been given a *nonliteral equivalent*."[154]
—*Gary A. Anderson*

Here's an important word for understanding sin that appears over six hundred times in the Bible:

	English	Hebrew	Hebrew Transliteration
42.	lift, carry, forgive	נָשָׂא	*nasa*

Often, this word refers simply to "lifting" or "carrying" something. David uses it when talking about shepherding: "When a lion or a bear came and carried off [*nasa*] a sheep from the flock, I went after it, struck it and rescued the sheep from its mouth" (1 Sam 17:34-35 NIV). In Exodus, God speaks about carrying the Israelites out of the land of Egypt: "You saw what I did to the Egyptians, and how I lifted [*nasa*] you up on eagles' wings and brought you to me" (19:4 CEB).

The Bible also uses *nasa* to talk about both humans and God carrying sins. At times, it envisions sinners bearing the weight of sin. Already in Genesis 4:13, Cain cries to God, "My iniquity is too great to bear [*nasa*]!" (translation mine).[155] Later in Ezekiel, we read: "You will be held accountable for your betrayals, and you will bear [*nasa*] the sins of your idols" (23:49 CEB). The Psalms use similar expressions, as in the following verse in which the word "burden" (*massa*, מַשָּׂא) is closely related to the Hebrew word for "lift" (*nasa*, נָשָׂא): "For my iniquities have gone over my head; they weigh like a burden [*massa*] too heavy for me" (Ps 38:4 [5 Heb.] NRSV).

The idea, then, is that sin and iniquity are not just abstract concepts. They are visualized as weights bearing down on a person, as burdens that the sinner carries (see also Lev 24:15 and Mic 7:9). In this context, forgiveness means: SOMEONE LIFTS THIS BURDEN OFF OF THE SINNER. Most often, God is described as the one doing this lifting. For example, Exodus 34:7 talks of God as "one who carries [*nasa*] iniquity, rebellion, and sin" (translation mine).[156] The idea is that by God's carrying away this sin, the people no longer need to carry it.

The Psalms similarly talk of God's forgiving nature with this imagery. Psalm 25:18 calls on God to see trouble and to bear this weight: "Consider my affliction and my trouble, and forgive [*nasa*] all my sins" (NRSV). Although the NRSV here gets at the right idea, the Hebrew imagery suggests that the person praying had previously been bearing (*nasa*) these sins. The bold prayer is for God to bear (*nasa*) them instead.

Once a year, on the Day of Atonement, a special activity took place symbolizing the removal of sins from the people. Leviticus 16 explains:

> [The high priest] is to lay both hands on the head of the live goat and confess over it all the wickedness and rebellion of the Israelites—all their sins—and put them on the goat's head. He shall send the goat away into the wilderness in the care of someone appointed for the task. The goat will carry [*nasa*] on itself all their sins to a remote place; and the man shall release it in the wilderness. (16:21-22 NIV)

In this symbolic act, the high priest transfers the burden of sin from the people to the animal, who carries it far away from the people. Their burden is gone.

So, the Old Testament assumes:

- Sin is a burden.
- After sinning, the sinner bears the weight of this burden.
- God can instead bear this weight.
- On the Day of Atonement, an animal sacramentally carries the weight of sin away from the people.

I wonder what would happen if people reframed sin in these terms. Perhaps sin would seem less enticing, given the ways it weighs us down. Perhaps we would be less likely to trivialize God's grace when we realize that God bears the weight of sin when it is taken off us.[157] Perhaps Christian imagery about Jesus bearing our sins would come to life in new ways.

Repent

For centuries, the church has said that to receive forgiveness, people need to do something called "repent." Unfortunately, that word is hardly ever used outside of church circles today. What does it actually mean?

Hebrew has two key words that mean "repent."[158] The first (נִחַם, *nikham*) is fairly straightforward and less metaphorical: it means changing one's mind. At times, it can carry overtones of having regret and being sorry.[159]

The second word is more interesting in terms of evoking a concrete image. Here it is:

	English	Hebrew	Hebrew Transliteration
43.	turn, return, repent	שׁוּב	*shuv*

The Bible uses this word more than one thousand times. Frequently, the sense pertains to changing directions:

- "Then Joseph returned [*shuv*] to Egypt, he, his brothers, and everyone who left with him to bury his father." (Gen 50:14 CEB)
- "When Samson drank, his energy returned [*shuv*]." (Judg 15:19 CEB)
- "The king returned [*shuv*] from the palace garden to the banquet room." (Esth 7:8 CEB)

When the Bible uses *shuv* to talk about repentance, it's talking about returning to God. People should walk in "the way of the Lord." They should stay with and protect (*shamar*) God's instruction. When they pass through (*avar*) God's instruction, moving on to something else, it's necessary to return (*shuv*) to God's covenant.

Consider Psalm 7:12 [13 Heb.]. It reads, "If one does not repent [*shuv*], God will whet his sword; he has bent and strung his bow" (NRSV). It's a frightening verse, warning that God opposes evil (see 7:11 [12 Heb.]). It's even more frightening when people read it and don't know exactly what "repent" means. How do you avoid God's judgment if you aren't sure what the text is saying? The Common English Bible translation offers a useful correction: "If someone doesn't change their ways [*shuv*], God will sharpen his sword, will bend his bow, will string an arrow." It's much easier to obey the Bible when we know what it's actually saying.

Another important example is Hosea 11:5. In the NIV, readers find: "Will they not return to Egypt and will not Assyria rule over them because they refuse to repent?" Interestingly, the Hebrew uses *shuv* for both of the underlined words. It's saying that because the Israelites refused to *return to God*, they will *return to Egypt*—in other words, they'll face slavery or something similar. Unfortunately, the NIV doesn't capture this play on words, preferring the term "repent" at the verse's end when "return" is more visual.

With some verses, translations do a better job, rendering *shuv* with "return" or "turn," rather than going with the more obsolete word "repent": "If the wicked turn from their ways, they will live. Turn, completely turn from your wicked ways! Why should you die, house of Israel?" (Ezek 33:11 CEB; cf. Ezek 18:21-32). A similar idea appears in Hosea 14, which uses a variety of words and concepts we've discussed:

> Return [*shuv*], O Israel, to the LORD your God,
>   For you have fallen because of your sin.
> Take words with you
>   And return [*shuv*] to the LORD.
> Say to Him: "Forgive [literally "lift" or "bear," *nasa*] all guilt
>   And accept what is good...."
> I will heal their affliction,
>   Generously will I take them back in love;
>   For My anger has turned away [*shuv*] from them.
>   (Hos 14:1-4 [2-5 Heb.] NJPS)[160]

This text envisions Israel as falling under the weight of sin, and it asks God to lift the burden. At the same time, it also talks of repentance in terms of returning to God. When the people turn back to the Lord, God's anger will turn away from them.

The Hebrew Bible is often filled with these sorts of connections. The original language gives people concrete images that teach them about the dangers of sin and how to get back into a right relationship with God. Instead of making religion something abstract, it's about getting in "the zone" of a covenant with God. When we pass through (*avar*) God's covenant and find ourselves in sin, we need to turn (*shuv*) from wickedness and return to our Creator.

Bless

What happens to people who protect (*shamar*) God's instruction? What happens to people who turn back (*shuv*) to God?

In the Bible, God *blesses* these people.[161] But what does "bless" mean? Today, we tend to use this word only after hearing someone sneeze. In terms of concrete specifics, what is a blessing, and what does it mean for one party to bless another?

To answer these questions, we can think of God working in two primary ways.[162] The first way is miraculous interventions. God shows up and rescues people from imminent danger. When all hope seems lost, God overturns every last table. The perfect example: God rescues the Israelites from Egyptian slavery. I discuss this idea later in the book when talking about deliverance.

The second way God works has less to do with fireworks and miracles. It's about the slow and steady hand of God in our lives. It's the everyday goodness sprinkled among us. It's a child's smile, the taste of a strawberry just picked from the garden, a Sunday afternoon nap, success in work. It's life fully lived—with all the laughter and tears that go along with that.

This second way God works is called *blessing*. It's a welcome alternative to the drama and stress that too often crowd our lives. God has a way of gradually bringing good things into the lives of the faithful. Those good things are blessings. To bless someone is to acknowledge goodness and power in them. Sometimes, gifts accompany this acknowledgment. Here's how the word looks in Hebrew:

	English	Hebrew	Hebrew Transliteration
44.	bless	בֵּרֵךְ	*berakh*

This verb appears over three hundred times in the Bible.

This word for "bless" (*berakh*) is strikingly similar to the Hebrew word for "knee" (*berekh*, בֶּרֶךְ).[163] The connection? One possibility is that the Bible's prime example of a blessing is having children. The Bible talks about childbirth by referring to the knees of someone present at birth (Gen 50:23; Job 3:12). It also mentions knees when talking about kids on their parents' laps (Isa 66:12).[164]

Another possible connection between "blessing" and "knees" relates to prayer. People praying in the Bible often fell to their knees, acknowledging their submission to God. Prayer is a key context for exchanging blessings with God. So, during the dedication of the temple in 1 Kings 8:54-56, we read:

> When Solomon had finished praying this entire prayer and supplication to the Lord, he arose from before the altar of the Lord, from kneeling on his knees [*berekh*] with his hands spread toward heaven. And he stood and blessed [*berakh*] all the assembly of Israel with a loud voice, saying: "Blessed [*berakh*] be the Lord, who has given rest to His people Israel, according to all that He promised." (NASB)

Solomon stands after prayerful kneeling, and blessings flow out in every direction: from him to the people and from the people to God. (See **How Can People Bless God?**)

How Can People Bless God?

It's normal to think of God blessing people. But what does it mean for people to bless God? To bless someone is to acknowledge greatness in that person. So, when we join parts of the Bible in saying to God, "Blessed are you," we're confessing our faith in God's greatness (see 1 Chron 29:10; Ps 119:12). We're acknowledging how good God is. God desires such acknowledgments the same way God desires healthy relationships with people.

When chemists mix two things together, new compounds can emerge. The classic example is vinegar and baking soda—the perfect ingredients for a do-it-yourself volcano. Pour the vinegar over the baking soda, and fizzy liquid erupts everywhere. We smell the vinegar while hearing the hiss of a thousand popping bubbles. On the technical side, a chemist could tell you that water, carbon dioxide, and sodium acetate emerge (the last being an ingredient in some potato chips). The water and other ingredients weren't present when the vinegar and baking soda were safely in their own packages. Newness results when mixed together.

Curses

Today, we often think of a curse as someone saying a bad word like, "Goddammit!" In the Bible, curses are the opposite of blessings. They are a way of saying that something is fundamentally wrong with the person being cursed, and that horrible things should result. See Deuteronomy 28:15-68 for a frightening list of curses.[165]

In the Bible, when God and people are mixed together, new things emerge. "Blessing" is a good word to describe the by-products of divine-human reactions—at least when God and people are on good terms! (See **Curses**.) New things emerge for people and even for God that wouldn't be present otherwise.

As noted earlier, the Old Testament is primarily concerned with realities in this world. Its authors didn't bank everything on an afterlife. Instead, they believed that good things occurred in the here-and-now to those who held fast to God. These "good things" are "blessings." So, when God blesses a person, God and the person are in a close relationship, and the person ends up with valuable things as a result. The person becomes greater than she would otherwise be. Sometimes there's an increase in property. Other times, there's an increase in offspring. Still other times, there's an increase in power, hope, or holistic peace (see the discussion of *shalom* in chapter 8).[166]

Christians sometimes get nervous when talking about faith leading to good things in this lifetime. They know that good things don't always come to those who hope in God. Sometimes, people become Christians and then face persecution. Other times, they become Christians and realize they need to make huge sacrifices in their lives. Still other times, disaster strikes, despite a firm faith. How do we sort out this tension? (See **A Statement on Prosperity**.)

A Statement on Prosperity

"We affirm that there is a biblical vision of human prospering, and that the Bible includes material welfare (both health and wealth) within its teaching about the blessing of God. . . . However, we reject the unbiblical notion that spiritual welfare can be measured in terms of material welfare, or that wealth is always a sign of God's blessing (since it can be obtained by oppression, deceit or corruption)."[167]

—*The Lausanne Movement*

For starters, it's useful to remember that the Bible presents the world as less than perfect. We no longer live in the garden of Eden. The world we inhabit retains a memory of the good God who made it. However, this world has also fallen from God's original intent. So, faithfulness doesn't always lead to material blessings. Sometimes, evildoers prosper while the faithful go without.

Yet, because creation retains God's fingerprints, there are moments when evil catches up with the wicked and blessings shower down on the faithful. We can't predict when it will happen. Life's too complicated for reduction to a mathematician's formula. But goodness does come to those who place their trust in the Lord.

Abraham is the classic example of someone blessed by God. The Lord tells him to leave his homeland, adding these words: "I will make of you a great nation and will bless [*berakh*] you. I will make your name respected, and you will be a blessing [a noun form of *berakh*]. I will bless [*berakh*] those who bless [*berakh*] you, those who curse you I will curse; all the families of earth will be blessed [*berakh*] because of you" (Gen 12:2-3 CEB). Abraham is obedient. He leaves his home. Although he's seventy-five years old, he moves across the known world. He does other crazy things like cut up animals for God (Gen 15) and make sure that both he and others around him are circumcised (Gen 17).

But God's blessings always seem a long way off. God promises from the outset to make Abraham a great nation. Presumably, he'd be having kids left and right. But he has none. He and his wife are older than the hills. At one point, his wife Sarah and he tragically decide he should sleep with Sarah's slave. The hope is that the slave will bear a son to carry on the family name. That plan falls to pieces.

For twenty-five years, God's promised blessing shows no sign of materializing. But one day (or more likely, one night), a miracle happens. Nine months later, Sarah gives birth to a son. Isaac. The one who would carry on the family name. The one whose son would have twelve more sons, becoming the twelve tribes of Israel. The people of Israel who would bless all the peoples of the earth.

As with Abraham, it may take a long time before God's blessing come our way. But a central affirmation of the Bible is that blessings are a natural by-product of being in a faithful relationship with God.[168]

Conclusion

Most of us live in post-Christian societies. Denominations dwindle while people are increasingly biblically illiterate. We can no longer assume that people come into church knowing "Christianese." Words like "transgression," "sin," "forgiveness," "repentance," and "blessing" need to be explained and translated.

Abstract definitions help in only limited ways. People think on concrete levels. With the technological revolution brought about by the internet, people are drawn to visual images more than ever before. (See **The Age of Visualcy**.)

The Age of Visualcy

"We are entering the age of 'visualcy,' the third great transformation in the way that human beings engage and interpret their world. The first was orality, when the most culturally…significant information was communicated and passed from one generation to another in the form of oral tradition, especially stories.…The second age was the age of literacy, when significant information was written down and oral information became secondary in importance.…

"But now the age of literacy is waning. Today the most compelling and significant information is communicated visually—neither through speech nor in writing, but in still and moving images."[169]

—Andy Crouch

Hebrew is an enormous resource in this context. Its theological words frequently invoke concrete images that can help people access the content of faith. By looking past centuries of abstract layers, we find a vocabulary that is fresh and engaging.

Chapter 6

Blinded by the Past

Abandoning Old Words

Since the third century BCE, people have translated the Bible.[170] Almost every new translation builds upon earlier translations. Even today, biblical scholars consult ancient and modern translations to assist with their work.

Sometimes, problems arise. Earlier translations can influence translators to use words that were popular in earlier times but have fallen into disuse today. So, whereas the biblical writers usually used words that connected in straightforward ways with their audiences, today's translations sometimes use old words that are no longer popular.[171]

> **A Word about the KJV**
>
> It's over four hundred years old, and it remains one of the most popular versions of the Bible. Why is this version so popular?
>
> The KJV does a nice job conveying the beauty of poetic texts like the Psalms. It's also attractive to people who grew up memorizing the KJV.
>
> This translation's popularity is also partially due to it being in the public domain. Publishers can use it without paying royalties.

Recent Bible translations no longer use words like "thee," "thou," and "passeth," which are found in the King James Version of the Bible (and even as late as the 1952 RSV; see for example Ps 23:4). However, other words found in the KJV persist in Bible translations today, even though people rarely use such language in everyday conversation. (See **A Word about the KJV**.) Here are the words that we will examine in this chapter:

- "behold"
- "woe" and "alas"
- "atone"
- "deliver" (when it means more than moving something someplace)
- "redeem"
- "host" (as in "the LORD of hosts")

This chapter looks at these words, examining the underlying Hebrew. It makes alternate proposals, hoping to make the Bible sound as fresh for readers today as it did for its original audiences. Here's how to envision the primary concept of this chapter:

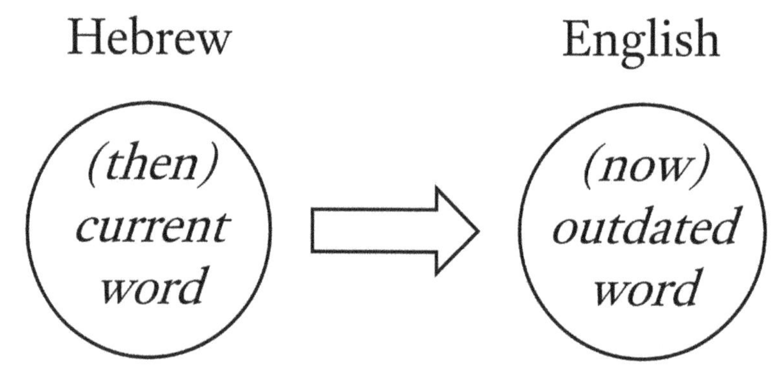

Figure 8

Behold

When I was growing up, my mom had a rather unique word when she wanted to draw my sister's and my attention to something. She'd say, often in a stern whisper, "Keetah!"[172] The moment she did so, we looked around. Rarely were we let down. We'd see a man walking down the sidewalk with a pet pig or someone wearing shorts in January in sub-zero Michigan. My mom didn't want to point and say, "Hey, kids, look at that guy who's going to have frostbitten shins." So, she stealthily drew our attention to something we didn't want to miss, using a word that only we understood.

Hebrew has its own attention-grabbing word. It worked a lot like "keetah," except it was very popular, something everyone knew and would say from time to time. In fact, the word appears over 1,100 times in the Bible. The word has two spellings in Hebrew:

	English	Hebrew	Hebrew Transliteration
45.	Behold! Hey!	הִנֵּה	*hinneh*
	Behold! Hey!	הֵן	*hen*

Traditionally, this word has been translated "behold." That word was popular in the time of Shakespeare. Today, however, no one says "behold" in everyday conversation.

What alternatives exist? Outside of my family, "keetah" won't work. "Indeed" is sometimes used, but that's not a particularly prevalent word outside of formal circles. However, English has plenty of attention-grabbing words: Hey! Wow! Shazam! Check it out! Boom! Look at me! Listen up![173]

Many of these words sound informal. An unfortunate assumption made by many Bible publishers is that the Bible should always sound formal. Sunday mornings—about the only time the Bible is read in public anymore—are often formal affairs for churchgoers. It makes no sense, however, for the Bible to sound proper and stiff when the original language consists of everyday speech.

Sadly, many translations today either stick with the obsolete word "behold" or leave the Hebrew untranslated. Consider, for example, Genesis 1:31. After God creates the universe, readers are supposed to be taken aback by the wonder and beauty of creation. The Hebrew word *hinneh* appears to make this point clear. But English translations struggle. Here's the NASB (1995): "God saw all that He had made, and **behold**, it was very good" (boldface mine). The NRSV (1989) is a little better: "God saw everything that he had made, and **indeed**, it was very good" (boldface mine). The NIV (1984–2011) ignores the attention-grabbing word altogether: "God saw all that he had made, and it was very good." A better approach would be this: "God looked at all he had made, and—*wow!*—it was supremely good."[174] It's a shame that published translations do so little to capture such an exciting and vivid word. Sadly, this tendency to leave *hinneh* untranslated is very common. According to one study, the NIV neglects to translate *hinneh* 588 of the 1,161 times it appears in the Hebrew Bible.[175]

One place the word appears is Amos 6–7. There, the prophet says that God has grown enraged with Israel's greed. In a short while, God's wrath will materialize in horrifying forms. When Amos speaks these words in Hebrew, he uses *hinneh* five times in a bold attempt to shock his audience out of their complacency with sin.[176]

When Amos speaks via translation, however, this word with its bold, attention-grabbing demands is too often lost. The NRSV, for example, translates this word "see" once (6:11), "indeed" another time (6:14), and leaves it untranslated three times (twice in 7:1, once in 7:4). In the text below (Amos 6:11, 14; 7:1, 4), I've altered the NRSV so that *hinneh* is translated in ways that grab attention (see underlines):

> Brace yourselves! The Lord commands, and the great house shall be shattered to bits, and the little house to pieces.... Watch out! I am raising up against you a nation, O house of Israel, says the Lord, the God of hosts, and they shall oppress you.... This is what the Lord God showed me: Listen up! He was forming locusts at the time the latter growth began to sprout. Yes! It was the latter growth after the king's mowings.... This is what the Lord God showed me: Boom! The Lord God was calling for a shower of fire, and it devoured the great deep and was eating up the land.

First, a brief word of explanation: the fertile season in ancient Israel yielded two cycles of crops. However, the first went to the king, meaning that the people needed to eke out enough from the second harvest to survive for the coming year. This second harvest would typically be followed by about six months with no rain. A locust plague destroying "the latter growth" would be especially devastating.[177] (See **Figure 9**[178] and **Death by Insect**.)

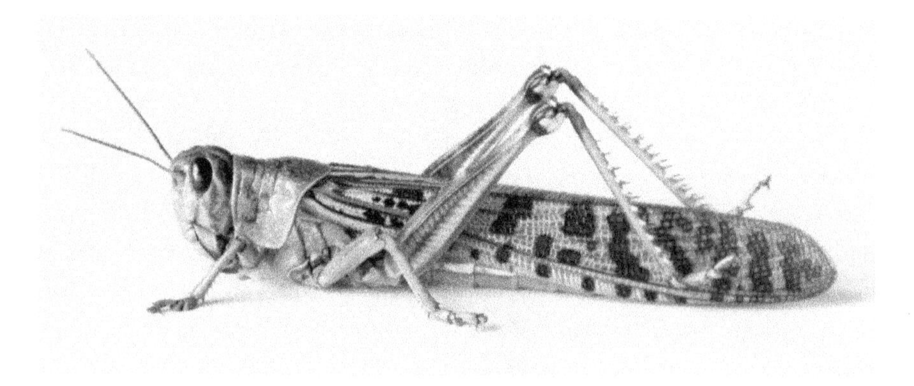

Figure 9

Without a doubt, the prophet uses the word *hinneh* to communicate the terrifying reality of an angry God. If Amos spoke in English today, perhaps he'd even use an obscene word, not to be profane or make the Bible any less holy, but to grab people's attention.

Death by Insect

"The recurrent appearance of locust swarms was one of the most dreadful plagues that afflicted the population of the ancient East. When the swarm made their ravenous way across the land, the face of the earth was stripped of every green plant. Nothing was left but the suffering and death of famine and the despair of [people] in the face of menace against which they were helpless. The horror was the greater in Israel because the locust was regarded as the plague of Yahweh, instrument of his curse upon Israel (Ex. 10.12ff.; Deut. 28.38, 42; Joel 1; Amos 4.9)."[179]

—*James Luther Mays*

The word *hinneh* reminds us that our faith isn't so much about abstract concepts as it is about shattering expected realities. The God of the Bible refuses to sit back and let the world spin in circles. This God acts, moves, shocks, moves mountains, changes the world, and leaves us in awe.[180] Biblical faith is a relationship with this wonder-making, excitement-spreading, and fear-inspiring God. According to the Bible, we live in a world where, at any moment—*hinneh!*—God may knock our socks off.

Woe, Alas

I'm not sure I've ever used the word "woe" in a sentence with my friends. The same goes with the word "alas." *The Oxford English Dictionary* notes that "alas" is now "chiefly archaic." It simply isn't uttered today.

Yet, "alas" makes about fifty appearances in recent Bible translations like the NIV and NRSV. Meanwhile, "woe" shows up about a hundred times in each of those two translations. When found in the Bible, what do they actually mean?

Several Hebrew words are at play. Here are the two most popular[181]:

	English	Hebrew	Hebrew Transliteration
46.	woe	אוֹי	*oy*
47.	alas	הוֹי	*hoy*

People sometimes use these Hebrew words today.[182]

The Dead

"My primary point is that when those to whom the prophets preached heard the initial exclamation, '*hoy!*', they would have immediately associated this mentally and emotionally with mourning for the dead. The association of *hoy* with lamentation would have been especially striking to the listeners, for it would have brought into vivid relief the pronouncement of Israel's death."[184]

—*James Williams*

In the Bible, these words are screams of fright.[183] They're used when people stare death in the face. (See **The Dead**.) They're spoken when ordinary words won't get the job done. *Hoy* is a cry that people utter when burying those they love. Thus, the prophet Jeremiah tells Jerusalem's King Zedekiah about his coming death: "You shall die in peace. And as spices were burned for your ancestors, the earlier kings who preceded you, so they shall burn spices for you and lament for you, saying, '*Hoy!* Ruler!' For I have spoken the word, says the LORD" (Jer 34:5 NRSV, alt.; cf. 1 Kgs 13:30; Jer 22:18). Like the words discussed in chapter 3, there isn't a great English equivalent for *hoy*. In deep lament, we might cry out, "No!" However, the word "no" suggests that the speaker is in denial of what has happened or at least opposes it. The Hebrew word, however, isn't first and foremost about denying the reality of death. It's a cry from deep within when staring at profound loss and separation created by death.

When a Foot Isn't a Foot

A *euphemism* is a pleasant-sounding word used instead of an unpleasant-sounding word. In English, for example, we often say that people "slept together" rather than saying they "had sexual intercourse." Hebrew has its euphemisms, too. With sex, it sometimes says that a couple "knew" each other. With sexual organs, it sometimes talks of a man's "feet." When describing the seraphim in Isaiah 6, the text says that these creatures covered their "feet," but it's likely referring to what's at the top of their legs, not the bottom. A similar euphemism is likely used in Ruth 3:4, 7, 8, 14.

Although *hoy* and *oy* have connections with burying the dead, they sometimes show up elsewhere. For example, in Isaiah 6, the prophet stands in God's temple. Suddenly, the hem of God's garment fills the place. Supernatural creatures called seraphim fly around. They have six wings, and they use two to fly. With the other four, they cover themselves, using two wings to cover their faces and two wings to cover their genitalia. (See **When a Foot Isn't a Foot**.) These creatures cry out "Holy! Holy! Holy!" Even these supernatural beings know they shouldn't be near such an awesome and holy God.

Isaiah, meanwhile, feels completely out of place. He has a tongue of venom.[185] As a sinner so close to God's holiness, he feels like someone caught within the blast radius of a nuclear bomb. Isaiah says something very important. Most translations render his words as "Woe is me!" The Hebrew is more of a guttural yell. It's a scream of fright: *Oy!* Isaiah feels like he's been invited to his own funeral. The New Living Translation perhaps comes the closest to approximating Isaiah's words: "*It's all over!* I am doomed, for I am a sinful man. I have filthy lips, and I live among a people with filthy lips. Yet I have seen the King, the LORD of Heaven's Armies" (Isa 6:5 NLT, italics mine).

As Isaiah prepares to be vaporized, one of these seraphim grabs a burning coal and touches it to his lips. Isaiah is purified. He is transformed. He can now do God's work. A dirty mouth is cleansed. It now brings God's message.

God's prophets are the ones most likely to use the Hebrew words *hoy* and *oy*. In fact, sixty-eight out of seventy-seven times the Bible uses these words, it's in the Prophetic Books. Why are they found so frequently there?

As we saw in chapter 4 while discussing the word *raah*, a common theme in the Old Testament is that evil actions bring evil results. The prophets lived in an evil time. Idolatry stole people away from the Lord, while people loved possessions more than each other. The prophets knew that such evildoing would lead to disaster. So, they forecasted impending doom.

People often doubted the prophets. They thought that God's love ensured they would never face judgment. They kept speaking of "the day of the LORD," much as Christians today talk about Jesus's second coming. However, the prophet Amos knew that the people's actions were fundamentally unjust and harmful to the most vulnerable in society. So, this is what he says: "*Hoy!* You who desire the day of the LORD! Why do you want the day of the LORD? It is darkness, not light; as if someone fled from a lion, and was met by a bear; or went into the house and rested a hand against the wall, and was bitten by a snake. Is not the day of the LORD darkness, not light, and gloom with no brightness in it?" (Amos 5:18-20 NRSV, alt.). Amos begins with this attention-grabbing word associated with death and destruction. As he proceeds, he tells people that God would indeed visit them, but due to their unrelenting wickedness, it would be a time of punishment and not rejoicing.

It's easy for modern readers to gloss over words like "alas" and "woe." No longer commonly used, they mean little to us today. However, they were as vivid as spilled blood for the Bible's original audiences. They captured attention and focused it on disturbing events.

Atone

Sometimes, relationships sour. Maybe we did something wrong. Maybe the other person did. Maybe simple misunderstandings accumulated. But there's a lack of peace. An uneasiness lingers whenever we think of that person.

The Bible knows full well that relationships can go this direction. We get off track in relating to God and other humans. Fortunately, the Bible describes ways to pacify anger and set things right again.

When describing how to make things right, English Bibles often use the verb "atone." This word shows up about a hundred times in the NRSV and NIV. However, it's rarely used outside of the Bible. What does it actually mean?

This verb once referred to two parties being united or set "at one."[186] Here's the Hebrew word:

	English	Hebrew	Hebrew Transliteration
48.	atone, reconcile, set right	כִּפֶּר	*kipper*

This word appears in a variety of contexts. One of them is shortly after the Israelites worship the golden calf at Mount Sinai. Although God had forbidden such practices in the Ten Commandments, they created this idol. After disastrous consequences unfold, Moses says to the people: "You have sinned a great sin. But now I will go up to the LORD; perhaps I can make atonement [*kipper*] for your sin" (Exod 32:30 NRSV). This obscure language of "make atonement" is unfortunate because few people talk about atonement these days. The idea is that Moses is trying to find a way for reconciliation or forgiveness between the people and God (see CEB, NJPS). He wants things to be set right again.[187] Through honest prayer, he does just that.

One interesting thing about the word *kipper* is *how* to set things right again. The Bible gives many examples. First, as we've just seen, a level of restoration can be achieved when a leader or prophet like Moses intervenes between the estranged parties.

A second path to reconciliation is that God works in decisive ways. We saw this pattern earlier with the prophet Isaiah. He knows he's a man with filthy language. He thinks he'll be incinerated by the power of God's holiness. But after the heavenly creature brings the coal to Isaiah, the text says, "See [*hinneh*], this has touched your lips; your guilt is taken away and your sin atoned [*kipper*] for" (Isa 6:7 NIV). Things are set right not because Isaiah grits his teeth and censors his bad language. God performs an act that sets things right. Isaiah's sins are covered over. The relationship is now okay.

A third path to reconciliation involves inner attitudes. As Proverbs 16:6 puts it, "Through love and faithfulness sin is <u>atoned</u> [*kipper*] for; through the fear of the LORD evil [or "disaster," *ra*] is avoided" (NIV). Sometimes, when others see virtue in us, they realize that we aren't the scoundrels we once made ourselves out to be.

A final path to reconciliation involves giving gifts and making sacrifices. (See **Too Spiritual**.)

Too Spiritual

The problem with Christianity today is that it has become overly spiritualized. We act as if faith were a matter pertaining to another spiritual realm. But at its heart, biblical faith is innately physical, forever focused with the here and now. Concrete gifts to God and others can be wonderful expressions of faith.

In Genesis, we read about twin brothers named Jacob and Esau. For much of his young adulthood, Jacob was an absolute villain. He manipulated his starving brother, Esau, out of his inheritance (Gen 25:29-34). He deceived his dying father into giving him Esau's blessing (Gen 27:1-40).

In response to a brother hell-bent on making his life miserable, Esau plans cowboy-style justice. He's ready to kill Jacob. Jacob catches wind of Esau's plan and flees (Gen 27:41-45). Twenty years later, life circumstances force Jacob to return toward Esau. What awaits? Esau advances with four hundred armed men (Gen 32:6 [7 Heb.]).

Jacob has matured and is, quite frankly, desperate. He sends nearly everything he owns—hundreds of animals—in front of him as gifts for Esau. His servants go with these animals. They're instructed to tell Esau that Jacob hopes to *kipper* with these gifts so that Esau will look kindly upon him and forgive him (Gen 32:20 [21 Heb.]).[188] Some translations say that Jacob wants to "appease" Esau with these presents (NASB, NRSV). Others say that Jacob wants to "pacify" him (CEB, NIV) or even "propitiate" him (NJPS). The basic idea is that Jacob wants things set right again. He wants reconciliation, peace, and a restored relationship.

At a climactic moment, when Esau meets Jacob, the brothers embrace. The gifts have communicated that Jacob is a different person than he was twenty years earlier. Jacob is no longer going to rob Esau. He is instead one to make amends and give back what was wrongfully taken.[189]

This story illustrates an important point: gifts can often heal ruptured relationships. Particularly when the gift is something valuable, it can communicate in concrete terms that we wish the other person well. Whatever happened previously, gifts say, "From this point on, we are no longer at odds. We may have seen each other as enemies or at least causes of tension, but that's no longer the case. I have goodwill for you. You can see it in what I now give you." As a result, anger often dissipates. Peace swells up. Things are set right.

Gifts can improve relationships between humans—and between humans and God. The Bible talks repeatedly about sacrifices that atone for one's sin. For example, in Numbers 15:24-25, we read: "The whole congregation shall offer one young bull for a burnt offering, a pleasing odor to the LORD, together with its grain offering and its drink offering, according to the ordinance, and one male goat for a sin offering. The priest shall make atonement [*kipper*] for all the congregation of the Israelites, and they shall be forgiven" (NRSV). Here, the Bible's saying that these sacrifices—gifts—serve to set things right with God. The anger that God may have toward us dissipates. The relationship can start afresh. The sacrifice is an outward and visible sign of our inner desire to be at peace with God. (See **Jesus and Atonement**.)

Jesus and Atonement

Christians have often thought of Jesus's death on the cross as the ultimate sacrifice, one that forever sets things right between God and humanity. There have been different thoughts on how exactly Jesus's death sets things right between God and us. Given the connections between gift-giving and atonement, we shouldn't lose sight of the ways that Jesus's death communicates God's desire to make things right with us: however much we may feel cheated by God and the events of life, God giving "his only begotten Son" was a supreme gift for humanity—a sign that God forever wishes us well and wants to live in harmony with us.

Does this idea of sacrifice and giving gifts to God mean that forgiveness can be bought? Not at all. In fact, many prophets condemn those who think they can sin and then make up for it in an instant by offering a sacrifice (e.g., Hos 6:6).

The Bible is also aware of the immense problems that occur when gift-giving degenerates into bribery (1 Sam 12:3; Amos 5:12).[190] Gifts for others should never be an excuse for us to engage in deplorable behavior in the future. Instead, they should be outward extensions of inward virtue.

So, what we find with the word *kipper* is that we don't need to rely on obscure language like "atonement." Instead, the word has to do with restoring a relationship that went awry. This reconciliation often occurs after a mediator intervenes (like Moses between the people and God), after God miraculously intervenes (as with Isaiah), after positive inward qualities like love come to light (as in Proverbs), or after gifts or sacrifices are given (as with Jacob and Esau).

Deliver

"The delivery guy's here." I hear these words, and immediately my mouth begins to salivate in anticipation of the pizza I'm about to devour.

I receive a work e-mail from the mailroom: "You have a delivery." I make my way to get the package, wondering if it's something exciting. It's usually a book I forgot I had ordered.

When we hear of someone *delivering* something, we usually think of an object being shipped somewhere. It seems odd, then, when the word "deliver" shows up in church. One of my favorite things to do in worship is participate in a responsive reading called "The Great Liturgy." On nine different occasions, the congregation responds, "Good Lord, deliver us."[191] This metaphor, however, seems quite strange when we use our normal definition of "deliver." The metaphor would seem to suggest:

WE ARE PACKAGES.

JESUS CHRIST IS A UPS WORKER.

Obviously, the church has something else in mind when it talks about deliverance. The Bible was written long before modern shipping services came on the scene.

Outside of churches, when people talk of a *person* being delivered, they usually speak of birth. *She's in the delivery room now.* Such a sentence is very exciting, as people ready themselves for a new baby in the world. However, when the Hebrew Bible speaks of *people* being delivered, it never describes newborns or births.[192]

Instead, the word "deliver" in the Bible usually comes out of military contexts. The act of deliverance was akin to a combat search and rescue mission where special operatives entered foreign territory, grabbed those who had been captured by enemies, and brought them back to their homes. In short, "to deliver" meant "to rescue." Here it is:

	English	Hebrew	Hebrew Transliteration
49.	deliver, rescue	הִצִּיל	*hitsil*

This word appears nearly two hundred times in the Bible.

It's used in 1 Samuel 30. There, David and his troops return home only to find that the Amalekites have razed their city and kidnapped their wives and children. After David and his troops locate their enemies, the text reads:

> David attacked [the Amalekites] from twilight until evening of the next day. He killed them all. No one escaped except four hundred young men who got on camels and fled. David rescued [*hitsil*] everything that the Amalekites had taken, including his own two wives. Nothing was missing from the plunder or anything that they had taken, neither old nor young, son nor daughter. David brought everything back. (1 Sam 30:17-19 CEB)

Like the English word "deliver," the Hebrew *hitsil* describes David's moving things and people: he *takes back home what was stolen*. However, the idea of transporting things is only the most basic of meanings. In this context—as well as most others where this Hebrew word shows up—the emphasis is on *rescuing someone from a clear and present danger*.

> **Collocations**
>
> Languages tend to pair words with one another. "Peanut butter" often shows up with "jelly." The technical term for word pairings is "collocations." One language's collocations don't necessarily transfer to another language. So, it's important to remember that Hebrew words like *hitsil* have an entirely different set of associations and collocations than the English word "deliver."

Many words work well in some places, but not in others. For example, in English, "yellow" is used to describe the color of things like houses, but "blond" is used to describe the color of hair, and "golden" is used to describe the color of metal. While "yellow," "blond," and "golden" appear at similar places on a color spectrum, we naturally associate them with certain objects. (See **Collocations**.)

In English, the word "deliver" often shows up in the context of shipping. Packages are what's normally delivered. The focus is on a movement from Point A to Point B without much emphasis on whether Points A and B are particularly good or bad places.

In Hebrew, the word *hitsil* is quite different. It shows up in the context of dangers, attacks, and violence. Instead of objects, it's usually people who are delivered.[193] There's a movement from Point A to Point B, but Point A is clearly a place of danger, while Point B is a place of safety.

Many people in America never worry about being captured by enemy forces. The people of the Bible did not have the luxury of living without such concerns. They dwelled in the shadow of different superpowers and hostile neighbors that rarely were happy with Israel's or Judah's independence.

A Closely Related Word

The word *hitsil* often shows up with one of its synonyms, הוֹשִׁיעַ or *hoshia*. This word means "to save."

Christians have long associated acts of deliverance and salvation with forgiveness of sins. Both the Old and New Testaments do sometimes make such connections (e.g., Ps 79:9; Rom 5:8-10). However, deliverance and salvation are by no means limited to forgiveness. Both words consistently have to do with surviving a danger-filled situation.

Biblical scholar Terence Fretheim puts it this way:

> To answer the question, "What are you saved from?" entails a response as comprehensive as the world's needs: guilt and shame; social chaos, war, and other types of violence; abuse in its many forms; mental and physical illness; famine; the rape of the environment. Put positively: it includes forgiveness, mental and physical health, peace, safety in every life setting, harmonious family relationships, community stability and well-being, and a healthy natural order.[195]

The Hebrew Bible spoke directly to the concerns of people living in that time. It not only described war heroes rescuing people. It also used this idea of "rescue" to describe the activity of God.

On a national scale, the Hebrew Bible frequently uses the word *hitsil* to describe the exodus: "This is what the LORD God of Israel says: I brought Israel up out of Egypt, and I delivered [*hitsil*] you from the Egyptians' power and from the power of all the kingdoms that oppressed you" (1 Sam 10:18 CEB).[194] In other words, God "rescued" Israel from oppressors. God snatched Israel out of their hands. (See **A Closely Related Word**.)

On a smaller scale, the Hebrew Bible uses this word to describe God's personal intervention to save individual lives. Thus, the psalmist prays:

> Please protect my life! Deliver [*hitsil*] me!
> Don't let me be put to shame because I take refuge in you. (Ps 25:20 CEB)

Some Psalms go so far as to say that people shouldn't trust in human forces to rescue them—no matter how powerful such military forces may be. On the day of danger, the faithful rely on God, not their arsenals[196]:

> A king is not saved [related to *hoshia*] by his great army;
> a warrior is not delivered [related to *hitsil*] by his great strength.

> The war horse is a vain hope for victory [related to *hoshia*],
> and by its great might it cannot save.
> Truly the eye of the LORD is on those who fear him,
> on those who hope in his steadfast love,
> to deliver [*hitsil*] their life [*nephesh*] from death,
> and to keep them alive in famine.
> Our soul [*nephesh*] waits for the LORD;
> he is our help and shield. (Ps 33:16-20 NRSV)

Praying these psalms is a bold act of faith in God. It's trusting that God will rescue when all looks hopeless, when dangers abound, and when all seems lost. As our deliverer, God has more in common with a firefighter than a delivery person.

A Prayer for Deliverance

The following prayer comes from the *Book of Common Prayer* (1928, alt.). It appropriately links deliverance to God's rescuing power:

> ALMIGHTY God, you are a strong tower of defense for your servants against their enemies: we give you praise and thanksgiving for our deliverance from those great dangers that encircled us: it was your goodness that we were not handed over as prey to them. We ask you to continue these mercies towards us, that the entire world may know that you are our Savior and mighty Deliverer; through Jesus Christ our Lord. Amen.[197]

When we pray, "Good Lord, deliver us," we're praying to be "rescued" from powers too great for us. (See **A Prayer for Deliverance**.)

Redeem

Outside of church, I don't hear the words "redeem" and "redemption" very much. When I do, it's usually to talk about coupons, gift certificates, or lottery tickets. When the Bible talks about God redeeming Israel, it's obviously not suggesting that Israel is like a coupon that gives God a discount on something! So, what's going on? I fear that for many Christians, "redemption" is a positive word, but also an empty word whose basic meaning is filled willy-nilly with whatever comes to mind.

Hebrew can help. Here's the word:

	English	Hebrew	Hebrew Transliteration
50.	redeem	גָּאַל	*gaal*

This word appears about a hundred times in the Bible.[198]

To understand this word, it's helpful to think about bankruptcy. What happens when people incur debts too great to pay off? In the United States, under certain conditions, individuals or businesses can declare bankruptcy. At that point, they're no longer liable for their debts, and creditors can no longer take action against them. The purpose is to give people fresh starts. Here's how the Supreme Court described this practice in 1934: "It gives to the honest but unfortunate debtor... a new opportunity in life and a clear field for future effort, unhampered by the pressure and discouragement of preexisting debt."[199] Declaring bankruptcy provides a new way for those facing enormous debt.

In the Bible, there was no bankruptcy court. Under ordinary circumstances, if landowners faced unbearable debt, they would have to give up their land. If a debtor didn't have any land to surrender, then either the landowner or a family member would have to become a slave.

Redemption in Ruth

The responsibility for redemption typically fell to one's closest male relative. In fact, sometimes, the nearest male relative is simply called a "redeemer." For example, in Ruth 2:20, Naomi describes Boaz as "one of our close relatives... one of our redeemers [from *gaal*]" (CEB). Boaz hasn't yet done anything to buy land or freedom. However, he's called a redeemer because he's a close male relative. Later in the book (e.g., 4:4), when there's talk of land being purchased, the book shifts gears and talks about redeeming the land in the sense described here.[202]

However, deep within biblical law is a provision that gives people a fresh start. A rich uncle could buy back the foreclosed family farm. This person, also called a redeemer, could similarly purchase freedom for enslaved family members. To redeem (*gaal*) people is to give them their land back or to buy their freedom. The word is found several times in Leviticus 25 and 27, such as 25:25: "When one of your fellow Israelites faces financial difficulty and must sell part of their family property, the closest relative [a noun form of *gaal*] will come and buy back [*gaal*] what their fellow Israelite has sold" (CEB). It's difficult to overstate how important redemption would be for people. Many parts of ancient Israel practiced what's called subsistence farming, which means that villagers lived off the land, producing enough to survive and for taxes, but without much excess.[200] There were no savings accounts for "rainy days" (though biblical writers would probably call them "days of drought").[201] When a landowner couldn't pay debt or taxes, land would often be confiscated. Without land to provide crops, slavery could quickly follow. Having a rich relative, then, could mean all the difference in the world. (See **Redemption in Ruth**.)

Several times in the Bible, God redeems. Exodus 6:6 and 15:13 say that God, like a redeemer rescuing a loved one from slavery, rescues the Israelites from the Egyptians.

The image of God as redeemer is especially prominent in Isaiah 40–66. This text addresses people from Jerusalem who saw their land destroyed and entered exile. As refugees living in foreign territory, they had lost their land, and they felt like slaves. In this context, the Bible boldly portrays God as the rich relative who buys back the family farm and rescues people from slavery. Here are some examples:

> But now thus says the Lord,
> he who created [*bara*] you, O Jacob,
> he who formed you, O Israel:
> Do not fear, for I have redeemed [*gaal*] you;
> I have called you by name, you are mine. (Isa 43:1 NRSV)

> I have swept away your transgressions like a cloud,
> and your sins like mist;
> return [*shuv*] to me, for I have redeemed [*gaal*] you.
> Sing, O heavens, for the Lord has done it;
> shout, O depths of the earth!...
> For the Lord has redeemed [*gaal*] Jacob,
> and will be glorified in Israel.
> Thus says the Lord, your Redeemer [from *gaal*],
> who formed you in the womb:
> I am the Lord, who made all things,...
> who says of Jerusalem, "It shall be inhabited,"
> and of the cities of Judah, "They shall be rebuilt,
> and I will raise up their ruins." (Isa 44:22-24, 26 NRSV)

> Go out from Babylon, flee from Chaldea,
> declare this with a shout of joy, proclaim it,
> send it forth to the end of the earth;
> say, "The Lord has redeemed [*gaal*] his servant Jacob!" (Isa 48:20 NRSV)

> In [God's] love and in His mercy He redeemed [*gaal*] them,
> And He lifted them and carried [*nasa*] them all the days of old.
> (Isa 63:9b NASB)

Given the importance of a word like *gaal* in Isaiah, it's not surprising that the New Testament invokes similar language to describe the work of Jesus: "[God] has rescued us from the power of darkness and transferred us into the kingdom of his beloved Son, in whom we have redemption, the forgiveness of sins" (Col 1:13-14 NRSV). The powerful Hebrew metaphor of redemption is picked up and applied in new ways to Jesus in the New Testament.

We could summarize different parts of the Bible by saying this:

- In Exodus, God *redeems* the enslaved Israelites and gives them freedom from the Egyptians.
- In Leviticus, a relative *redeems* those enslaved or made landless by their financial debt, giving them freedom and livelihood again.
- In Isaiah, God *redeems* those exiled and made landless by their sin, giving them freedom and the promised land again.
- In Colossians, Jesus *redeems* those in darkness by their sin, giving them God's kingdom and forgiveness.

Redemption in the Bible, then, has nothing to do with coupons. And it's far from being an empty word. Instead, it's about unrepayable debts and how redeemers bring about freedom on good land once again.

Host

Most English Bibles talk of "the LORD of hosts" over two hundred times. In fact, this name for God is one of the most popular ways of talking about God in all of the Bible.[203] It's been called "the loftiest and grandest and... the royal name of God."[204] However, the name raises an obvious question: what exactly is a "host"?

Typically, I think of a host as the counterpart to a guest. It's someone who entertains company, giving food or lodging.

As it turns out, when the Bible talks about "the LORD of hosts," it never has hospitality in view. However, when English Bibles first became popular with the King James Version and the Geneva Bible, the word "host" had an additional meaning that is no longer very popular. A "host" was a great army. That definition actually matches the Hebrew rather well. Here's the word:

	English	Hebrew	Hebrew Transliteration
51.	hosts, armies	צְבָאוֹת	*tsevaot*

Some of us know Martin Luther's hymn "A Mighty Fortress Is Our God." A verse of that hymn actually uses this Hebrew word:

> Did we in our own strength confide, our striving would be losing,
> were not the right man on our side, the man of God's own choosing.
> Dost ask who that may be? Christ Jesus, it is he;
> Lord *tsevaot*, his name, from age to age the same, and he must win the battle.[205]

By calling Jesus "Lord *tsevaot*," the hymn equates Jesus of the New Testament with the God of the Old Testament.

This word *tsevaot* is the ordinary Hebrew word for "army" in the plural form. This word is quite popular. It shows up nearly five hundred times in the Hebrew Bible, and about half of these occurrences are part of the phrase "the LORD of hosts."

Several biblical texts portray God as willing to execute justice through violence. For example, the end of Isaiah 31:4 reads, "the LORD of hosts [*tsevaot*] will come down to fight [*tsava*, a word related to *tsevaot*] upon Mount Zion and upon its hill" (NRSV). (See **A Violent God?**)

Who are these armies? Many answers have been suggested. Here are five of the most common.[207]

A Violent God?

It's disturbing to think about God as violent.

However, it's important to keep in mind that biblical writers often assumed that God's violence meant that humans should *not* be violent. So, Exodus 14:14 says, "The LORD will fight for you; you need only to be still" (NIV).

Elsewhere, it's obvious that many biblical writers didn't embrace a warrior culture precisely because they believed God, far more than their own military, would provide success in battle (e.g., Judg 7; Ps 20:7 [8 Heb.]).[206]

First, some people think that "the LORD of armies" refers to Israel's armies. When David comes before Goliath, he talks about God in such a way, saying to Goliath: "You come against me with sword and spear and javelin; but I come against you in the name of the LORD *tsevaot*, the God of the ranks of Israel, whom you have defied" (1 Sam 17:45 NJPS, alt.). Here, it seems that David clarifies the meaning of "the LORD *tsevaot*" by associating God with the ranks of Israel's armies.

A second possibility is much broader. It sees God's armies as every living being in God's creation. In Genesis 2:1, at the conclusion of a creation story, we read, "Thus the heavens and the earth were finished, and all their multitude" (NRSV). The word translated "multitude" here is *tsevaot*. So, it's possible that the name "the LORD of hosts" means most basically "the LORD of armies," but more generally "the LORD of every living thing."

The third and fourth options pertain less to earth and more to heaven. The third possibility is that the armies are the heavenly bodies that we all can see: the sun and stars. Several texts talk about the stars with precisely this word that usually means "army."[208] For example, in Jeremiah 33:22, God says, "As the host [*tsevaot*] of heaven cannot be counted and the sand of the sea cannot be measured, so I will multiply the descendants of David My servant and the Levites who minister to Me" (NASB). In this case, it's clear that *tsevaot* refers to stars. It's possible that such a meaning is also in view when used alongside "the LORD" as well.

A fourth possibility is that the phrase refers to a council of heavenly beings. Several texts make clear that God is a God of community. In addition to humans and animals on earth, there are angels and celestial beings in heaven. The seraphim, discussed earlier in this chapter, would be one type of them. The Bible doesn't tell us much about who makes up the heavenly court—presumably, so that readers don't end up worshipping them instead of God. Nevertheless, the Bible assumes that God is in fellowship with other beings in heaven. Sometimes, these angels show up on earth as fierce warriors (e.g., Josh 5:13-15). So, it's quite possible that "the LORD of armies" refers to "the LORD of heavenly forces," which is how the CEB chooses to translate this term.

The fifth and final possibility is the most abstract. It appeals to a feature of Hebrew grammar. In many languages, there are ways of changing a word to talk about that word's essential quality. For example, consider the following:

creative + -ity = creativity = the essential feature of being creative

In Hebrew, you could accomplish something similar. Naturally, you didn't add the English "-ity" suffix to the end of Hebrew words. However, you could make words plural. And while that often meant you had more than one of the noun, it could also mean you were talking about the essential feature of that noun.[209] So, it's possible that *tsevaot* doesn't refer to literal armies, but rather to the essential feature(s) of armies: their strength, their power, and their ability to shape history. Thus, the name "the LORD *tsevaot*" may be a way of talking about God Almighty:

the God of strength and power who shapes history. One of the earliest known translations of the Hebrew Bible, the Septuagint, tended to take this approach when translating "the LORD *tsevaot*" into Greek.

Which possibility is the most likely? In most cases, it depends on context. The Old Testament came together over several centuries. In certain periods, particular meanings were probably more prevalent than others.[210] Nevertheless, in almost all cases, God's power and strength are in view, frequently with military overtones. The idea of hospitality, however, isn't being emphasized, even though popular translations put forth the translation "host."

Conclusion

Most of our English Bibles lack words like "thee" and "thou." However, they continue to use words that aren't very common any longer like "behold," "woe," "alas," and "atone." Other times, they use words like "deliver," "redeem," and "host," even though they aren't talking about packages, coupons, or guests. Returning to the Hebrew allows us to understand what the Bible itself envisions. We can recapture meanings that are lost in translation.

Chapter 7
Practices and Objects

Dictionary Versus Encyclopedia Definitions

I've heard of locusts. However, having lived in North America my entire life, I couldn't tell you anything about different types of them. My knowledge about their life cycle is limited to what I've seen on a documentary. Generally, I think of locusts as a type of bug I don't personally need to worry about.

For biblical writers, however, locusts meant destruction. Locusts meant starvation. Locusts meant death. Locusts could even be eaten: after a locust plague destroyed all vegetation, the bodies of dead locusts were one of the few food sources that remained.[211] Biblical writers and their original audiences knew about different types of locusts, as well as the different phases of locusts' life cycles. Whereas I only know one English word for locust, there are about eight Hebrew words for these insects.[212] Even though the English word "locust" does little to scare me, these various Hebrew words evoked fear among the Bible's first audiences.

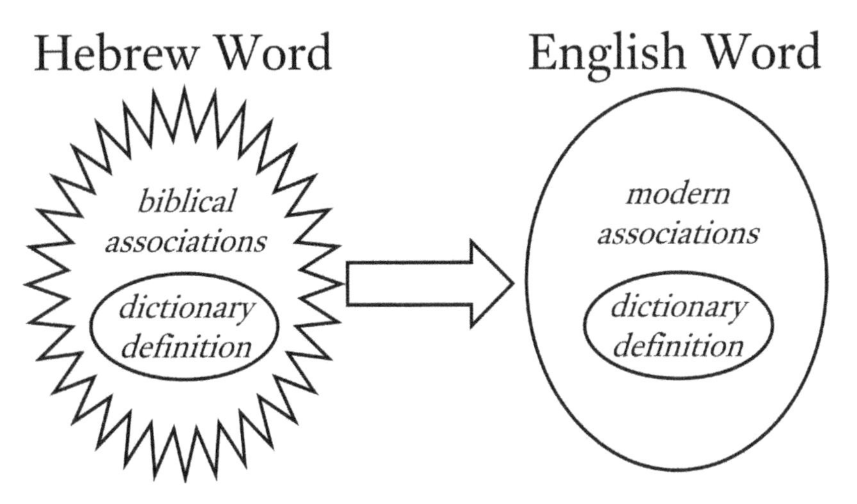

Figure 10

All this to say, the English word "locust" and its various Hebrew counterparts refer to the same type of insect. Yet, these words carry different overtones in each language and time. Associations differ even when Hebrew and English words have the same dictionary definitions: even though dictionary definitions often work across cultures, a word's encyclopedic range of connections frequently does not. (See **Encyclopedic View of a Word**.)

> **Encyclopedic View of a Word**
>
> "The dictionary-like attitude to word meaning... is not very satisfactory. Instead, one must be committed to discovering the *encyclopaedic* view of a word."[213]
>
> —*Kurtis Peters*

People who study communication often use the term "social construction" to talk about how societies construct meaning around particular words. These scholars have made an important distinction between *that it is* and *what it is*. Whereas people from different cultures will readily agree *that locusts exist*, they typically have different ideas about *what locusts are*: Are they a food source? a life-threatening danger? a bug evolved from the same insect as the grasshopper? When it comes to these broader meanings, cultures differ considerably.[214]

This chapter explores Hebrew words whose associations don't transfer well into contemporary English. It gives particular attention to words for:

- remembering
- covenants
- walking
- horses
- gates
- houses

As we'll see, it's often easy to find an English word that accurately replaces the dictionary definition of Hebrew words. However, surrounding associations are often lost in such acts of translation. (See **Words and Worlds**.)

Remember

To "remember" obviously means to call something from the past to mind. In modern society, we associate remembering with certain things: we try to recall facts for an exam, where we put our car keys, and the directions to places we haven't been in a while.

Words and Worlds

"We cannot study words... without their cultural context, information insufficiently undertaken in our currently available lexica.

"What I think the field could truly use is an encyclopedia of words and their usages that include the specific cultural context of the word, whether it is political, economic, social or material.

"[A] word without their worlds, without their internal literary contexts and external cultural realities, is not a word, as any user would have understood it."[215]

—*Mark Smith*

The Hebrew word for "remember" has the same basic meaning, but it carries an entirely different set of associations.[216] It appears over two hundred times in the Bible. Here it is:

	English	Hebrew	Hebrew Transliteration
52.	remember	זָכַר	*zakhar*

The Bible presents remembering as a core component of a right relationship with God. In fact, as part of their relationship together, it goes so far as to present *both* God *and* people as actively involved in remembering.

The story of Noah's ark is so familiar that we can miss how it oddly talks of the way the rainbow in the sky will cause God to remember the covenant. God says:

> When I bring clouds over the earth and the bow is seen in the clouds, I will remember [*zakhar*] my covenant that is between me and you and every living creature of all flesh; and the waters shall never again become a flood to destroy all flesh. When the bow is in the clouds, I will see it and remember [*zakhar*] the everlasting covenant between God and every living creature of all flesh that is on the earth. (Gen 9:14-16 NRSV)

What's going on here? Doesn't God know everything? Why does God need reminders—a sticky note in the sky?

These questions take on added significance when we discover that about seventy times in the Bible, God is the subject of the verb *zakhar*. Repeatedly, the psalmists pray that God will remember them: "Remember [*zakhar*] me, O Lord, when you show favor to your people; help me when you deliver them" (Ps 106:4

NRSV). They also pray that God will remember compassion while not remembering human sin. Psalm 25:6-7 is typical:

> LORD, remember [*zakhar*] your compassion and faithful love—
> they are forever!
> But don't remember [*zakhar*] the sins of my youth or my wrongdoing.
> Remember [*zakhar*] me only according to your faithful love
> for the sake of your goodness, LORD. (CEB)

This emphasis on God remembering the bond with people but forgetting sin is similar to what is found as the book of Leviticus draws to a close. Speaking about Israel, God says:

> But if they confess their and their ancestors' guilt for the wrongdoing they did to me, and for their continued opposition to me... then I will remember [*zakhar*] my covenant with Jacob. I will also remember [*zakhar*] my covenant with Isaac. And my covenant with Abraham. And I will remember [*zakhar*] the land.... For their sake I will remember [*zakhar*] the covenant with the first generation, the ones I brought out of Egypt's land in the sight of all the nations, in order to be their God; I am the LORD. (Lev 26:40-45 CEB)

While there are many examples like this one in the Bible, questions remain. Why does God need to remember the covenant? Doesn't God know everything? Wouldn't God always have the covenant in mind? What's going on?

It's helpful to keep a few things in mind. First, the Old Testament loves talking about God in human terms. Verbs for remembering are no exception. As Christians who believe that God became human, such portrayals shouldn't disturb us any more than the incarnation. Presumably, God is capable of anything, including not needing reminders. However, the Bible implies that God has self-imposed limitations for the sake of relating to humanity in genuine ways.

Second, the associations linked to the English word "remember" differ from those linked to the Hebrew word *zakhar*. We usually talk about remembering impersonal objects: concepts, ideas, facts, where we put something, where we heard something, or how a joke goes. In the Bible, the verb *zakhar* is linked more to people than objects. God remembers people, as well as relationship concepts, like covenants. As we will see, people are also called to remember God.

Finally, while the basic meaning of *zakhar* is "remember," we're not talking about momentarily recalling a fact. The verb relates to reflection that usually leads to action. As one scholar puts it, "God's remembering has to do with his attention and intervention, whether in grace or judgment."[217] Another scholar goes even further, saying, "When God is challenged to 'remember' the meaning is better taken as 'pay attention to.'"[218] So, while "remember" often works to translate *zakhar*, there are times when it means "reflectively call to mind and act accordingly." For example, Psalm 74:2 reads: "Remember [*zakhar*] your congregation that you took as your own long ago" (CEB). This prayer asks God to thoughtfully consider the chosen people and to act powerfully on their behalf. Similarly, when God remembers people like Samson and Hannah, God considers them and answers their prayers (Judg 16:28; 1 Sam 1:11-20).

The previous discussion has focused on God remembering God's people. When we read the Old Testament carefully, a matter of highest importance is the people remembering God. The Bible even suggests that salvation depends on remembrance. God's people need to engage in two types of remembering.

First, they need to remember all that God has done for them: how they were once slaves, how God rescued them from slavery, how God has acted decisively on their behalf. This type of remembering appears repeatedly in Deuteronomy. Here are some examples:

> You may say to yourselves, "These nations are stronger than we are. How can we drive them out?" But do not be afraid of them; remember well [literally, "remembering, remember!"; *zakhar* appears twice in a row for emphasis] what the LORD your God did to Pharaoh and to all Egypt. (Deut 7:17-18 NIV)

> Remember [*zakhar*] the LORD your God! He's the one who gives you the strength to be prosperous in order to establish the covenant he made with your ancestors. (Deut 8:18 CEB)

> Remember [*zakhar*] that you were slaves in Egypt and the LORD your God redeemed you from there. That is why I command you to do this. (Deut 24:18 NIV)

The Benefits of Remembering

"Remembering God's laws brings encouragement (Ps 119:52). Remembering his name at night means turning to him in prayerful meditation (Ps 119:55; cf. 63:6[7]). To remember God's greatness is an antidote to fear (Neh 4:14 [8]; cf. Deut 7:18)."[219]

—*Leslie C. Allen*

Remembering what God has done explains why we should be faithful. (See **The Benefits of Remembering**.) In fact, it's precisely when people forget God's goodness that they chase false gods. Judges 8 talks about this idea, describing the time after Israel's leader Gideon: "No sooner had Gideon died than the Israelites again prostituted themselves to the Baals. They set up Baal-Berith as their god and did not remember [*zakhar*] the LORD their God, who had rescued them from the hands of all their enemies on every side" (Judg 8:33-34 NIV; cf. Neh 9:17; Ps 106:7; Isa 17:10). When we forget the ways God has rescued and provided for us, false gods prove too attractive.

God's people are called, secondly, to remember God's commandments. At times, people need to remember particular holy days, like Sabbaths (Exod 20:8) and the day when they came out of Egypt (Exod 13:3). Other times, remembering is more general, extending to all of God's commandments.

We previously discussed how the rainbow served as a reminder for God of the covenant with Noah. People, of course, need reminders as well. The book of Numbers explains how that should work for the Israelites:

> Speak to the Israelites and say to them: Make fringes on the edges of your clothing for all time. Have them put blue cords on the fringe on the edges. This will be your fringe. You will see it and remember [*zakhar*] all the LORD's commands and do them. Then you won't go exploring the lusts of your own heart or your eyes. In this way you'll remember [*zakhar*] to do all my commands. Then you will be holy to your God. (Num 15:38-40 CEB; cf. Deut 6:8-9)

As with God, remembering isn't merely bringing something to mind. It also entails reflecting on what comes to mind and then acting accordingly. In this case, the fringes remind the Israelites of God's commands so that they'll then act in accordance with those commands. (See **What about Christians Today?**)

What about Christians Today?

"Jewish prayer shawls have fringes attached to the corners. Our Lord wore fringes, i.e. tassels on his clothes, and the sick touched them to obtain healing (Matt. 9:20; 14:36). This Old Testament requirement finds no equivalent in the New Testament. Christians, however, have frequently taken to wearing various badges and signs of their faith; the most popular and significant has undoubtedly been the cross, a reminder to its owners to deny themselves, take up their crosses daily and follow Christ (Luke 9:23)."[220]

—*Gordon Wenham*

Remembrance, then, constitutes a core component of faithful living. God remembers people in an expanded sense of the word "remember." God brings people to mind and acts according to their requests and commitments. People remember both what God has done for them and what God expects of them. In the Bible, remembering is essential to the life of faith.[221]

Covenant

In English, the word "covenant" refers to a binding agreement between two parties. That definition works well for the Hebrew word as well, which makes nearly three hundred appearances in the Bible:

	English	Hebrew	Hebrew Transliteration
53.	covenant	בְּרִית	*berit*

The English word has connections with contracts, negotiations, deals, and pacts. They are often made official when documents are signed. Many covenants in the United States involve real estate, stipulating what land can and cannot be used for. Lawyers draw them up. When one party violates the terms of a covenant or contract, courts often get involved. That's true not only of land covenants but also of marriage covenants.

In the Bible, the word *berit* also describes a binding agreement. Occasionally, it refers to a marriage arrangement (Mal 2:14). More commonly, the Bible talks about a *berit* as a treaty, alliance, or trade agreement between two leaders. For example, King Solomon of Israel enters into a trade agreement or *berit* with King Hiram of Tyre, in which Israel sends wheat and olive oil to Tyre in exchange for cedar and pinewood (1 Kgs 5:10-12 [24-26 Heb.]).

The Bible speaks about these agreements between people dozens of times, but it most frequently uses the word *berit* to describe the relationship between God and God's people. The fundamental idea here is that God and the covenant people are bound together in the closest imaginable ways. Many signs and symbols can accompany a *berit* to drive home its significance. For example, Abraham and his male offspring are commanded to be circumcised as a sign of their covenant with God (Gen 17). In other words, at a central point on their bodies—and one of the most sensitive places—they are to be physically and irreversibly marked as belonging to God. In essence, their penises are branded as God's property. Later texts will pick up on this idea of circumcision and talk about the circumcision of the heart (e.g., Jer 4:4). The idea is that our hearts should be different: vulnerable and sensitive to God and God's ways.

Today, we talk about signing a contract. In the Bible, a *berit* wouldn't be signed. Instead, it would be "cut." In fact, most of the time when our English Bibles talk about someone "making a covenant," the Hebrew literally talks about someone "cutting a *berit*." This idea of cutting comes to the forefront not only with circumcision but also with another practice mentioned a couple of times in the Bible.

Here, "cutting a *berit*" meant cattle were killed and the animals' bodies sliced in two.[222] The halves of these carcasses would face each other. Next, those making the covenant would walk between the bleeding corpses. The idea was that those who violate the covenant deserve to become like the corpses.[223] The Bible talks about this practice with regard to both people (Jer 34:18-20) and God (Gen 15:17-18).

It's amazing that God willingly enters into such an agreement. However, we see something similar in the covenant with Noah. Hebrew doesn't have a word for "rainbow." It simply uses the word for "bow"—a weapon that shoots arrows. When God commits never to flood the earth again, the bow in the sky stands as a reminder. And as commentators have pointed out at least since the Middle Ages, this bow points toward heaven, toward God.[224] It's as though God is saying, "If I again destroy the earth in this way, may I be shot."

Thus, covenant making wasn't something taken lightly. It created a powerful bond between two parties. (See **Oaths, Commitment, Love, Friendship**.) *Berit*-breakers could expect death. The word *berit* thus carried considerably more weight than the English word "covenant."

Oaths, Commitment, Love, Friendship

"The terms for 'covenant'...are distributed according to two semantic fields: *oath and commitment* on the one hand, *love and friendship* on the other.... [The] basic terms for 'covenant' in Hebrew...express pledge and commitment, which actually create the covenant. On the other hand, any settlement between two parties is conditioned by good will or some kind of mutual understanding which enables the conclusion of an agreement, and this is why covenantal relations were expressed by terms like 'grace,' 'brotherhood,' 'peace,' 'love,' 'friendship,' etc."[225]

—*Moshe Weinfeld*

Berit also had an interesting connection with food. When two people made a covenant together, they would often share a meal (Gen 26:28-31; 31:44-55 [31:44-32:1 Heb.]). Meanwhile, a covenant between God and people could involve animal or grain sacrifices (e.g., Ps 50:5). These rites were somewhat akin to a meal with God (and an early precursor to the Eucharist). Salt plays an important role with covenants at times (Num 18:19; 2 Chron 13:5). The biblical world obviously lacked refrigeration and freezers. To make something last, you covered it with salt. So, as a symbol of how covenants were to last, salt was used in offerings.

One remarkable feature of the Bible is just how frequently God enters into covenants with people. Because the term "Old Testament" means "Old Covenant," people sometimes assume that the Old Testament describes just one old covenant that is then replaced in the New Testament. However, the Old Testament actually talks about God making new covenants with a wide variety of people and even animals:

- Noah, his family, "and every living being" (Gen 6:18; 9:9-17)
- Abraham (Gen 15:18, 17:2-21)
- The first generation of Israelites to leave Egypt (Exod 19:5; 23:32; 24:7-8; 31:16; 34:10-28; Lev 26:9-45)
- Phinehas (Num 25:12-13) and Levitical Priests (Neh 13:29; Jer 33:21; Mal 2:4-8)
- The second generation of Israelites to leave Egypt (Deut 4:13–5:3; 29:1-29 [28:69–29:28 Heb.]; Josh 24:25)
- David (2 Sam 23:5; 2 Chron 21:7; Ps 89; Jer 33:21)
- The Judahites and Israelites under Asa (2 Chron 15:12)
- Joash and the people (2 Kgs 11:17)
- Hezekiah (2 Chron 29:10)
- Josiah and residents of Jerusalem (2 Kgs 23:3; 2 Chron 34:31)
- People under Ezra (Ezra 10:3)
- Large animals, birds, and small animals (Hos 2:20)

It's worth noting that these covenants differ from one another. Sometimes, God seems to do all the work with little expected of humans (as with Noah in Gen 9). Other times, the terms of the covenant entail (1) God working decisively on the people's behalf, (2) God expecting the people to be exclusively committed to God in return, and (3) God promising blessings for obedience and curses for disobedience. Such features show up in a book like Deuteronomy, and they bear some similarities with other international agreements found in the ancient world.

A Covenant Prayer in the Wesleyan Tradition

I am no longer my own, but thine.
Put me to what thou wilt, rank me with whom thou wilt.
Put me to doing, put me to suffering.
Let me be employed by thee or laid aside for thee,
Exalted for thee or brought low for thee.
Let me be full, let me be empty.
Let me have all things, let me have nothing.
I freely and heartily yield all things
To thy pleasure and disposal.
And now, O glorious and blessed God,
Father, Son, and Holy Spirit,
Thou art mine, and I am thine. So be it.
And the covenant which I have made on earth,
Let it be ratified in heaven. **Amen.**[226]

Many Christians today believe that God still calls them into a covenant relationship. The Wesleyan tradition, for example, often celebrates covenant renewal services near the first of the calendar year. (See **A Covenant Prayer in the Wesleyan Tradition**.) Circumcision and animal sacrifices aren't part of these New Year's services. While I'm relieved that they aren't, it's worth noting that biblical covenants involved shocking (think of the blood!) practices that drove home the covenant's significance.

Walk

My wife and I like to go for walks after supper. It keeps us active, lets us talk to each other, and puts us both in better moods. We live in Iowa, so we rarely walk in winter months.

Hebrew has its own word for walking, and at its most basic level, it means the same thing as the English word "walk." It shows up over 1,400 times in the Bible:

	English	Hebrew	Hebrew Transliteration
54.	walk, go	הָלַךְ	*halakh*

Both "walk" and *halakh* refer to moving on your feet.

However, walking in the Bible is different from walking today. I see walking largely as a pastime. For people of the Bible, however, walking was their main mode of transportation. They obviously lacked cars. Furthermore, the average person didn't use horses, as we'll see later in this chapter. At times, a donkey might walk alongside a person, though these animals were often used to carry goods rather than people (e.g., Gen 42:26).[227]

In the Bible, walking was a way of life, and not an easy one. People rarely had the luxury of moving on level ground. In fact, topographically, biblical lands display an incredible amount of diversity in a very small area.[228] Consider the strip of land running from the Mediterranean Coast through Jerusalem to the Dead Sea. This strip of land is only about fifty miles wide. Yet, it is home to several ecological zones with their own climates and vegetation[229]:

	Name	Elevation	Average Annual Rainfall	Features
A	Coastal Plains	Begins at Sea Level	20 in or 50 cm (dryer than about 80 percent of US states)	Home to the Philistines
B	Low Hills (or Shephelah)	Highest Points: 1,500 ft or 460 m (comparable to the elevation of some inland US cities like Pittsburgh)	23.5 in or 60 cm (dryer than about 75 percent of US states)	A place of conflict between Philistines and Israelites
C	Central Highlands	Jerusalem: 2,400 ft or 730 m (similar in altitude to US cities in or near mountains, like Asheville, NC; Spokane, WA; and Las Vegas, NV)	27.5–31.5 in or 70–80 cm (near the average precipitation of the entire US)	Home to Jerusalem and much of the biblical story
D	Jordan Valley and Dead Sea	1,200 ft or 370 m *below sea level* (the lowest place on earth, about 1,000 ft lower than Death Valley, CA)	Less than 4 in or 10 cm (about half the rainfall of Nevada, the driest US state)	Desert land with few inhabitants

Here's a map showing these areas with corresponding letters.[230]

As you can see, in a relatively small amount of space, the land displays considerable hills, mountains, and valleys. In fact, from Jerusalem to the Dead Sea is about fifteen miles. In that short span, the land drops about two-thirds of a mile.

All this to say, walking this land wasn't an easy matter of moving forward. It often entailed traveling up or down as well. Hebrew vocabulary reflects this. Common verbs mean "go up" or "go down."

Texts like the introduction to Jonah are filled with verbs of motion:

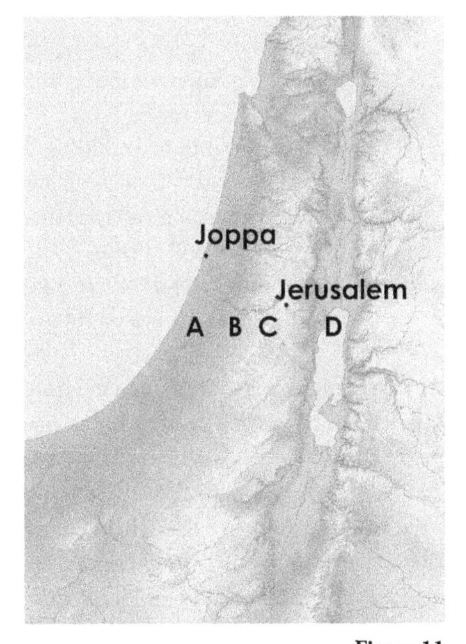

Figure 11

> The word of the LORD came to Jonah…"Arise, go [*halakh*] to Nineveh the great city and cry against it, for their wickedness has come up before Me." But Jonah rose up to flee to Tarshish from the presence of the LORD. So he went down to Joppa, found a ship which was going to Tarshish, paid the fare and went down into it to go with them to Tarshish from the presence of the LORD. (Jonah 1:1-3 NASB)

The text doesn't say exactly where Jonah starts. Most inhabitants of Israel and Judah lived in the Central Highlands. So, when the text says, "he went down to Joppa," it's likely talking about the prophet moving from the central mountainous region to the coastal city of Joppa (also in the map on the previous page).

There's also a sense in which God's presence is in the heavens (thus the talk of Nineveh's wickedness *coming up* before God). So, Jonah's going down, first to Joppa and then into the hold of a ship, signals his trying to flee from God—albeit rather foolishly.

As this brief text illustrates, we can understand the Bible more easily when we understand walking and what it entailed on biblical lands. Isaiah 40 is another good example. The text proclaims a message of hope to refugees forced out of Jerusalem and into Babylon:

> A voice is crying out:
> "Clear the LORD's way in the desert!
> Make a level highway in the wilderness for our God!
> Every valley will be raised up,
> and every mountain and hill will be flattened.
> Uneven ground will become level,
> and rough terrain a valley plain.
> The LORD's glory will appear,
> and all humanity will see it together;
> the LORD's mouth has commanded it." (Isa 40:3-5 CEB)

At first glance, this text may seem confusing: why fill in valleys and level mountains? Aren't valleys and mountains places of beauty? Some people even talk of personal encounters with God in terms of "mountaintop experiences."

When we keep in mind that transportation took place on foot in biblical times, these verses from Isaiah make more sense. Amid the tumultuous terrain, there's a vision of a highway that can be easily traveled. Moreover, it will be traveled by none other than God! The idea is that this pathway should be fitting for Israel's king, the Lord their God. There are even hints in this text of the refugees themselves returning from exile to Jerusalem.[231] They travel along this path with easy walking. The people move with God on the smooth road home from exile.

While the preceding passage is one of great hope, earlier passages in Isaiah talk of God's judgment and punishment on wickedness. Several times, the text uses images of thorny plants covering the land to talk about God's judgment (Isa 5:6; 7:23-25; 34:13). To modern eyes, such images might seem out of place alongside images of destruction and desolation. I certainly don't like thorn bushes, but I have plants with thorns on my property, some of which I've planted myself, like raspberry bushes. So why are thorns seen as images of God's judgment?

Again, it's important to keep in mind that people traveled primarily on foot. Commoners usually wore sandals while the poor went barefoot.[232] Clothes were typically made of wool or linen, not leather.[233] Thorns and briars made walking painful, even dangerous. They were a sign that a land was abandoned and neglected.

Other dangers accompanied the simple act of walking. In Genesis 21, Abraham and Sarah force Hagar and Ishmael out of their house:

> Early next morning Abraham took some bread and a skin of water, and gave them to Hagar. He placed them over her shoulder, together with the child, and sent her away. And she wandered [*halakh*] about in the wilderness of Beer-sheba. When the water was gone from the skin, she left the child under one of the bushes, and went [*halakh*] and sat down at a distance, a bowshot away; for she thought, "Let me not look on as the child dies." And sitting thus afar, she burst into tears. (Gen 21:14-16 NJPS)

In what follows, it takes nothing short of an act of God to save Hagar and Ishmael. Although walking was the primary mode of transportation in biblical times, it could quickly become life-threatening.

On the Road Again

God's people are often on the move:

- from Ur to Canaan with Abraham
- from Canaan to Egypt with Joseph
- from Egypt to the wilderness with Moses
- from the wilderness to the promised land with Joshua
- from the promised land to Assyria and Babylonia in different exiles
- from Babylon to Jerusalem as told in Ezra and Nehemiah

The author of Hebrews writes, "For this world is not our permanent home; we are looking forward to a home yet to come" (13:14 NLT). Perhaps Old Testament travelogues can inspire us as we journey to our home that awaits us.

Dangers come not only from the environment but also from other people. In Numbers 20, the Israelites are trying to make their way from Egypt to the land of promise. They approach the king of Edom, asking his permission to pass through his land: "Please let us cross through [*avar*] your land. We won't pass through [*avar*] any field or vineyard, or drink water from any well. We will walk [*halakh*] on the King's Highway and not turn to the right or to the left until we have crossed [*avar*] your border" (20:17 CEB). Edom refuses. When Israel again requests to pass through on foot, Edom comes out heavily armed, prepared to go to war against any trespassers. Israel takes the long route around Edom. (See **On the Road Again**.)

Life Spent Wandering

"For nomadic groups it is not surprising that *halakh* should represent the focus of activity. They live 'on the move'; their life is mostly spent wandering. This experience may lead to an understanding of human life as a way or a pilgrimage.... The word *halakh*—above and beyond its concrete spatial meaning—takes on the meanings 'conform to a norm, follow someone, behave.'"[234]

—*F. J. Helfmeyer*

Walking, then, was no easy task. Yet, it was a way of life for most people in the Bible. Walking could even be used as a metaphor to talk about one's religious life. (See **Life Spent Wandering**.) We read in Jeremiah:

The LORD proclaims:
Stop at the crossroads and look around;
ask for the ancient paths.
Where is the good way?
Then walk [*halakh*] in it
and find a resting place for yourselves.
But you said, "We won't go [*halakh*]!" (6:16 CEB)

The prophet later returns to the same imagery, saying that the people have neglected God's paths to the point that the whole country has become ruined. It's like a land without reliable roads:

Yet my people have forgotten me;
they have offered sacrifices to a lie.
And so they have stumbled along the way,
even along the ancient paths.
They have taken [*halakh*] side roads,

not the main roads.
They have ruined their country
and brought utter shame on it. (Jer 18:15-16 CEB)

Meanwhile, the Psalms present the enormous benefits of walking in God's paths:

Those whose way is blameless—
who walk [*halakh*] in the LORD's Instruction [*torah*]—are truly happy!
Those who guard God's laws are truly happy!
They seek God with all their hearts [*lev*].
They don't even do anything wrong!
They walk [*halakh*] in God's ways. (119:1-3 CEB)

Although walking was no doubt challenging in ancient times, happiness and rest could be found by walking God's ways. By remembering the different associations that *halakh* evokes, we can gain a better understanding of the biblical text.

Horses

It's not just practices like walking that pick up a variety of associations based on the culture in view. It's also physical objects and organisms. (See **Objects and Cultures**.)

Objects and Cultures

"Words which refer to concrete physical objects must be defined in ways which reflect their symbolic value to a particular culture."[235]

—*Carolyn Leeb*

This even includes horses. Many Hebrew students learn the following Hebrew word early in their studies because it's useful in noun paradigms:

	English	Hebrew	Hebrew Transliteration
55.	horse	סוּס	*sus*

There's little doubt that this word is best translated "horse." Both *sus* and "horse" refer to the same animal. Yet, this animal serves very different purposes in biblical and modern societies.

Today, horses are associated with racing and hobbies. Traditional societies including the Amish use horses for transportation and farming. However, in developed cultures cars and tractors have replaced much of what horses used to accomplish. Consequently, for most people, horseback riding is more likely to take place while vacationing in a scenic area rather than amid everyday life. Horses may be ridden on dude ranches out west, or by police in busy cities, but they typically are connected with sport and entertainment today.

Horses: Then and Now

"In the Bible, the horse functioned only as a military machine and not as a power source for agricultural or other daily tasks."[236]

—*Oded Borowski*

In biblical times, horses were rarely connected with races or hobbies. (See **Horses: Then and Now**.) In fact, they weren't even used first and foremost as instruments of transport or agriculture.[237] Instead, horses served military purposes.[238] They were the closest thing to a tank in the biblical world. The Hebrew word *sus* commonly appears in verses that talk about swords, arrows, bows, shields, weapons, warriors, or battles.[239] (See **Figure 12**, which depicts King Assurbanipal of the Assyrians [a superpower to Jerusalem's north] using a spear to defeat a lion in the seventh century BCE.[240])

Figure 12

So, rather than seeing horses as racing or hobby animals, the Bible presents horses as a means of warcraft. Theologically, the Bible makes three very important and related statements about horses. First, God has given Israel victory over enemies with horses. Many verses talk about God rescuing Israel from enemy warhorses. Exodus 15:19 is typical: "When the horses [*sus*] of Pharaoh with his chariots and his chariot drivers went into the sea, the LORD brought back the waters of the sea upon them; but the Israelites walked through the sea on dry ground" (NRSV). A number of verses commemorate these sorts of victories (Exod 14:9, 23; 15:1, 21; Deut 11:4; Josh 11:4, 6, 9; Ps 76:6 [7 Heb.]).

The second theological statement regards not the past but the future. People should trust God to provide victory, not depend on horses: "Some trust in chariots and some in horses (*sus*), but we trust in the name of the LORD our God" (Ps 20:7 [8 Heb.] NIV). People wanting to live out the Bible today might say, "Some trust in tanks and some in military drones, but we trust in the name of the Lord our God."[241] (See **YHWH Versus Horses**.)

YHWH Versus Horses

"In all parts of the biblical tradition, it is affirmed that the power of Yahweh will defeat oppressive kings who have horses and chariots."[242]

—*Walter Brueggemann*

In the prophets, the worst thing people could do is trust in the military might that comes from horses, rather than rely on God:

Doom [*Hoy*] to those going down to Egypt for help!
They rely on horses [*sus*],
trust in chariots because they are many,
and on riders because they are very strong.
But they don't look to the holy one of Israel;
they don't seek the LORD.
But God also knows how to bring disaster [*ra*];
he has not taken back his words.
God will rise up against the house of evildoers [*raa*]
and against the help of those who do wrong.
Egypt is human and not divine;
their horses [*sus*] are flesh and not spirit [*ruakh*].
The LORD will extend his hand;
the helper will stumble,
those helped will fall,
and they will all die together. (Isa 31:1-3 CEB; cf. Deut 20:1; Ezek 17:15)

Although horses were immensely attractive militarily, they did not compare to the power that comes from God.

Third and related, horses are forbidden in Israel (Deut 17:16). In an act of apostasy, King Solomon boldly disobeyed this command (1 Kgs 4:26 [5:6 Heb.]; 10:25-29). Subsequent kings did as well, so that Isaiah later mourns how the land is filled with not only idols but also horses (Isa 2:7b–8a). Micah's vision of God purifying Israel includes these words: "'In that day,' declares the LORD, 'I will destroy your horses [*sus*] from among you and demolish your chariots'" (Mic 5:10 [9 Heb.] NIV). Just as Jesus refuses to take up the sword in the New Testament (Matt 26:52; Luke 22:51; John 18:11; cf. Matt 5:39), God wants Israel free of horses in the Old Testament.

Essential to understanding these Old Testament passages is that horses served a very different function in biblical Israel than in the modern world. The words "horse" and *sus* refer to the same animal: dictionary definitions fit perfectly. However, the function of a horse in each society differs markedly. The Hebrew word *sus* belonged to a similar field of ideas as words like "tank," "missile," "bomber," and "drone" today. The challenging message of the Bible—especially for those who live in countries with advanced militaries—is that we should neither trust in our nation's military might nor invest in military weaponry but instead rely on the God who is more powerful than any weapon.

Gates

When I think of a gate, I think of my grandparents' farm in Wisconsin. Around the barnyard was an electric fence. An old gate was there if you needed to enter. You'd undo the chain, and it would creakily swing open. It was big enough that a car or tractor could fit through. I also have a couple of gates on my backyard fence. They keep pets and toddlers inside.

Here's the Hebrew word for gate:

	English	Hebrew	Hebrew Transliteration
56.	gate	שַׁעַר	*shaar*

This word is quite common, popping up 375 times in the Old Testament.

When we read about gates in the Bible, it's clear that they usually refer to a type of door or entrance structure on an open-air wall or fence. However, important differences persist beyond these basic similarities with the English.

The first reference to a gate is in Genesis 19:1, which talks of Abraham's nephew Lot "sitting in the gate [*shaar*] of Sodom" during the evening. None of the gates I regularly encounter would be places for sitting *inside* of.

The next reference occurs a couple of chapters later. God promises many wonderful things to Abraham: "I will indeed bless [*berakh*] you, and I will make your offspring as numerous as the stars of heaven and as the sand that is on the seashore [literally "the lip of the sea"]. And your offspring shall possess the gate [*shaar*] of their enemies" (Gen 22:17 NRSV). The verse is powerful and moving. However, the talk of possessing gates seems odd. Why doesn't the text talk about possessing enemies' treasures? Why is there an emphasis on gates?

Both of these passages, as well as dozens of other biblical texts, make more sense when we understand the cultural function of gates in the biblical world. Although "gate" and *shaar* have similar *dictionary* definitions, their *encyclopedia* definitions differ.

Most of the time, biblical gates didn't belong on fences.[243] They belonged on city walls. These city walls were absolutely massive, big enough to keep out invading armies. Capital cities frequently had walls made out of solid rock. Other cities usually had casemate walls, meaning there were chambers in the walls that could be used for rooms or storage.

Unless fortified, gates were the weakest part of city walls. Invading armies tended to focus their attacks there (cf. 2 Sam 11:14-25). If an invading army could take possession of the city gate, the rest of the city would fall, too. That's why Genesis 22 talks of Abraham's descendants possessing the gates of their enemies. There's no reason to talk about the enemies' treasures, houses, or valuables. If the gate fell, everything else would, too. Isaiah 24:12 drives this point home, equating a city's ruin with its destroyed gates: "The city is left in ruins, its gate [*shaar*] is battered to pieces" (NIV). The fate of ancient cities depended on their gates.

Given the importance of gates, people developed certain ways of fortifying them. Instead of a single door between the city walls, they developed a system of defenses, often with multiple doors. As Figure 13 illustrates, they elongated the gate opening, giving it several chambers so that any invading army who made it through the outermost door would then have to face troops, more doors, and additional obstacles before making it into the city itself.[244] Defenders would construct the doors out of thick wood and overlay it with metal so that it couldn't catch on fire. Horizontal bars held these doors in place (cf. Ps 147:13).

Figure 13 provides an aerial view of what many gates would have looked like in biblical times. The place marked 1 represents the area just outside the gate system. The various chambers marked 2 would provide places for troops to gather and attack anyone making it through an outside door. Meanwhile, 3 would be the area in the city just inside the gate system. Lastly, 4 represents the beginning of a (casemate) wall that would extend around the entire city.

Because of this type of structure, we have verses in the Bible like 2 Samuel 18:24: "Now David was sitting between the two gates [*shaar*]" (NASB). The idea here is that there would have been an outside door (near #1) and a city door (near #3). David was between them, near or in the chambers marked #2.

Aside from biblical scholars, hardly anyone thinks of this elaborate structure when they see the word "gate." Yet, the Hebrew word *shaar* would refer to such a system—even though it's typically translated with the English "gate." (See **Heads on Gates**.)

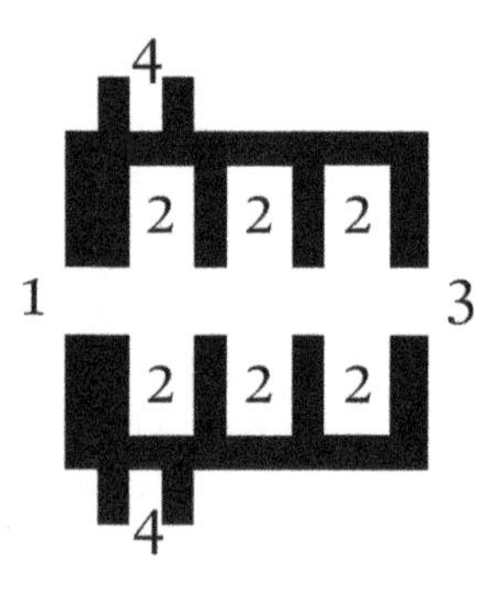

Figure 13

What happened to these biblical gates in times of peace? At night, gates would often be closed (Josh 2:5). However, during the daytime, people would pass through the gates into or out of the city.[246] Meanwhile, the gate's chambers would serve as centers for public activities.

Sometimes, these gates functioned like marketplaces (e.g., 2 Kgs 7:1). Additionally, a city's older population would gather in these chambers, uphold community standards, and administer justice. This group of elders would, for example, decide what to do when someone was killed (Josh 20:4).[247] Archaeologists have even discovered the benches on which such elders would sit.[248]

Heads on Gates

Psalm 24:7 (cf. 24:9) talks about gates having heads: "Lift up your heads, O ye gates; and be ye lift up, ye everlasting doors; and the King of glory shall come in" (KJV). If this verse sounds familiar, it provides the words to a memorable chorus in Handel's *Messiah*. But what could it envision when it talks of gates having heads?

As we've just discussed, gates were part of massive stone wall structures. At times, the tops of gateposts would be connected by a horizontal crossbeam called a "lintel." The idea here is that the King of glory could not fit beneath these crossbeams. The King is simply too great. So, the poet imagines the gates lifting their heads—these lintels—as the heavenly King enters.[245]

As the book of Isaiah draws to a close, the prophet paints hope-filled images of what God has in store for Jerusalem—which had previously been looted and destroyed. Former inhabitants will return, along with riches of every kind. Even kings will travel to Jerusalem to share their wealth and service. At a climactic moment, we read: "Your gates [*shaar*] shall always be open; day and night they shall not be shut, so that nations shall bring you their wealth, with their kings led in procession" (Isa 60:11 NRSV). In the past, Jerusalem's gates were barred shut to keep out invading armies. Now, in a grand reversal, they shall remain open day and night so that all peoples may come and experience Jerusalem's joy.

Without better alternatives, the English word "gate" is the best way to translate *shaar*. The dictionary definitions of each word roughly overlap. However, "gate" doesn't carry all the meanings and significance attached to the Hebrew *shaar*. By paying attention to the encyclopedia definitions surrounding Hebrew words, we can better understand God's word.[249]

Houses

Students learning biblical Hebrew often have an easy time with its word for "house." The word sounds like something a zealous realtor might say: "Buy it!"

	English	Hebrew	Hebrew Transliteration
57.	house	בַּיִת	*bayit*

This word is very popular, showing up over two thousand times in the Hebrew Bible.

The Bible uses this word in a variety of ways. It can describe:

- a palace: "the king's house [*bayit*]" (e.g., 2 Sam 11:2)
- a temple or shrine: "the house [*bayit*] of God" (e.g., Judg 18:31)
- a household, descendants, or dynasty: "David's house [*bayit*]" (e.g., 2 Sam 3:1)
- a place where people live: "Elisha's house [*bayit*]" (e.g., 2 Kgs 5:9)

This last use is similar to how the English word "house" is commonly used.

In other words, the dictionary definitions of "house" and *bayit* largely overlap. Yet, important differences remain. Obviously, a house twenty-five hundred years ago would lack some of the amenities we've come to enjoy and expect today. Air conditioning, electricity, and usually plumbing would be missing.[250] However, houses in the biblical periods were usually more than simple huts.

Archaeologists in Israel have uncovered many dwellings made of bricks, clay, and stones.[251] They're often called "four-room houses."[252] This name, however, is somewhat misleading because these structures didn't necessarily have four rooms. The house's door led to a central room. In the back there frequently was a room. Then pillars or walls tended to divide the remainder of the first floor, sometimes giving the bottom level four rooms. Among other things, the first floor was used for storing commodities and food preparation. (See **Figures 14 and 15**.[253])

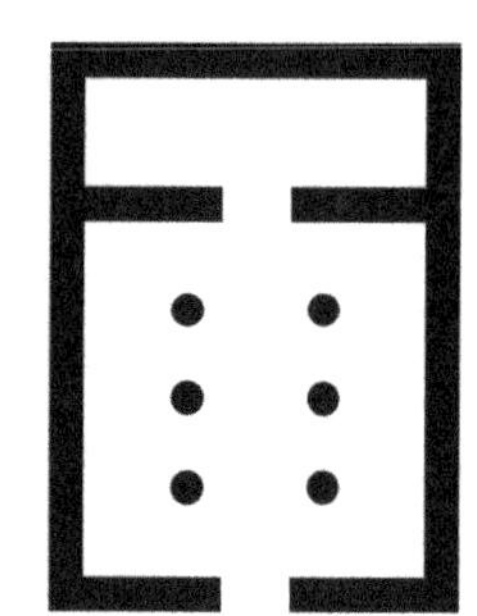

Figure 14

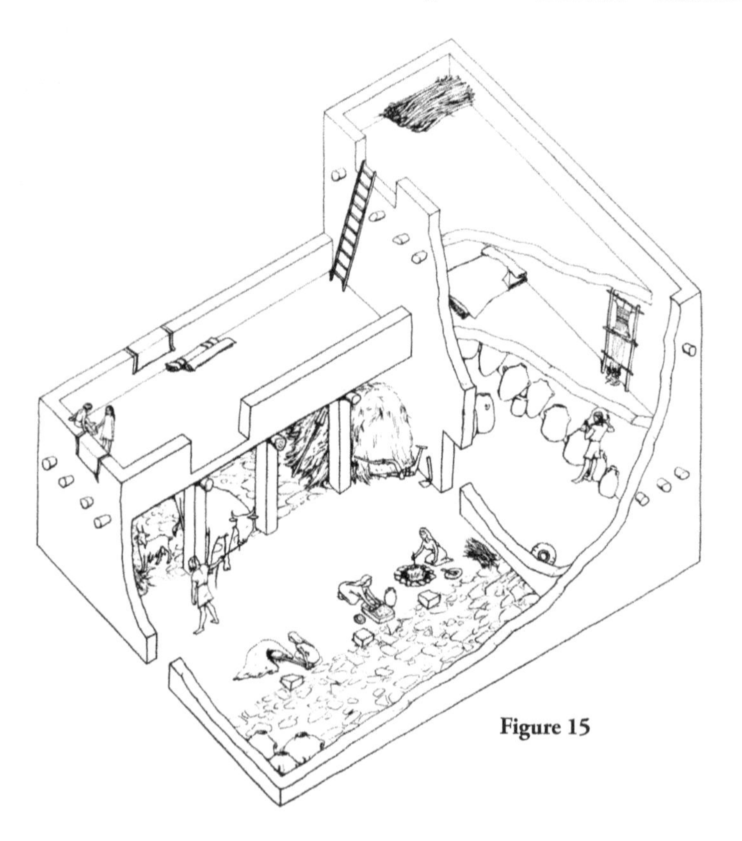

Figure 15

A ladder or staircase often led to a second floor (sometimes even a third floor). Many scholars think that the main living area was on this second floor, where there would be greater access to light and the open air.[254] We find references to the second floor in different parts of the Bible. For example, the prophet Jeremiah denounces those who build houses corruptly, failing to give workers what they deserve: "Woe [*hoy*] to him who builds his house [*bayit*] without righteousness [*tsedeq*, related to *tsedaqah*] And his upper rooms without justice [*mishpat*], Who uses his neighbor's services without pay And does not give him his wages" (Jer 22:13 NASB). The phrase "upper rooms" refers to the second level of the *bayit*.

Quite a few people could stay inside these houses: grandparents, parents, children, slaves, hired hands, and guests. However, given high mortality rates, one might find only a pair of parents and two or three children in a house. Frequently, farm animals stayed inside the *bayit* as well: sheep, goats, and cattle.[255] They would naturally stay on the first floor. (Donkeys don't do well on ladders!) Keeping farm animals inside a house strikes most of us as odd, if not stinky. However, it kept the animals protected, and animals were often the most valuable possessions people had. Additionally, the animals gave off heat—serving as furry furnaces—which was helpful, given how cold things could get at night (cf. Gen 31:40).

When studying biblical texts carefully, the practice of keeping animals inside a house becomes apparent. For example, the warrior Jephthah strikes many readers as one of the stupidest people in the Bible. Desperate for military victory, he makes what seems like the dumbest vow ever. In Judges 11:30-31, we read: "Jephthah made a solemn promise to the LORD: 'If you will decisively hand over the Ammonites to me, then whatever comes out the doors of my house [*bayit*] to meet me when I return victorious from the Ammonites will be given over to the LORD. I will sacrifice it as an entirely burned offering'" (CEB). Jephthah defeats the Ammonites and goes home, and his daughter comes out of the doorway of his house. The text says that Jephthah had no other children. Yet, he seems terribly grieved and disturbed that she comes out of the house to meet him because he now is bound by his vow to sacrifice her to God. I've often wanted to shout at Jephthah, asking, "Well, who on earth did you expect to exit your house?!"

More on Judges

The book of Judges is a confusing and disturbing part of the Bible. Part of the problem is that people do horrible things, such as Jephthah killing his own daughter.

Ironically, Leviticus 27 explains that if a human being ever vows to sacrifice another human being, a cash amount can be donated instead. Jephthah appears ignorant of such a law.

One of Judges's purposes is to explain how lawless and reckless things were when "there was no king in Israel" (17:6; 18:1; 19:1; 21:25). The monarchy brought great problems for Israel (like idolatry and exile). However, Judges shows that anarchy was even worse.[256]

When we remember that animals were frequently kept inside houses, Jephthah's actions are a little more understandable. Presumably, he thought that a sheep or goat would exit his house and that such an animal would be the one sacrificed. Obviously, there was risk that a human would come out instead. Yet, the presence of animals in the home helps readers understand why Jephthah seems shocked and disturbed when his only child exits his home (Judg 11:35). (See **More on Judges.**)

We don't know much about what types of furniture would be found in a *bayit.* Wood items usually don't last long enough for archaeologists to study today.[257] However, the Bible does provide us some clues about furniture. For example, we read the following in 2 Kings:

> One day Elisha went to Shunem. A rich woman lived there. She urged him to eat something, so whenever he passed by, he would stop in to eat some food. She said to her husband, "Look, I know that he is a holy man of God and he passes by regularly. Let's make a small room on the roof. We'll set up a bed, a table, a chair, and a lamp for him there. Then when he comes to us, he can stay there." (4:8-10 CEB)

Again, we see a reference to the second floor of a *bayit.* We also find references to the types of furniture we might today find in a dorm room, minus computers and speakers: a bed, table, chair, and lamp.

So, the biblical word *bayit* refers to more than a mere hut. It had several rooms and even furniture somewhat comparable to what's used today. However, there are also differences. Unlike many houses in the United States, biblical houses often contained farm animals.

Conclusion

A well-respected biblical scholar named Mark Smith writes, "Generally I think of words as evoking all kinds of worlds, of different realms of experience and worldview."[258] As we've seen, the worlds evoked by biblical words frequently differ from the worlds evoked by their English counterparts. Remembering wasn't a matter of finding car keys but a central component of faith. Covenants weren't signed; they were sealed with blood. Walking was a dangerous but everyday activity. Gates were focal points of city life. Houses were more complex than we might assume for ancient peoples—even if they were homes to both animals and people. Modern cultures and biblical cultures may agree on the dictionary definitions of these words. But beyond basic meanings, very different worlds exist. The Bible invites us to explore these worlds, and knowledge of Hebrew is the passport to visiting them.

Chapter 8

Cultural Values

Dictionary Versus Encyclopedia Definitions

The last chapter examined words that have similar dictionary definitions in Hebrew and English but have very different encyclopedia definitions. It focused on three cultural practices (remembering, cutting covenants, and walking) and three cultural objects (horses, gates, and houses). This chapter continues to look at the dictionary and encyclopedia definitions of Hebrew words, but it focuses attention on cultural values, examining peace, love, holiness, honor, cleanliness, fear, and wisdom. (See **Cultural Identity**.)

> **Cultural Identity**
>
> "The simple fact of translation presupposes contact between at least two cultures, and does so in relation to language use, the social activity that perhaps most effectively and insidiously weaves complex relations of cultural identity."[259]
>
> —*Anthony Pym*

Shalom

A favorite Hebrew word among churchgoers is *shalom*. Here it is:

	English	Hebrew	Hebrew Transliteration
58.	shalom, peace	שָׁלוֹם	*shalom*

This word shows up nearly 250 times in the Bible. At its most basic level, it means "peace." It doesn't always work to translate this word as "peace," however, because the Hebrew encompasses a wider meaning.

In English, two nations might be at peace with each other when bombs no longer drop and bullets no longer fire. Yet, people who have just suffered the ravages of war would still lack *shalom* in the broadest sense of the word. They would be a people in mourning, trying to pick up the rubble of their lives. Trauma would persist. Fear of more violence would haunt their lives.

Shalom, however, refers to a peace of body, mind, spirit, and relationship. A person who feels *shalom* is complete and whole. We see this in Leviticus 26, where God promises rewards for obedience.[260] God says: "I will give *shalom* in the land, so that you can lie down without anyone terrifying you. I'll destroy dangerous animals from the land. No sword will cross your land" (26:6, translation mine). The presence of *shalom* means not only the *absence* of swords and wild beasts but also the *presence* of worry-free rest. (See **Peace and Happiness**.)

Peace and Happiness

"Peace has come to mean the time when there aren't any wars or even when there aren't any major wars. Beggars can't be choosers; we'd most of us settle for that. But in Hebrew peace, *shalom*, means fullness, means having everything you need to be wholly and happily yourself."[261]

—*Frederick Buechner*

The people of the Bible knew how fragile life could be. They knew how *shalom* could escape our grasp. So, when people asked how others were doing, they didn't keep it on a generic level of "How's so-and-so?" Instead, they cut to the chase: "Does so-and-so have *shalom*?" (e.g., Gen 29:6). The implication is, on the one hand, that people who have *shalom* have all they need. If people lack *shalom*, on the other hand, then it doesn't matter what else they may have; things aren't right.

The Bible is very realistic about the tendency of human relationships to sour, even among family members. In Genesis 37, Joseph's brothers grow jealous that their dad favors Joseph over them. Most translations say something like, Joseph's brothers "couldn't say a kind word to" Joseph (Gen 37:4 NLT). That translation certainly reads well in English. However, the Hebrew there could more literally be rendered: "They couldn't speak to him in the direction of *shalom*" (translation mine[262]). And as the story unfolds, we see how far away from *shalom* things end up. The brothers eventually plot to kill Joseph and then decide to sell him into slavery. They go in the opposite direction of *shalom*.

Some words related to *shalom* can mean "prosperity." That's not to say that everyone who has *shalom* also has riches.[263] However, the overtones of *shalom* include economic well-being (e.g., Ps 37:11). *Shalom* is a peace not only with enemies but also with oneself, one's body, one's family, one's friends, and even one's economy. Those who have *shalom* have God's blessing.[264] (See **Peace and Prosperity**.)

Peace and Prosperity

"*Shalom* is...'fullness,' 'completeness.' So it's well-being. It's prosperity: not in a cheap...making-a-profit sense of possibility, but in a deep sense of 'my well-being is integrated with the well-being of all around me, human and non-human and the earth on which our lives depend.'"[265]

—*Ellen Davis*

Several texts talk about God wanting to enter a covenant of *shalom* with God's people. The idea is that God wants to invade every part of our lives with *shalom*, complete peace that entails a freedom from all types of harm. *Shalom* can entail friendship, harmony, and even reconciliation.[266] Using the word *shalom* twice, God in Isaiah 54 says it better than I ever could:

> The mountains may shift,
> and the hills may be shaken,
> but my faithful love won't shift from you,
> and my covenant [*berit*] of peace [*shalom*] won't be shaken,
> says the Lord, the one who pities you.
> Suffering one, storm-tossed, uncomforted,
> look [*hinneh*], I am setting your gemstones
> in silvery metal
> and your foundations with sapphires.
> I will make your towers of rubies,
> and your gates [*shaar*] of beryl,
> and all your walls of precious jewels.
> All your children will be disciples of the Lord—
> I will make peace [*shalom*] abound for your children.
> You will be firmly founded in righteousness [*tsedaqah*].
> You will stay far from oppression because you won't fear,
> far from terror because it won't come near you. (54:10-14 CEB)

God's vision of *shalom* entails riches beyond comprehension, peace from foreign and inner demons.

Chapter 8

Love

Today, churches emphasize that Christianity is all about love. Jesus quotes the Old Testament in saying that the most important commandments are to love God with all that we are and to love our neighbors as ourselves (Matt 22:37-40; cf. Deut 6:5; Lev 19:18). Later in the New Testament, readers find the expression "God is love" (1 John 4:8), which has clear continuity with many Old Testament verses (e.g., Exod 34:6).

While there's good reason to talk about love, there's also a problem here. Love can be defined in many different ways. It can refer to a strong liking. However, sometimes people talk about how they love people even though they don't like them—when they grit their teeth and hope the person starts acting in better ways. Love can also refer to infatuation—an intense head-over-heels feeling during which it's hard to stop thinking about the other person. Sometimes love is equated with sex or at least sexual desire.

Consider the following statements:

- I love spaghetti.
- I love cassette tapes.
- I love the Coen Brothers' movie *A Serious Man*.
- I love my job.
- I love my wife.
- I love my infant son.

All of these statements are true for me. But I relate to these objects of affection in very different ways. Spaghetti tastes delicious and makes me feel great—at least when I don't eat too much. I like the feel, look, and sound of cassette tapes because they remind me of my childhood—plus in our digital age they strike me as ridiculous and therefore funny. I'm enraptured by *A Serious Man* because of its memorable lines, colorful characters, and intense connections with the Bible. I love my job because I find teaching and writing great fun; these activities make me a better person. My wife is the one person I've committed to stick with no matter what the rest of my life, and she's the one person with whom I'm romantic. My infant son can't talk to me yet, and he wakes everyone up wanting to be fed in the middle of every night—which is hard—but then he smiles, and my heart melts. I have love for each of these objects and people, but very different types of love.

When we talk about God's love for us and our love for God, things can naturally become confusing. What does divine love have to do with the above types of human love? Is "love" just a hollow shell of a word that can be filled with nearly any positive meaning?

Hebrew can help. It has several words related to love. Here's the most popular one:

	English	Hebrew	Hebrew Transliteration
59.	love, loyalty	חֶסֶד	*khesed*

This word appears about 250 times in the Hebrew Bible.

Unlike the English word "love," *khesed* is fairly specific about the type of love envisioned. It's not primarily romantic, sexual, or about gushy feelings. In fact, it's never found in the Song of Songs, the Bible's most romantic book.[267] *Khesed* has to do less with infatuation and more with faithfulness. It's about loving someone, come what may. It's about commitment. It's about tenacity and stick-with-it-ness.

The word *khesed* is translated many ways by English translations: lovingkindness, kindness, steadfast love, love, loyalty, devotion, faithfulness, and mercy.[268] Some scholars even suggest the word can't be adequately captured in English, like words in chapter 3.[269] Perhaps the word that comes closest to *khesed*'s meaning is "loyalty." (See ***Khesed* and Kindness?**)

Khesed and Kindness?

Khesed "has been rendered as 'kindness.' But this rendering is a pale reflection of the multivalent richness of this term. Indeed, when God is a subject of *khesed*, its relation to 'kindness' is extremely remote. Rather, it refers to God's fidelity to His commitments, that is, to His covenant."[270]

—*Jacob Milgrom*

Because *khesed* has connections with commitment, it sometimes shows up with the word *berit* ("covenant").[271] Deuteronomy 7:9 is a good example: "Know therefore that the Lord your God, He is God, the faithful [*aman*, which is related to *amen* and *emet*] God, who keeps [*shamar*, literally "protects"] His covenant [*berit*] and His lovingkindness [*khesed*] to a thousandth generation with those who love Him and keep [*shamar*] His commandments" (NASB). The idea of God protecting the covenant with Israel is completely congruent with God's intense loyalty to Israel.

Another word that occurs even more frequently with *khesed* is *emet*, which as we saw in chapter 2 refers to truth, faithfulness, and reliability. We see *khesed* and *emet* in Psalm 40:10b-11 [11b-12 Heb.]:

> I have not concealed your steadfast love [*khesed*] and your faithfulness [*emet*]
> from the great congregation.
> Do not, O LORD, withhold
> your mercy from me;
> let your steadfast love [*khesed*] and your faithfulness [*emet*]
> keep me safe forever. (NRSV)

In the context of this psalm, it's clear that the person praying faces life-threatening danger. Frequently in the Psalms, people mention God's *khesed* when their own strength won't suffice.

At times, the Bible stretches the limits of language to express the size of God's *khesed*. Psalm 103:11 puts it this way: "As high as heaven is above the earth, that's how large God's faithful love [*khesed*] is for those who honor him" (CEB; see also Pss 57:10 [11 Heb.]; 108:4 [5 Heb.]). I've often heard people say things like, "I like the loving God of the New Testament so much more than the angry God of the Old Testament." I try to remind people that the New Testament talks about a burning lake of fire (Rev 20:15; 21:8) while the Old Testament contains verses like the above one.

At the same time, there's a valid question: how do we balance God's love with God's anger? A recurrent statement in the Bible is that God is slow to anger and abounding in *khesed*. We see it in Exodus 34:6-7:

> And [God] passed in front of Moses, proclaiming, "The LORD, the LORD, the compassionate and gracious God, slow to anger, abounding in love [*khesed*] and faithfulness [*emet*], maintaining love [*khesed*] to thousands, and forgiving [*nasa*, literally "lifting"] wickedness, rebellion and sin. Yet he does not leave the guilty unpunished; he punishes the children and their children for the sin of the parents to the third and fourth generation." (NIV)

Similar statements can be found in about two dozen other texts.[272] In fact, many biblical scholars think that this statement provides the Old Testament's central portrait of who God is.[273]

We find similar statements balancing God's anger and love elsewhere. For example, Isaiah 54:8 addresses people who have experienced God's wrath and judgment. Notice what God says here:

"In a surge of anger
  I hid my face from you for a moment,
but with everlasting kindness [*khesed*]
  I will have compassion on you,"
  says the LORD your Redeemer [from *gaal*]. (NIV; cf. Mic 7:18)

God becomes angry over wrongdoing. That's a good thing: the alternative is a God who does nothing in the face of evil. So, the Bible says with great clarity that God can and does grow angry. However, it balances such statements by reminding people of God's *khesed*. It contrasts the momentary nature of God's anger with the enduring nature of God's *khesed*.

In fact, one of the Bible's most popular statements is this: "God's *khesed* is everlasting." Hebrew's word for "everlasting" shows up in the same verse as *khesed* fifty-eight times in the Hebrew Bible.[274] Over and over again, the Bible reminds us that God's love is one that endures. In that sense, *khesed* differs dramatically from many forms of human love.

The vast majority—more than three-quarters—of the Bible's references to *khesed* describes God's love for humanity. When human *khesed* is in view, it's often when two people make an alliance with each other (e.g., Gen 21:23; 1 Sam 20:15). Interestingly, there aren't many cases in which the Bible talks of human *khesed* for God. The Bible knows all too well just how fickle and sinful we can be.

Yet, when the Bible does talk about human *khesed* for God, it's often in very significant places. One place is the book of Hosea. This small book envisions the relationship between God and Israel as a marriage relationship. Israel has broken the wedding vows, forsaking *khesed*: "Hear [*shama*] the word of the LORD, O people of Israel; for the LORD has an indictment against the inhabitants of the land. There is no faithfulness [*emet*] or loyalty [*khesed*], and no knowledge of God in the land" (Hos 4:1 NRSV). Yet, God still holds out hope that the people will turn around and enter again into a relationship of mutual love and faithfulness: "But you must return [*shuv*] to your God; maintain love [*khesed*] and justice [*mishpat*], and wait [*qavah*, cf. 'hope'] for your God always" (Hos 12:6 NIV [7 Heb.]). A similar statement is found in one of the most popular verses of the Bible[275]: "He has told you, human one [*adam*], what is good and what the LORD requires from you: to do justice [*mishpat*], embrace faithful love [*khesed*], and walk [*halakh*] humbly with your God" (Mic 6:8 CEB). As Katharine Doob Sakenfeld puts it at the conclusion of a book-length study of *khesed*, "God continues to honor whatever acts of loyalty frail mortals are able to perform."[276] Although we are imperfect, sinful, and broken, the Bible urges us to attempt this steady, faithful love for God.

Chapter 8

Cleanliness

One of the most confusing parts of the Old Testament is its regulations on what's clean and unclean. Several times, the Old Testament says that people should avoid eating or touching unclean animals like vultures (Lev 11, Deut 14). Individuals themselves can become unclean if they:

- have certain diseases, particularly those involving the skin (Lev 13–14)
- have bodily discharges like menstruation and semen (Lev 12, 15)
- touch a corpse (Lev 21; Num 19)
- engage in morally problematic behavior such as incest or child sacrifice (Lev 18:1-30; 20:3; Num 35:34)

What's at the heart of this discussion?

Many Hebrew words can be discussed when treating this topic, but here are three of the most important:

	English	Hebrew	Hebrew Transliteration
60.	(be) unclean, impure	טָמֵא	*tame*
61.	be clean, pure	טָהֵר	*taher*
62.	clean, pure	טָהוֹר	*tahor*

The first word (*tame*) appears about 250 times in the Hebrew Bible, while the last two (*taher* and *tahor*) show up nearly 200 times. They play an especially important role in the texts just discussed. For example, in the five chapters of Leviticus 11–15, these words (and closely related ones) show up over 150 times—an average of almost once per verse.

What are the core concepts here? To begin, there's a reason that these words have often been translated with the English words "(un)clean" and "(im)pure." Every society has its own regulations about what's clean and orderly, on the one hand, and what's dirty and disgusting, on the other hand. In fact, there are general areas of overlap between what we consider disgusting and what the Israelites thought of as unclean:

- When it comes to *animals*, we see some of them as disgusting. Cockroaches, for example, aren't something people usually want to touch, much less eat, even when sterilized.[277] Biblical Israelites, meanwhile, would have been mortified by the American fascination with bacon (Lev 11:7).

- Similarly, many *diseases* are considered disgusting today. When people sneeze, for example, we hope to God they cover their faces. Biblical Israelites, meanwhile, were especially concerned with skin disorders (Lev 13–14).
- *Bodily discharges* are both a natural part of life and something that we tend to clean up in socially acceptable ways, whether we're talking about nasal mucus, semen, or menstruation. When it comes to these last two, the Bible tells people how to clean themselves before going to the tabernacle (Lev 15:16-24).
- *Corpses* are something that we don't tend to touch. They were similarly avoided in the biblical world (cf. Num 19).
- *Morally problematic behavior* can be repulsive even in today's world. Who wants to live in a house where a murder took place? For the people of the Bible, some morally problematic behaviors were seen as disgusting as well (see Lev 18).

While the specifics can differ, it's clear that modern and ancient societies alike operate with cultural norms that govern what's acceptable and what's disgusting. The biblical words *tame* and *taher*/*tahor* relate to these categories.

Generally speaking, most types of behaviors described as "unclean" (*tame*) weren't actually sinful. In the course of life's events, people would become sick, have sex, menstruate, and even touch the dead. Becoming unclean in these ways wasn't innately wrong. What was wrong would be entering God's temple while you were in an unclean state. To come into the house of worship, you'd need to become clean (*tahor*), usually by bathing, waiting, or making a sacrifice.

The idea here is that God, on the one hand, is pure, holy, undefiled. We humans, on the other hand, can be disgusting. So, some type of purification was necessary before coming into the presence of a holy and pure God. (See **Physical Cleanliness**.)

Physical Cleanliness

"God was *physically present* with ancient Israel in the tabernacle; therefore, *physical purity laws* were important for the proper maintenance of the Lord's physical presence in their midst (cf. 2 Chron 34:8)."[278]

—*Richard E. Averbeck*

You could say that the Israelites made hygiene a sacrament. They cared for their bodies as ways of honoring God. They entered God's temple with respect.

Similarly, they watched what entered their bodies. Avoiding unclean animals, they ate animals they deemed fit for both God and themselves: mostly beef and mutton. They kept away from certain types of food, just as they hopefully kept away from practices like idolatry.

One thing that makes the Bible's language about being "unclean" difficult to understand is that *sometimes* it does refer to sin.[279] In these instances, we're then talking *not* about things that naturally happen in the course of life's events, but rather about behaviors that biblical authors saw as extraordinarily problematic. So, having sex with animals or engaging in child sacrifice could also be classified as "unclean" (*tame*). However, the Bible typically uses additional language letting people know that we're not talking about your normal run-of-the-mill, stay-home-from-the-tabernacle stuff. Hebrew has additional words like "abomination" (תּוֹעֵבָה, *toevah*) and "pollute" (חָלַל, *khalal*) that tend to show up in these places (e.g., Lev 18:26-30; 20:1-5).

So, we find that cleanliness is an important biblical value. However, rather than having to do with sparkling floors and pleasant smells, it has to do with the opposite of disgust. Three primary ideas are in view:

1. People shouldn't enter God's house while they're ceremonially unclean (*tame*). As a sign of respect, they should only enter it when clean (*tahor*)—just as we usually take showers before going to church today.

2. People should avoid animals considered unclean (*tame*). They should only eat those that are clean (*tahor*). This practice reminded people of the importance of avoiding things like idolatry.

3. People should avoid morally disgusting behaviors, especially those described as an abomination or pollution.

As with so many words, there are not only basic similarities between biblical and English words but also vastly different networks of association.[280]

Holiness

Many of the churches I encounter today show little interest in holiness. Yet, in the Bible, words for "holiness" appear more frequently than words for "love."[281] Here is the Hebrew:

	English	Hebrew	Hebrew Transliteration
63.	holiness	קֹדֶשׁ	*qodesh*
64.	be holy	קָדַשׁ	*qadash*
65.	holy	קָדוֹשׁ	*qadosh*

These three words appear over 750 times in the Bible.

When something is holy, it's pure, sacred, perfect, honored, and set apart.[282] It belongs to God. In many parts of the Bible, holiness describes not only God, but also God's home—the tabernacle, temple, or Mount Zion where the temple stood.

In fact, it's interesting what happens before these sanctuaries are built. In Exodus 3, Moses is a shepherd east of Egypt. He discovers a bush on fire that doesn't burn up. Wondering why the shrub doesn't turn into ash, Moses approaches it, only to hear God's voice calling to him. God says, "Don't come any closer! Take off your sandals, because you are standing on holy [*qodesh*] ground" (Exod 3:5 CEB). Given that Moses was a shepherd, it's not too difficult to imagine what he might have stepped on earlier that day. Such dirt and muck doesn't belong in the presence of a pure and holy God. By the time Moses speaks, his words are filled with how he feels out of place, unworthy for the tasks this holy God asks of him. (See **Encountering the Holy**.)

Encountering the Holy

Building on several theories of holiness including Old Testament ideas, biblical scholar John Rogerson explains features of encountering the holy:

> Reality cannot ultimately be totally comprehended in terms of human rationality; ...particular times and places can (but not necessarily do or must) assume a significance that points beyond themselves;...experiences of the sublime can induce human feelings of insignificance, uncleanness and danger;...people can feel themselves to be grasped by an unseen reality that becomes something to be after for its own sake and which in this way liberates seekers from self-interest.[283]

Some parts of the Bible emphasize the holiness of God, God's sanctuary, God's offerings, and God's priests. Other parts make clear that all of Israel is invited to reflect God's holiness. (See **Holiness and Godliness**.) Leviticus 19 is perhaps the clearest example. Even though Leviticus is an unpopular book of the Bible, its nineteenth chapter contains material of highest importance to the life of faith. Here's how it begins: "You must be holy [*qadosh*], because I, the Lord your God, am holy [*qadosh*]" (Lev 19:2 CEB; cf. 20:7).[285] As this statement suggests, being holy means imitating God. In the rest of Leviticus 19, readers find a combination of commandments about loving neighbor and loving God. The text echoes many of the Ten Commandments (19:3, 11, 16, 30). People should provide for the most vulnerable in society (19:9-11, 13-15, 32-36). They are told to love their neighbors, and the text implies that neighbors will sometimes be enemies (19:18). By upholding the Ten Commandments, caring for those in need, and loving others, the people bear marks of belonging to God. They become holy. They embody God's nature. (See **Holiness, Justice, Compassion**.)

Holiness and Godliness

"That which humanity is *not*, nor can ever fully be, but that which humanity is commanded to emulate and approximate, is what the Bible calls *qadosh*, 'holy.' Holiness means imitating God—the life of godliness."[284]

—*Jacob Milgrom*

I don't hear much about holiness today. A current encyclopedia wouldn't claim that holiness is one of today's society's most important values. But within the world of the Bible, things are different. Holiness names who God is and who God's people should be.

Holiness, Justice, Compassion

"Holiness in Israel was a summons to Israel to aspire to the justice and compassion characteristic of her summoning God."[286]

—*John Gammie*

Glory

I could have treated the Hebrew word for "glory" in a number of earlier chapters. Like the words in chapter 5, this word often carries an abstract meaning, but it may derive from a much more concrete idea, as we'll see. Like the words examined in chapter 6, "glory" finds its way into hymns and worship songs, but its meaning isn't always fully understood. However, I've chosen to treat it here because it's an important part of biblical values. Here's the breakdown:

	English	Hebrew	Hebrew Transliteration
66.	(be) glorious, honorable, weighty	כָּבֵד	*kaved*
67.	glory, honor	כָּבוֹד	*kavod*

These words show up over 350 times in the Hebrew Bible.

On a concrete level, *kaved* and *kavod* refer to matters that are weighty, substantive, heavy, intense, great, severe, and massive. Isaiah 32:2 uses *kaved* to talk about a "massive" or "weighty" rock—one so big that it provides people with shade. Other things described with this word include the "severe" famines of Genesis and the "momentous" plagues of Exodus.[287] The word also describes Pharaoh's stubborn heart in Exodus. English translations often say that Pharaoh (and later God) hardened Pharaoh's heart. However, a more literal translation would say that Pharaoh and God made Pharaoh's heart heavy.[288] In English, a "heavy heart" is a sad heart. However, the Hebrew communicates that Pharaoh made his heart heavy in the sense of making it unmovable. He would not change even though great signs and wonders took place around him.

In chapter 5, we examined how the Bible presents sin and transgression as something that creates a burden. Such an idea appears with the word *kaved* in Isaiah 24:20: "The earth reels to and fro like a drunkard And it totters like a shack, For its transgression is heavy [*kaved*] upon it, And it will fall, never to rise again" (NASB). Obviously, things like famines, plagues, stubborn hearts, and transgressions are very negative.

It's a mistake, however, to assume that the words *kaved* and *kavod* always refer to something problematic. This word's emphasis falls on weightiness and significance, not what's undesirable. In fact, it's often used figuratively to talk about a person's social standing. The more weight or *kavod* ascribed to a person, the more esteemed, respected, and honored the person was. Not surprising, then, many kings are described as "honorable" or at least have some connection with *kaved* or *kavod*:

- Saul (1 Sam 15:30)
- David (2 Sam 6:20, 22; 1 Chron 17:18; 29:12, 28)
- Solomon (1 Kgs 3:13; 2 Chron 1:11-12)
- Jehoshaphat (2 Chron 17:5; 18:1)
- Hezekiah (2 Chron 32:27, 33)
- Ahasuerus (Esth 1:4)

Although neither Joseph nor Moses served as kings, they both functioned as leaders and are similarly described with these words.[289] Power and authority thus have close connections with *kavod*.[290] Wealth and riches also appear alongside this word for "glory."[291] Those who have "glory" also receive praise and blessings.[292] Shame, however, is the opposite of *kavod*.[293]

Even though the Bible attaches positive value to power, riches, praise, and honor, it doesn't tell people to seek them selfishly. Solomon receives these things only because he humbly seeks understanding on how to govern (1 Kgs 3:5-13).

Meanwhile, many proverbs emphasize humility, not selfishness, as the path to honor.[294]

So far, we've focused on human honor. What does a word like *kavod* mean when it's applied to God? The Hebrew word is often translated "glory." There are two primary meanings here.

First, the term can, like human *kavod*, refer to honor. God reigns from the heavens as the supreme king who displays power throughout the earth. As such, God deserves more honor than any human. For this reason, the psalms speak powerfully about God's glory (*kavod*). Even human kings acknowledge God's greatness: "Let all the earth's rulers... sing about the LORD's ways because the LORD's glory [*kavod*, or 'honor'] is so great!" (Ps 138:4-5 CEB). Repeatedly, the psalms make similar points, saying that God's glory and honor are on display for all to see.[295]

Second, the Bible talks of "God's glory [*kavod*]" to talk about God's presence. As the previous verses make clear, many parts of the Bible envision God interacting with the whole earth, which implies that God is everywhere (cf. Ps 139:7-12). Yet, there are also verses that connect God's presence with very specific places and times. God may be everywhere, but there's a weight and significance to what's sometimes experienced. In these cases, the Bible talks about God's "glory" or "weightiness" to communicate God's palpable presence.[296]

For example, when the Israelites leave Egypt, God travels with them. The text says: "The LORD went [*halakh*] in front of them in a pillar of cloud by day, to lead them along the way, and in a pillar of fire by night, to give them light, so that they might travel [*halakh*] by day and by night" (Exod 13:21 NRSV). Rather than saying that the Israelites fully glimpsed God, the Bible says that the Israelites saw God's *kavod* in this cloud and fire (Exod 16:7, 10; 24:16-17).

Later, Israelites experience God most strongly at the tabernacle and temple. Here also, the Bible talks of God's presence in terms of God's *kavod* or "glory."[297]

Why talk about God's presence in terms of God's glory? Why not simply talk about God being present? A couple of answers can be given.[298] The first pertains to the nature of the word *kavod*. Because it carries a sense of intensity, it works well to describe places where God feels intensely present to humans.

Second, the Bible tells the story of a profound tension in how humans experience God. On the one hand, God is accessible and understandable to humanity. God draws near. God appears. God speaks. Creation displays God's handiwork. In this sense, we can think of the nearness of God—divine immanence.

But on the other hand, God is also distinct from humanity. God isn't a creature. God won't be confined to human expectations. God is holy and set apart. God is mysterious, even dangerous. God can feel very distant. In this sense, we can think of God existing beyond anything we could ever imagine. This idea is sometimes called divine transcendence.

This tension between God's immanence and transcendence nears a snapping point when the Bible expresses intimacy between humans and God. God's love means that God wants to be in deep, abiding, and real fellowship with humanity. However, the Bible makes clear that human sin doesn't mix well with God's holiness. So, several times, the Bible makes clear that a real danger exists in seeing God face-to-face. We saw it earlier when Isaiah encounters God in the temple and thinks he's going to die (Isa 6:5). We also see it when God passes before Moses on Sinai. Moses hides in the cleft of a rock, able only to see God's back (Exod 33:18-23). Other examples could be given.[299]

The point here is that the Bible expresses both the desire of God to be in fellowship with humanity and the realization that mixing sinful humans with a holy God can have disastrous consequences. One way that it navigates this tension is by saying that the people experience not God's direct presence but rather God's glory (*kavod*). For example, the opening chapter of Ezekiel features a vivid and complicated glimpse into what heaven looks like. There's talk of bizarre creatures that look something like human beings but have wings and four faces each: that of a human, lion, bull, and eagle (1:5-10). There's a glittering dome above (1:22), as well as a blue throne on which sits "a form that looked like a human being [*adam*]" (1:26 CEB). But then—instead of saying that this human being is how God appeared to Ezekiel, the text says, "This was how the form of the LORD's glory [*kavod*] appeared" (1:28 CEB). Rather than talking about the direct appearance of God, the text reminds readers that this is what God's glory looked like.

So, whether talking about God's appearance in the wilderness, God's appearance in the tabernacle and temple, or God's appearance in visions, the Bible often says that the people see God's glory (*kavod*) rather than God's face.

While English uses of the word "glory" have some overlap with biblical uses of *kavod*, there's obviously more going on with the biblical word *kavod* than contemporary English uses of "glory." Although the word "glory" is found in hymns and praise choruses, many people don't realize that biblical glory refers not only to honor, praise, and fame but also to what we experience when in close contact with the divine.

Wisdom

We live in the information age. At no point in history has humanity had access to so much information so quickly. What was once confined to dusty encyclopedias, the backs of baseball cards, and the *Guinness Book of World Records* is now only a few clicks away. People today even talk of being on "information overload." There simply is too much data for our small brains to absorb.

We value quantitative data over qualitative data. In other words, people want to see numbers. They want things that can be put on graphs. They want assured results. They want what's calculable, predictable, controllable, and efficient.[300]

With access to so much knowledge, we've achieved incredible things. We've made it to the moon and sent spacecraft into the outer reaches of our solar system. Medicine has allowed people to live longer than ever before.

We've gained much, but we've also lost something. We've lost a sense of beauty. A sense of mystery. A sense of awe. A sense of conviction. A sense that it's good to come to terms with our own finitude, ignorance, and mortality. A sense that even with all our information, we still desperately need each other. Google alone won't suffice.

What we've lost is wisdom. We have unimaginable information, but we don't know how to use it wisely. We've figured out how to split an atom, but we've used that knowledge to kill more people than our brains can comprehend. We've figured out how to make electricity readily available, how to mass produce cars, and how individuals can each travel thousands of miles, but the resultant global warming has made our planet less inhabitable. We have so much information and so little wisdom.

Here are the Hebrew words for "wise" and "wisdom"[301]:

	English	Hebrew	Hebrew Transliteration
68.	wise	חָכָם	*khakham*
69.	wisdom	חָכְמָה	*khokhmah*

Together, these words appear almost three hundred times in the Bible.

Khokhmah has several definitions. (See **Other Meanings of *Khokhmah*.**) However, the most common has ethical and religious overtones. As one of my mentors put it, "The goal of all wisdom was the formation of character."[302] It's closely associated with righteousness (*tsedaqah*, a word mentioned in chapter 1 with Isaiah 5:7 and in chapter 4 with "Justice and Judgment").[303] Righteousness here can be seen as the moral order of our world. The basic idea is that a good God created the universe, and God's fingerprints are all over creation. By doing God's will, we live in harmony with the created order.[304]

Words for wisdom appear most commonly in Proverbs, Ecclesiastes, and Job. In fact, over half of the Bible's uses of these words show up in these books. The book of Proverbs urges readers to pursue wisdom with all they have (4:7;

8:11; 16:16). This book overflows with short but substantive sayings that prize what pleases God. It teaches that the moral life requires a great deal of attention to what we say.[305] It teaches the importance of humility.[306] It draws a sharp contrast between the wise and the fool. Here, we need to keep in mind that these terms ("wise" and "fool") have more to do with upright living than with basic intelligence (e.g., 14:8, 16, 24, 33). The "fool" is simply another word for the "wicked"—those who act in harmful ways.

Other Meanings of *Khokhmah*

Like many words, these terms related to wisdom can be used in several different ways. There are times when the Bible talks about being wise with respect to a particular skill. Those who build the tabernacle, for example, are described in these terms: "All who are skillful [*khakham*] among you shall come and make all that the LORD has commanded" (Exod 35:10 NRSV). On other occasions, people try to become wise in either their own eyes or the eyes of other people—something quite foolish compared with wisdom in God's eyes: "You felt secure in your wickedness; you said, 'No one sees me.' Your wisdom [*khokhmah*] and your knowledge led you astray, and you said in your heart [*lev*], 'I am, and there is no one besides me'" (Isa 47:10 NRSV; cf. Job 5:13; Prov 3:7; 26:12). While these other definitions exist, wisdom in the Bible is often an ethical term related to faithfully obeying God.

While Proverbs emphasizes the wisdom of righteous living, Ecclesiastes and Job sound another important note: wisdom ultimately belongs to God more than humanity. We see this type of statement with crystal clarity in Job: "With God are wisdom [*khokhmah*] and strength; he has counsel and understanding" (12:13 NRSV). With vivid poetry, Job 28 names wisdom as God's domain:

> But wisdom [*khokhmah*], where can it be found;
>   where is the place of understanding?
> Humankind doesn't know its value;
>   it isn't found in the land of the living.
> The Deep says, "It's not with me";
>   the Sea says, "Not alongside me!"
> It can't be bought with gold;
>   its price can't be measured in silver....
> Neither gold nor glass can compare with it;...
>   the price of wisdom [*khokhmah*] is more than rubies....
> But wisdom [*khokhmah*], where does she come from?
>   Where is the place of understanding?...
> God understands her way;
>   he knows her place;

for he looks to the ends of the earth
    and surveys everything beneath the heavens.
In order to weigh the wind [*ruakh*],
    to prepare a measure for waters,
when he made a decree for the rain,
    a path for thunderbolts,
then he observed it, spoke of it,
    established it, searched it out,
and said to humankind [*adam*]: "Look [*hen*],
    the fear of the LORD is wisdom [*khokhmah*];
        turning from evil [*ra*] is understanding."
(Job 28:12-15, 17a, 18a, 20, 23-28 CEB)

These words foreshadow what comes at the end of the book of Job, where God shows up and tells Job and his friends that their debate over why Job suffers is absurd. They pretend to know the ways of the world and of God, but they are simply too small and insignificant to fathom such realities. As God asks at one point:

Can you send forth lightnings, so that they may go [*halakh*]
    and say to you, "Here we are"?
Who has put wisdom [*khokhmah*] in the inward parts,
    or given understanding to the mind?[307]
Who has the wisdom [*khokhmah*] to number the clouds?
    Or who can tilt the waterskins of the heavens? (Job 38:35-37 NRSV)

In comparison with God, humans are insignificant. They lack the wisdom belonging to God alone.

The speaker of Ecclesiastes, often called Qohelet or "the Teacher," similarly stresses how little wisdom humans can obtain: "All this I have tested by wisdom [*khokhmah*]; I said, 'I will be wise [*khakham*],'[308] but it was far from me" (Eccl 7:23 NRSV). Such sentiment is reiterated in the next chapter: "I observed all the work of God—that no one can grasp what happens under the sun. Those who strive to know can't grasp it. Even the wise [*khakham*] who are set on knowing are unable to grasp it" (Eccl 8:17 CEB). What little wisdom can be obtained by human beings is insufficient to stave off death, which comes to the wise and fool alike (Eccl 2:13-16).

Because human wisdom can only take people so far, several diverse parts of the Bible stress that wisdom ultimately comes from God's instruction.[309] It's there that we gain a sense of what is right and wrong. It's there that we find what beauty really is. It's there that we come to see the expectations of the Creator:

"Your commandments make me wiser [*khakham*] than my enemies; they always stand by me" (Ps 119:98 NJPS; cf. Ps 19:7 [8 Heb.]). Similar words appear in Deuteronomy, where Moses says to the people:

> See, I have taught you statutes and judgments [*mishpat*] just as the LORD my God commanded me, that you should do thus in the land where you are entering to possess it. So keep [*shamar*, literally "protect"] and do them, for that is your wisdom [*khokhmah*] and your understanding in the sight of the peoples who will hear [*shama*] all these statutes and say, "Surely this great nation is a wise [*khakham*] and understanding people." (Deut 4:5-6 NASB)

Verses like this one suggest that the goal of God's law and instruction is to become wise (cf. Prov 4:7; 8:11; 16:16).

For Christians, it's easy to see how these words from Deuteronomy speak today. In a world saturated with information but short on wisdom, God's word contains what we so desperately need.

Fear

A popular verse of the Bible connects wisdom with fear: "The fear of the LORD is the beginning of wisdom [*khokhmah*]" (Prov 9:10 NASB; cf. 1:7; 15:33). Other verses similarly cast fear in a positive light. Isaiah 33:6, for example, says that "the fear of the LORD is Zion's treasure" (NRSV). These statements puzzle readers. Who embraces fear? Who wants to be afraid? This emotion is associated with teasing, embarrassment, bullying, and shame. Many of us are taught from an early age to conceal our fears. (See **Cosmic Cop**.)

Cosmic Cop

"Try as I may, I cannot altogether shake off my habitual awe of the Church nor completely dissociate it from the far more fearful God to whom the Church makes its ritual obeisances. I still think of God... as a watchful, vengeful, enormous, omniscient policeman, instantly aware of the slightest tinge of irreverence in my innermost thought, always ready to pounce (though with ominous patience he might hold his hand for a time) if I curse, if I mention him in anger, fun or mere habit, if I (O hell-fire and horror!) blaspheme his holy name."[310]

—*T. S. Matthews*

Not all cultures are so averse to fear, however. Anthropologists have studied indigenous peoples in the Southwest Pacific, finding that their cultures actually celebrate fear.[311] Instead of feeling shame about being afraid, peoples from this part of the globe will often share and even treasure stories of experiencing fear. They do so, in part, because it communicates to others that they are not a threat. They reveal their own vulnerability to one another as a way of saying, "I'm human like you. We are one in facing fears."

The Hebrew Bible similarly sees fear as a potentially good thing. Here is the key word[312]:

	English	Hebrew	Hebrew Transliteration
70.	be afraid, fear	יָרֵא	*yare*

This word appears nearly four hundred times in the Hebrew Bible. Over eighty times, the Bible talks specifically about "fearing God" or "fearing the LORD."[313] Sometimes, the Bible even describes God as "awesome"; and the meaning of "awesome" here has less to do with being "cool" and more to do with inspiring awe and fear.[314]

I've heard many people suggest that biblical talk about "fearing God" simply means respecting or revering God. Such language even makes it into widely respected Bible translations. For example, the Common English Bible translates 2 Chronicles 19:9 as follows: "[King Jehoshaphat] instructed them, 'You must respect the LORD at all times, in truth, and with complete integrity.'" The part translated "You must respect the LORD" reads more literally in the Hebrew, "You must act in the fear of the LORD" (see NASB, NRSV, NIV, NJPS).

Does the Bible's talk of fearing God simply mean respecting God? Or, are the CEB translators trying to sugarcoat a difficult teaching?

On the one hand, there are cases in which the Hebrew verb *yare* means "to respect." Thus, Leviticus 19:3 gives this command: "Each of you must *yare* your mother and father" (NIV, alt.).[315] The image evoked is *not* one of fearing abusive parents, but rather of giving respect and honor to one's father and mother. A similar idea with paternal imagery surfaces in Psalm 103:13, which talks about fearing God: "As a father has compassion for his children, so the LORD has compassion for those who fear [*yare*] him" (NRSV). Both this verse and the surrounding ones emphasize God's compassion and forgiving nature. The passage as a whole presents God as merciful, not mean. In such a context, it makes perfect sense to translate *yare* as "respect."

Another good example is Psalm 33:18. It uses the verb *yare* in the context of talking about God's goodness and God providing in difficult times: "Truly [*hinneh*] the eye of the LORD is on those who fear [*yare*] him, on those who hope in his steadfast love [*khesed*]" (NRSV). Here, fearing God is connected with awaiting God's love, not awaiting divine punishment. Instead of saying that people fear God because God is capricious, it says that those who fear God expect to receive God's loyal love. In such a verse, *yare* obviously means respect for God. Elsewhere, the word similarly has to do with respecting God, as in Psalm 112:1 and Nehemiah 1:11, which talk of those who revere [*yare*] God also experiencing delight.

There are times, however, when the biblical idea of fearing God entails more than simply respecting God. Sometimes, God supernaturally breaks into the world and shocks us. Humans are left frightened by what's happened. Thus, many texts talk about fearing God in the context of supernatural occurrences—times when God makes the hair on the back of the neck stand up. Thus, when Jacob dreams of a ladder reaching to heaven and realizes he is in the presence of God, the text says, "He was terrified [*yare*] and thought, This sacred place is awesome [i.e., 'a place to fear' from *yare*]. It's none other than God's house [*bayit*] and the entrance to heaven" (Gen 28:17 CEB). God's signs and wonders can startle people and evoke awe if not fear (e.g., Exod 9:20).

In other texts, fearing God entails a belief that God holds people accountable for their actions. Thus, Abraham worries that the Philistines will kill him to get his wife because, in his words, "there is no fear of God in this place" (Gen 20:11 NASB). In contrast, Joseph later in Genesis assures others that they can trust his word. Why can they trust him? Because as he puts it, "I fear God" (Gen 42:18 NASB). Elsewhere, texts make clear that God-fearers will avoid various types of wrongdoing presumably because they fear what consequences God will send if they commit evil.[316] Perhaps the most explicit text is Proverbs 16:6b: "And by the fear [a noun related to *yare*] of the Lord one keeps away from evil [*ra*]" (NASB). Knowing that evil actions lead to calamity, those who fear God embrace goodness. They know that God's covenant (*berit*) and instruction (*torah*) offer rewards to those most concerned with what God wants.[317]

A particularly interesting text is Exodus 1:15-22. It provides background for the story of Moses's birth, and it says that the Pharaoh of Egypt told midwives to kill all newborn Israelite boys. In verse 17, we read, "The midwives, fearing [*yare*] God, did not do as the king of Egypt had told them; they let the boys live" (NJPS). What's so interesting about this verse is that most people would be scared to death to disobey Pharaoh's orders. Yet, what's stressed is that the midwives feared God. They clearly act in accordance with their fear of God, rather than acting in fear of Pharaoh (see also Exod 1:21).

This story drives home an important biblical message: aside from the self-absorbed, most people fear something. The ultimate question is, will you act fearing God, or will you act fearing something else? Later in Exodus, as the Israelites are leaving the land and approaching the Sea of Reeds, Pharaoh draws near with his armies. There, the people fear Pharaoh (Exod 14:10). However, Moses commands the people not to be afraid (14:13). By the chapter's end, after God rescues them, the people fear God—as they should (14:31; cf. 20:20).

In Samuel, we read that Saul, Israel's first king, failed to sacrifice animals even though God specifically told him to do so (1 Sam 15:3, 21). Saul loses the throne as a result of his actions. As Saul comes to his senses, he confesses exactly what he did wrong: "Saul said to Samuel, 'I have sinned; for I have transgressed [*avar*] the commandment of the LORD and your words, because I feared [*yare*] the people and obeyed [*shama*] their voice'" (1 Sam 15:24 NRSV). When Saul should have been fearing and obeying God, he instead feared and obeyed the people, thus rendering himself unfit to lead the people (cf. Ps 56:11 [12 Heb.]).

A well-known commandment is to avoid worshipping other gods. Sometimes, the Hebrew behind this command literally says that people shouldn't bow down or serve these other gods. Other times, the text literally says that people shouldn't *fear* these gods.[318] The Bible suggests that aside from people who live serving only themselves, most of us fear something. It calls readers to give our fear not to humans or other gods but to a just God who loves righteousness and hates evil.

In fact, many texts emphasize that when things are right with God, there's no reason to be afraid.[319] Throughout Deuteronomy and Joshua, the Israelites are commanded not to be afraid, for God is with them (e.g., Deut 1:29-30). In the little-used book of Zephaniah, we read these comforting words: "The LORD has taken away your punishment, he has turned back your enemy. The LORD, the King of Israel, is with you; never again will you fear [*yare*] any harm [*ra*]" (3:15 NIV). Similar words are found in the second major part of Isaiah. For example:

> Do not fear [*yare*], for I am with you;
> Do not anxiously look about you, for I am your God.
> I will strengthen you, surely I will help you,
> Surely I will uphold you with My righteous right hand. (Isa 41:10 NASB)

> In righteousness [*tsedaqah*] you will be established:
> Tyranny will be far from you;
>   you will have nothing to fear [*yare*].
> Terror will be far removed;
>   it will not come near you. (Isa 54:14 NIV)

These words addressed refugees who had suffered the loss of their homes and cities. They of all people would have most reason to be afraid. Yet, the hopeful message of the Bible is that they need not fear any longer.

Saint Francis of Assisi writes, “It is in giving that we receive, it is in pardoning that we are pardoned, it is in dying that we are born again to eternal life.”[320] To this list of paradoxes, we could add, “It is in fearing God that we no longer need to be afraid.” It’s by respecting, revering, and even fearing a good God that we set things right. And when things are right with God, there’s nothing else to fear.

Conclusion

It’s easy to assume, especially in cultures in which Christianity has played a significant role, that contemporary values align with those in the Bible. However, when we look at concrete specifics, we see important differences. Biblical love isn’t the same thing as the love that’s sung about on the radio. Cleanliness functioned like a sacrament in biblical Israel. Glory and holiness are nearly extinct concepts today. Modern culture overflows with information but lacks wisdom. Fear differed then from now. Biblical Hebrew unlocks a new, transformational way of thinking.

Chapter 9

Conclusion

Like a steady, unnoticed heartbeat, language performs vital functions in our lives. With our language, we process our experiences, we understand our identity, and we make sense of our world. By learning a new language—or even parts of it—new worlds open up to us. As John Utz puts it, "Words constitute the very terms of our existence; they are the medium in which we exercise both our beliefs and our fears, our power and our contrition."[321]

Words form the building blocks of our thoughts. They are the raw materials we use to construct our understanding of the world. Our thoughts are in some ways dependent upon the words we know. Our understanding of the world hinges upon the language that we use. (See **Language and Knowledge**.)

Language and Knowledge

"Language... is... a repository of world knowledge, a structured collection of meaningful categories that help us deal with new experiences and store information about old ones."[322]

—*Dirk Geeraerts and Hubert Cuyckens*

When we learn a new language, a new world opens up to us. A new way of thinking about reality becomes available to us. When we learn how someone else speaks, we begin to understand how that person thinks.

Learning a language is like learning a worldview. Those who learn biblical Hebrew can better understand not only what biblical authors wrote but also how they thought.[323]

In the twelfth chapter of Romans, we read, "Do not be conformed to this world, but be transformed by the renewing of your minds, so that you may discern what is the will of God—what is good and acceptable and perfect" (12:2 NRSV). There are many ways this transformation, renewal, and discernment can take place.

One of them is learning the Bible's native tongue. At first glance, learning Hebrew seems like it's best left to specialists. However, learning a language can be a means of theological formation.

Romans talks specifically about the transformation and renewal of our minds. I know of no better way to transform our thinking processes than learning a new language. Language provides the building blocks out of which our thoughts take shape. Learn a new language, and new thoughts become more accessible. We can certainly understand the basic message of Christianity in any language, including English. However, Hebrew allows us to flourish in new ways. (See **Vocabulary and Theology**.)

Vocabulary and Theology

"Vocabulary is theologically useful, not as a mere list of words, but through an understanding of meanings. . . . Once we talk of 'meanings' of words like the words for God, for 'create', for 'right' or 'justice', we are already moving into something close to theology. Word meanings are not a basis for theology: they already involve us in theology."[324]

—*James Barr*

As we have begun to study this language, we have gained new ways of viewing the Bible, the world, and our lives. By learning Hebrew sounds, we've found new dimensions at work in old texts. As we learned the meaning of various Hebrew names such as "Adam" and "Eve," we've come to see foundational passages in new lights. We have come to understand some of the unique nuances of particular passages, such as those using the word *bara*, the type of creating that only God is capable of. We have realized some of the ways that Hebrew words have multiple definitions, so that *raah* isn't just an ethical category but also disastrous results. We have visualized sin as a burden and forgiveness as the lifting (*nasa*) of that burden. We have unlocked the shackles of the past, finding fresh alternatives to such words as "behold" that no one uses any longer. Remembering (*zakhar*) has become an important part of faithful living. Biblical love has become less about infatuation and more about loyalty, at least when *khesed* is in view.

Both in terms of how we see the world and how we study the Bible, Hebrew is invaluable. It might be three thousand years old, but its words have remarkable freshness, deep meaning, and evocative power.

Appendix

How the Hebrew Alphabet Works

One of the most challenging aspects of learning biblical Hebrew is mastering its alphabet. The language is one of the few that's read from right to left. The letters look unlike our English letters, and unfortunately, many are easily confused with one another.

To help, the website www.MatthewSchlimm.com contains pronunciation aids and a concordance that lists the verses containing the Hebrew words described in this book. The material below also provides assistance.

Consonants

There are twenty-two consonants in biblical Hebrew. The following chart explains each letter's appearance, name, transliteration, and sound. Transliteration is how the letter appears in italics when using English letters. There are many ways of transliterating; the one here follows the Society of Biblical Literature General-Purpose Style.[325]

Hebrew Consonant	Name	Transliteration	Sound	Star Wars Word with Same Sound
א	*alef*	[none because it's silent]	[none]	(Similar to how all *y*'s aren't pronounced in Kashyyyk)
ב; בּ	*bet*	*v* for ב; *b* for בּ	*v* for ב; *b* for בּ	Vader for ב; Boba Fett for בּ
ג	*gimel*	*g*	*g*	Galactic Empire
ד	*dalet*	*d*	*d*	Death Star

Hebrew Consonant	Name	Transliteration	Sound	Star Wars Word with Same Sound
ה	*he*	*h*	*h*	Hoth
ו	*vav*	*v*	*v*	Vader
ז	*zayin*	*z*	*z*	Ziro the Hutt
ח	*khet*	*kh*	*kh*	Chewbacca (note: this Hebrew sound is actually more like the hard "h" in Bach)
ט	*tet*	*t*	*t*	Tatooine
י	*yod*	*y*	*y*	Yoda
כ; כּ	*kaf*	*kh* for כ; *k* for כּ	*kh* for כ; *k* for כּ	Chewbacca for כ; Ben Kenobi for כּ
ך-	final *kaf* (i.e., how *kaf* looks at the end of a word)	*kh*	*kh*	Chewbacca
ל	*lamed*	*l*	*l*	Lando Calrissian
מ	*mem*	*m*	*m*	Millennium Falcon
ם-	final *mem* (i.e., how *mem* looks at the end of a word)	*m*	*m*	Millennium Falcon
נ	*nun*	*n*	*n*	Nien Nunb
ן-	final *nun* (i.e., how *nun* looks at the end of a word)	*n*	*n*	Nien Nunb
ס	*samek*	*s*	*s*	Leia Organa Solo
ע	*ayin*	[none because it's silent]	[none]	(Similar to how all *y*'s aren't pronounced in Kashyyyk)

Hebrew Consonant	Name	Transliteration	Sound	Star Wars Word with Same Sound
פ; פּ	*pe*	*ph* for פ; *p* for פּ	*ph* for פ; *p* for פּ	Bib Fortuna for פ; Jek Porkins for פּ
ף	final *pe* (i.e., how *pe* looks at the end of a word)	*ph*	*ph*	Chief Chirpa
צ	*tsade*	*ts*	*ts*	Lightsaber
ץ	final *tsade* (i.e., how *tsade* looks at the end of a word)	*ts*	*ts*	Spaceports
ק	*qof*	*q*	*q*	Kit Fisto
ר	*resh*	*r*	*r*	Rebel Alliance
שׂ	*sin*	*s*	*s*	Han Solo
שׁ	*shin*	*sh*	*sh*	Shadow Troopers
ת	*tav*	*t*	*t*	Grand Moff Tarkin

A few things to note:

1. Three consonants are pronounced differently when they have a dot (called a *dagesh*) in them: *bet*, *kaf*, and *pe*. The presence of this dot often means the consonant is doubled. So, הִנֵּה is transliterated with two *n*'s because of the *dagesh* in the *nun*: *hinneh*.
2. Five consonants appear differently when at the end of a word: *kaf*, *mem*, *nun*, *pe*, and *tsade*.
3. Unfortunately, some consonants are easily confused:
   - *Bet* is ב and כ is *kaf*. Notice the bottom right part of the letters.
   - *Dalet* is ד and ר is *resh*. Notice the upper right part of the letters.
   - *Gimel* is ג and נ is *nun*. Notice the bottom of the letters.
   - *He* is ה and ח is *khet*. Notice the upper left part of the letters.
   - *Vav* is ו and ז is *zayin*. Notice the top of the letters.
   - *Khet* is ח and ת is *tav*. Notice the bottom left part of the letters.
   - *Tet* is ט and מ is *mem*. Notice the bottom of the letters.
   - *Yod* is י and ר is *resh*. Notice the difference in size.

- *Kaf* is כ and נ is *nun*. Notice the difference in width.
- Final *mem* is ם and ס is *samek*. Notice that the bottom of *samek* has more curves.
- *Ayin* is ע and צ is *tsade*. Notice the bottom right part of the letters.
- *Sin* is שׂ and שׁ is *shin*. Notice the positions of the dots.

Vowels

Hebrew was originally written without vowels. In the Middle Ages, people began forgetting how to pronounce the words. So, scribes invented ways of adding vowels to the biblical text, typically by putting dots and symbols above and below particular consonants. In the chart below, I show how the vowels look with the letter *mem*.

Hebrew Vowel with *mem*	Vowel Name	Transliteration	Sound	Star Wars Word with Same Sound
מַ	*patakh*	*a*	*ah*	Chewbacca
מָ	*qamets*; occasionally *qamets khatuf*	*a* for *qamets*; *o* for *qamets khatuf*	*ah*	Chewbacca
מֶ	*segol*	*e*	short *e*	Boba Fett
מֵ	*tsere*	*e*	*ay*	Vader
מֵי	*tsere yod*	*e*	*ay*	Vader
מִ	*hireq*	*i*	short *i* or long *e*	Millennium Falcon or Ewok
מִי	*hireq yod*	*i*	long *e*	Ewok
מֹ	*holem*	*o*	long *o*	Yoda
מוֹ	*holem vav*	*o*	long *o*	Yoda
מֻ	*qibbuts*	*u*	*u* or *oo*	Jabba the Hutt or Luke
מוּ	*shureq*	*u*	*oo*	Luke
מֲ	*khatef patakh*	*a*	*a*	Imperial Assault
מֱ	*khatef segol*	*e*	*e*	Rebel Fleet
מֳ	*khatef qamets*	*o*	*o*	X-Wing Pilot
מְ	vocal *sheva*	*e*	*e*	Rebel Fleet

Abbreviations

This book uses the following abbreviations, especially in the Works Cited and Endnotes.

AB	Anchor Bible
ABD	*Anchor Bible Dictionary*. Edited by D. N. Freedman. 6 vols. New York: Doubleday, 1992
alt.	altered
ANESSup	Ancient Near Eastern Studies Supplement Series
ANET	*Ancient Near Eastern Texts Relating to the Old Testament*. Edited by James B. Pritchard. 3rd ed. Princeton: Princeton University Press, 1969
AThR	*Anglican Theological Review*
BDB	Brown, Francis, S. R. Driver, and Charles A. Briggs. *A Hebrew and English Lexicon of the Old Testament*
BibInt	*Biblical Interpretation*
BibInt	Biblical Interpretation Series
BT	*The Bible Translator*
BZAW	Beihefte zur Zeitschrift für die alttestamentliche Wissenschaft
CC	Continental Commentaries
CEB	Common English Bible
cf.	compare
ch.	chapter
ConBOT	Coniectanea Biblica: Old Testament Series
COS	*The Context of Scripture*. Edited by William W. Hallo. 3 vols. Leiden: Brill, 1997–2002
DCH	*Dictionary of Classical Hebrew*. Edited by David J. A. Clines. 9 vols. Sheffield: Sheffield Phoenix, 1993–2016
DDD	*Dictionary of Deities and Demons in the Bible*. Edited by Karel van der Toorn, Bob Becking, and Pieter W. van der Horst. Leiden: Brill, 1995
ed(s.)	editor(s), edited by, edition
e.g.	for example
esp.	especially
fig.	figure

GKC	*Gesenius' Hebrew Grammar*. Edited by Emil Kautzsch. Translated by Arther E. Cowley. 2nd ed. Oxford: Clarendon, 1910
Grk.	Greek
HALOT(se)	*The Hebrew and Aramaic Lexicon of the Old Testament*. Ludwig Koehler, Walter Baumgartner, and Johann J. Stamm. Translated and edited under the supervision of Mervyn E. J. Richardson. Study ed. 2 vols. Leiden: Brill, 2001
Heb.	Hebrew
HS	*Hebrew Studies*
HUCA	*Hebrew Union College Annual*
IBC	Interpretation: A Bible Commentary for Teaching and Preaching
IBHS	*An Introduction to Biblical Hebrew Syntax*. Bruce K. Waltke and Michael O'Connor. Winona Lake, IN: Eisenbrauns, 1990
ibid.	in the same place
IDBSup	*Interpreter's Dictionary of the Bible: Supplementary Volume*. Edited by K. Crim. Abingdon Press: Nashville, 1976
idem	the same
i.e.	that is
JETS	*Journal of the Evangelical Theological Society*
JBL	*Journal of Biblical Literature*
JHebS	*Journal of Hebrew Scriptures*
JPS	Jewish Publication Society
JSOTSup	Journal for the Study of the Old Testament: Supplement Series
KAI	*Kanaanäische und aramäische Inschriften*. Herbert Donner and Wolfgang Röllig. 2nd ed. Wiesbaden: Harrassowitz, 1966–1969
KJV	King James Version
LHBOTS	The Library of Hebrew Bible/Old Testament Studies
n	note
NASB	New American Standard Bible
NICOT	New International Commentary on the Old Testament
NIDB	*New Interpreter's Dictionary of the Bible*. Edited by Katharine Doob Sakenfeld. 5 vols. Nashville: Abingdon, 2006–2009
NIDOTTE	*New International Dictionary of Old Testament Theology and Exegesis*. Edited by W. A. VanGemeren. 5 vols. Grand Rapids: Zondervan, 1997
NIV	New International Version
NJPS	*Tanakh: The Holy Scriptures: The New JPS Translation according to the Traditional Hebrew Text*
NLT	New Living Translation
no.	number
NRSV	New Revised Standard Version
OBT	Overtures to Biblical Theology
OED	*Oxford English Dictionary*
OLA	Orientalia lovaniensia analecta
OTL	Old Testament Library
rev.	revised
RSV	Revised Standard Version
SBL	Society of Biblical Literature
SBLABS	Society of Biblical Literature Archaeology and Biblical Studies

SBLDS	Society of Biblical Literature Dissertation Series
SBLSymS	Society of Biblical Literature Symposium Series
SBT	Studies in Biblical Theology
SHBC	Smyth & Helwys Bible Commentary
SJOT	*Scandinavian Journal of the Old Testament*
StBibLit	Studies in Biblical Literature
SubBi	Subsidia biblica
s.v.	under the word
TDNT	*Theological Dictionary of the New Testament.* Edited by Gerhard Kittel and Gerhard Friedrich. Translated by Geoffrey W. Bromiley. 10 vols. Grand Rapids: Eerdmans, 1964–1976
TDOT	*Theological Dictionary of the Old Testament.* Edited by G. Johannes Botterweck and Helmer Ringgren. Translated by John T. Willis et al. 15 vols. Grand Rapids: Eerdmans, 1974–2006
TLOT	*Theological Lexicon of the Old Testament.* Edited by Ernst Jenni, with assistance from Claus Westermann. Translated by Mark E. Biddle. 3 vols. Peabody, MA: Hendrickson, 1997
TOTC	Tyndale Old Testament Commentaries
TWOT	*Theological Wordbook of the Old Testament.* Edited by R. Laird Harris, Gleason L. Archer Jr., and Bruce K. Waltke. 2 vols. Chicago: Moody Press, 1980
trans.	translated by
UMH	*United Methodist Hymnal.* Nashville: United Methodist Publishing House, 1989
v.	verse
vol.	volume
VTSup	Supplements to Vetus Testamentum
WBC	Word Biblical Commentary
WW	*Word and World*
ZAW	*Zeitschrift für die alttestamentliche Wissenschaft*

Works Cited

Administrative Office of the US Courts on Behalf of the Federal Judiciary. "Process —Bankruptcy Basics." *United States Courts.* http://www.uscourts.gov/services-forms/bankruptcy/bankruptcy-basics/process-bankruptcy-basics.

Aitken, J. K. *The Semantics of Blessing and Cursing in Ancient Hebrew.* ANESSup 23. Louvain: Peeters, 2007.

"Altitudes of Major U.S. Cities." *Red Oaks Trading.* Formerly available at http://www.altimeters.net/cityaltitudes.html.

American Colony (Jerusalem), Photo Department. "Locust from the Plague in Palestine, 1915.jpg." Wikimedia Commons. Uploaded by Maksim. https://commons.wikimedia.org/wiki/File:Locust_from_the_plague_in_Palestine,_1915.jpg.

Amin, Osama Shukir Muhammed. "Assyrian King Ashurbanipal on His Horse Thrusting a Spear onto a Lion's Head: Alabaster Bas-relief from Nineveh, Dating Back to 645–635 BCE and Is Currently Housed in the British Museum, London." Wikimedia Commons. https://commons.wikimedia.org/wiki/File:Assyrian_king_Ashurbanipal_on_his_horse_thrusting_a_spear_onto_a_lion%E2%80%99s_head._Alabaster_bas-relief_from_Nineveh,_dating_back_to_645-635_BCE_and_is_currently_housed_in_the_British_Museum,_London.jpg.

Andersen, Francis I. "Lo and Behold!" In *Hamlet on a Hill: Semitic and Greek Studies Presented to Professor T. Muraoka on the Occasion of His Sixty-Fifth Birthday*, edited by M. F. J. Baasten and W. Th. Van Peursen, 25–66. OLA 118. Leuven: Peeters, 2003.

Anderson, Gary A. *Sin: A History.* New Haven: Yale University Press, 2009.

Anderson, Stephen R. *Languages: A Very Short Introduction.* Very Short Introductions 320. Oxford: Oxford University Press, 2012.

"Average Annual Precipitation by State." *Current Results.* https://www.currentresults.com/Weather/US/average-annual-state-precipitation.php.

Barnhart, Robert K., ed. *Chambers Dictionary of Etymology*. London: Chambers, 1988.

Barr, James. *Biblical Faith and Natural Theology: The Gifford Lectures for 1991, Delivered in the University of Edinburgh*. Oxford: Oxford University Press, 1999.

———. *The Concept of Biblical Theology: An Old Testament Perspective*. Minneapolis: Fortress, 1999.

———. "Hebrew Lexicography: Informal Thoughts." In *Linguistics and Biblical Hebrew*, edited by Walter R. Bodine, 137–51. Winona Lake, IN: Eisenbrauns, 1992.

———. "The Position of Hebrew Language in Theological Education." *International Review of Mission* 50, no. 200 (1961): 435–44.

———. "Semantics and Biblical Theology—A Contribution to the Discussion." In *Congress Volume: Uppsala 1971*, edited by P. A. H. de Boer, 13–19. VTSup 22. Leiden: Brill, 1972.

———. *The Semantics of Biblical Language*. London: SCM, 1961.

Barton, John. *Understanding Old Testament Ethics: Approaches and Explorations*. Louisville: Westminster John Knox, 2003.

Bauckham, Richard. *Jesus and the God of Israel: God Crucified and Other Studies on the New Testament's Christology of Divine Identity*. Grand Rapids: Eerdmans, 2008.

Becking, Bob, and Marjo C. A. Korpel. "To Create, to Separate or to Construct: An Alternative for a Recent Proposal as to the Interpretation of ברא in Gen 1:1–2:4a." *JHebS* 10 (2010): doi:10.5508/jhs.2010.v10.a3.

The Bible Project. "Shema." *YouTube*. https://www.youtube.com/watch?v=6KQLOuIKaRA.

Blenkinsopp, Joseph. *Isaiah 40–55: A New Translation with Introduction and Commentary*. AB. New York: Doubleday, 2002.

———. "Life Expectancy in Ancient Palestine." *SJOT* 11 (1997): 44–55.

Blois, Reinier de. "Towards a New Dictionary of Biblical Hebrew Based on Semantic Domains." *A Semantic Dictionary of Biblical Hebrew*. Swindon, UK: United Bible Societies, 2013. http://www.sdbh.org/documentation/Paper_SBL_2000.pdf.

Borowski, Oded. *Daily Life in Biblical Times*. SBLABS 5. Atlanta: SBL, 2003.

———. "Horse." *NIDB*, 2:891–93.

Botterweck, G. Johannes, and Helmer Ringgren, eds. *Theological Dictionary of the Old Testament*. Translated by John T. Willis et al. 15 vols. Grand Rapids: Eerdmans, 1974–2006.

Breytenbach, C., and P. L. Day. "Satan." *DDD*, 726–32.

Brown, Francis, S. R. Driver, and Charles A. Briggs. *A Hebrew and English Lexicon of the Old Testament*. Oxford: Clarendon, 1907.

Brueggemann, Walter. *Divine Presence amid Violence: Contextualizing Violence in the Book of Joshua*. Eugene, OR: Cascade, 2009.

———. *Prayers for a Privileged People*. Nashville: Abingdon, 2008.

Buechner, Frederick. *Wishful Thinking: A Theological ABC*. New York: Harper & Row, 1973.

Carasik, Michael. *Theologies of the Mind in Biblical Israel*. StBibLit 85. New York: Peter Lang, 2006.

Carroll, Robert P. "Cultural Encroachment and Bible Translation: Observations on Elements of Violence, Race and Class in the Production of Bibles in Translation." *Semeia* 76 (1996): 39–53.

Casanowicz, Immanuel M. "Paronomasia in the Old Testament." *JBL* 12 (1893): 105–67.

Chamberi. "Four Room House, Israel Museum, Jerusalem." Wikimedia Commons. https://commons.wikimedia.org/wiki/File:Four_room_house._Israel_Museum,_Jerusalem.JPG.

Chardin, Jean Siméon. "Soap Bubbles." The Met. http://www.metmuseum.org/art/collection/search/435888.

Childs, Brevard S. *Isaiah*. OTL. Louisville: Westminster John Knox, 2001.

———. *Memory and Tradition in Israel*. SBT. Naperville, IL: Alec R. Allenson, 1962.

———. *Old Testament Theology in a Canonical Context*. Philadelphia: Fortress, 1986.

The Church of England. "Prayers and Thanksgivings." *Book of Common Prayer*. http://www.churchofengland.org/prayer-worship/worship/book-of-common-prayer/prayers-and-thanksgivings.aspx.

Clark, Gordon R. *The Word* Hesed *in the Hebrew Bible*. JSOTSup 157. Sheffield: Sheffield Academic, 1993.

Clines, David J. A. "Alleged Basic Meanings of the Hebrew Verb *qdš* 'be holy': An Exercise in Comparative Hebrew Lexicography." *Academia*. www.academia.edu/28065748.

———. "The Challenge of Hebrew Lexicography Today." In *Congress Volume: Ljubljana 2007*, edited by André Lemaire, 87-98. VTSup 133. Leiden: Brill, 2010.

———, ed. *Dictionary of Classical Hebrew*. 9 vols. Sheffield: Sheffield Phoenix, 1993–2016.

Crenshaw, James L. *Defending God: Biblical Responses to the Problem of Evil*. Oxford: Oxford University Press, 2005.

———. *Old Testament Wisdom: An Introduction*. Rev. and enlarged ed. Louisville: Westminster John Knox, 1998.

Cross, Frank Moore. *Canaanite Myth and Hebrew Epic: Essays in the History of the Religion of Israel.* Cambridge, MA: Harvard University Press, 1973.

Crossan, John Dominic, and Richard G. Watts. *Who Is Jesus? Answers to Your Questions about the Historical Jesus*. New York: HarperCollins, 1996.

Crouch, Andy. "The Future Shape of Theological Education." *Catalyst: Contemporary Evangelical Perspectives for United Methodist Seminarians* 39, no. 3 (2013): 1–3.

Davies, Philip R., and John Rogerson. *The Old Testament World*. 2nd ed. Louisville: Westminster John Knox, 2005.

Davis, Ellen F. "Blessing and Well-Being." *The Work of the People*. http://www.theworkofthepeople.com/blessing-and-well-being.

———. *Reading Israel's Scriptures* [working title]. Unpublished manuscript.

———. *Scripture, Culture, and Agriculture: An Agrarian Reading of the Bible*. New York: Cambridge University Press, 2009.

———. "Slaves or Sabbath-Keepers? A Biblical Perspective on Human Work." *ATbR* 83 (2001): 25–40.

Dever, William G. *The Lives of Ordinary People in Ancient Israel: Where Archaeology and the Bible Intersect*. Grand Rapids: Eerdmans, 2012.

Donner, Herbert, and Wolfgang Röllig. *Kanaanäische und aramäische Inschriften*. 2nd ed. Wiesbaden: Harrassowitz, 1966–69.

Edwards, Douglas R. "Dress and Ornamentation." *ABD*, 2:232–38.

Elnes, E. E., and P. D. Miller. "Elyon." *DDD*, 293–99.

Ewald, Heinrich. *Old and New Testament Theology*. Translated by Thomas Goadby. Edinburgh: T. & T. Clark, 1888. https://books.google.com/books?id=OV5BAAAAYAAJ.

Fee, Gordon D., and Mark L. Strauss. *How to Choose a Translation for All Its Worth: A Guide to Understanding and Using Bible Versions*. Grand Rapids: Zondervan, 2007.

Fokkelman, J. P. *Narrative Art in Genesis: Specimens of Stylistic and Structural Analysis*. 2nd ed. Eugene, OR: Wipf & Stock, 1991.

Francis of Assisi. "The Prayer of Saint Francis." *UMH* 481.

Freedman, David Noel. "The Aaronic Benediction (Numbers 6:24–26)." In *No Famine in the Land: Studies in Honor of John L. McKenzie*, edited by James W. Flanagan and Anita Weisbrod Robinson, 35–48. Missoula, MT: Scholars, 1975.

Fretheim, Terence E. *Exodus*. IBC. Louisville: Westminster John Knox, 2010.

———. "Salvation in the Bible vs. Salvation in the Church." *WW* 13 (1993): 363–72.

———. *The Suffering of God: An Old Testament Perspective*. OBT. Philadelphia: Fortress, 1984.

Frick, Frank S. *A Journey through the Hebrew Scriptures*. 2nd ed. Belmont, CA: Thomson Wadsworth, 2003.

Gaba, Eric. "Israel Relief Location Map-Blank." Wikimedia Commons. https://commons.wikimedia.org/wiki/File:Israel_relief_location_map-blank.jpg.

Gammie, John. *Holiness in Israel*. OBT. Minneapolis: Fortress, 1989.

Geeraerts, Dirk, and Hubert Cuyckens. "Introducing Cognitive Linguistics." In *The Oxford Handbook of Cognitive Linguistics*, edited by Dirk Geeraerts and Hubert Cuyckens, 3-21. Oxford: Oxford University Press, 2007.

Glueck, Nelson. Hesed *in the Bible*. Translated by Alfred Gottschalk. Cincinnati: Hebrew Union College Press, 1967.

Gossai, Hemchand. *Barrenness and Blessing: Abraham, Sarah, and the Journey of Faith*. Eugene, OR: Cascade, 2008.

"The Great Litany." In *The (Online) Book of Common Prayer*, 148-55. New York: The Church Hymnal Corporation. https://www.bcponline.org/GreatLitany/Litany.html.

Green, Joel B. *Why Salvation?* Reframing New Testament Theology. Nashville: Abingdon, 2014.

Greenstein, Edward L. "Wordplay, Hebrew." *ABD*, 6:968–71.

Grossman, Jonathan. "The Double Etymology of Babel in Genesis 11." *ZAW* 129 (2017): 362–75.

Ḥakham, Amos, and Israel V. Berman. *Psalms with the Jerusalem Commentary*. 3 vols. Jerusalem: Mosad Harav Kook, 2003.

Hallo, William W., ed. *The Context of Scripture*. 3 vols. Leiden: Brill, 1997–2002.

Hamilton, Victor P. *The Book of Genesis: Chapters 1–17*. NICOT. Grand Rapids: Eerdmans, 1990.

———. *Exodus: An Exegetical Commentary*. Grand Rapids: Baker Academic, 2011.

———. "Satan." *ABD*, 5:985–89.

Harris, R. Laird, Gleason L. Archer Jr., and Bruce K. Waltke, eds. *Theological Wordbook of the Old Testament*. 2 vols. Chicago: Moody Press, 1980.

Hays, Richard B. *Reading Backwards: Figural Christology and the Fourfold Witness*. Waco, TX: Baylor University Press, 2014.

Herrmann, W. "El." *DDD*, 274–80.

Herzog, Ze'ev. *Archaeology of the City: Urban Planning in Ancient Israel and Its Social Implications*. Nadler Institute of Archaeology Monograph 13. Tel Aviv: Tel Aviv University Press, 1997.

Heschel, Abraham Joshua. *Man Is Not Alone: A Philosophy of Religion*. New York: Farrar, Straus & Young, 1951.

Horne, Milton P. *Proverbs—Ecclesiastes*. SHBC. Macon, GA: Smyth & Helwys, 2003.

Howard, Jr., David M. "David." *ABD*, 2:41–49.

Jackson, J. B. *Dictionary of the Proper Names of the Old and New Testament Scriptures, Being an Accurate and Literal Translation from the Original Tongues*. New York: Loizeaux Brothers, 1909.

Jacobs, A. J. *The Year of Living Biblically*. New York: Simon & Schuster, 2007.

Jacobson, Rolf A. "Learning Hebrew by Writing in English." *Teaching Theology and Religion* 14 (2011): 125–36.

Jenni, Ernst, ed., with assistance from Claus Westermann. *Theological Lexicon of the Old Testament*. Translated by Mark E. Biddle. 3 vols. Peabody, MA: Hendrickson, 1997.

Jeremias, Jörg. *The Book of Amos*. Translated by Douglas W. Scott. OTL. Louisville: Westminster John Knox, 1998.

Jerome, Saint. *To Pammachius: On the Best Method of Translating (St Jerome, Letter 57)*. Translated by Louis G. Kelly. Ottawa: Ecole de Traducteurs et d'Interpretes, Université d'Ottawa, 1976.

Jobes, Karen J. "Relevance Theory and the Translation of Scripture." *JETS* 50 (2007): 773–97.

Jones, Alfred. *Jones' Dictionary of Old Testament Proper Names*. Grand Rapids: Kregel, 1990.

Jones, Ethan. "Direct Reflexivity in Biblical Hebrew: A Note on שׁנפ." *ZAW* 129 (2017): 411–26.

Kabergs, Valérie, and Hans Ausloos. "Paronomasia or Wordplay? A Babel-Like Confusion towards a Definition of Hebrew Wordplay." *Bib* 93 (2012): 1–20.

Kautzsch, Emil, ed. *Gesenius' Hebrew Grammar*. Translated by Arther E. Cowley. 2nd ed. Oxford: Clarendon, 1910.

Kittel, Gerhard, and Gerhard Friedrich, eds. *Theological Dictionary of the New Testament*. Translated by Geoffrey W. Bromiley. 10 vols. Grand Rapids: Eerdmans, 1964–1976.

Kitz, Anne Marie. *Cursed Are You! The Phenomenology of Cursing in Cuneiform and Hebrew Texts*. Winona Lake, IN: Eisenbrauns, 2014.

Klawans, Jonathan. *Impurity and Sin in Ancient Judaism*. Oxford: Oxford University Press, 2000.

Knauf, E. A. "Shadday." *DDD*, 749–53.

Koch, Klaus. *The Prophets*. 2 vols. Philadelphia: Fortress, 1983–84.

Koehler, Ludwig, Walter Baumgartner, and Johann J. Stamm. *The Hebrew and Aramaic Lexicon of the Old Testament*. Translated and edited under the supervision of Mervyn E. J. Richardson. Study ed. 2 vols. Leiden: Brill, 2001.

Lakoff, George, and Mark Johnson. *Metaphors We Live By*. Chicago: University of Chicago Press, 2003.

Lambert, David Arthur. "Refreshing Philology: James Barr, Supersessionism, and the State of Biblical Words." *BibInt* 24 (2016): 332–56.

Leeb, Carolyn. "Translating the Hebrew Body into English Metaphor." In *The Social Sciences and Biblical Translation*, edited by Dietmar Neufeld, 109-25. SBLSymS. Atlanta: SBL, 2008.

Levy, Robert I. *Tahitians: Mind and Experience in the Society Islands*. Chicago: University of Chicago Press, 1973.

Luther, Martin. "A Mighty Fortress Is Our God." Translated by Frederick H. Hedge. *UMH* 110.

———. "Sendbrief vom Dolmetschen." In *An den christlichen Adel deutscher Nation; Von der Freiheit eines Christenmenschen; Sendbrief vom Dolmetschen*, edited by Ernst Kähler, 151-73. 2nd ed. Stuttgart: Reclam, 1970.

Lutz, Catherine A. *Unnatural Emotions: Everyday Sentiments on a Micronesian Atoll and Their Challenge to Western Theory*. Chicago: University of Chicago Press, 1988.

MacDonald, Nathan. "Deuteronomy." In *The CEB Study Bible*, 259–324 OT. Nashville: Common English Bible, 2013.

———. *What Did the Ancient Israelites Eat? Diet in Biblical Times*. Grand Rapids: Eerdmans, 2008.

Matthews, T. S. *Under the Influence*. London: Cassell, 1977.

Matthews, Victor H. "Cloth, Clothing." *NIDB*, 1:691–96.

Mays, James Luther. *Amos: A Commentary*. OTL. Philadelphia: Westminster, 1969.

Merwe, C. H. J. van der. "A Cognitive Linguistic Perspective on הִנֵּה in the Pentateuch, Joshua, Judges, and Ruth." *HS* 48 (2007): 101–40.

Mettinger, T. N. D. "Yahweh Zebaoth." *DDD*, 920–24.

Milgrom, Jacob. *Leviticus*. CC. Minneapolis: Fortress, 2004.

———. *Numbers*. The JPS Torah Commentary. Philadelphia: JPS, 1990.

Mitchell, Christopher Wright. *The Meaning of* BRK *"To Bless" in the Old Testament*. SBLDS 95. Atlanta: Scholars, 1987.

Mueller, Enio R. "The Semantics of Biblical Hebrew: Some Remarks from a Cognitive Perspective." *A Semantic Dictionary of Biblical Hebrew*. Swinton, UK: United Bible Societies, 2000–2009. http://www.sdbh.org/documentation/EnioRMueller_SemanticsBiblicalHebrew.pdf.

Mundhenk, Norm. "Jesus Is Lord: The Tetragrammaton in Bible Translation." *BT* 61 (2010): 55–63.

Newsom, Carol. "Models of the Moral Self: Hebrew Bible and Second Temple Judaism." *JBL* 131 (2012): 5–25.

Nussbaum, Martha. *Upheavals of Thought: The Intelligence of Emotions*. Cambridge: Cambridge University Press, 2003.

OED Online. Oxford University Press. http://www.oed.com/.

Olson, Dennis. *Numbers*. IBC. Louisville: Westminster John Knox, 1996.

Ortberg, John. *The Life You've Always Wanted: Spiritual Disciplines of Ordinary People*. Grand Rapids: Zondervan, 2002.

Pardee, D. "Eloah." *DDD*, 285–88.

Parker, Evelyn L. "Honoring the Body." In *On Our Way: Christian Practices for Living a Whole Life*, edited by Dorothy C. Bass and Susan R. Briehl, 133–48. Nashville: Upper Room, 2010.

Parrot, André. *Assur*. Paris: Gallimard, 2007.

Peters, Kurtis. *Hebrew Lexical Semantics and Daily Life in Ancient Israel: What's Cooking in Biblical Hebrew*. BibInt 146. Leiden: Brill, 2016.

Peterson, Eugene H. *Christ Plays in Ten Thousand Places: A Conversation in Spiritual Theology*. Grand Rapids: Eerdmans, 2005.

Poirier, John C. "The Case for Italics in Bible Translation." *Stone-Campbell Journal* 16 (2013): 207–16.

Pritchard, James B., ed. *Ancient Near Eastern Texts Relating to the Old Testament*. 3rd ed. Princeton: Princeton University Press, 1969.

Pym, Anthony. *Negotiating the Frontier: Translators and Intercultures in Hispanic History*. New York: Routledge, 2000.

Rau, Andy. "The Top Ten Bible Verses of 2015 and More: Bible Gateway's Year in Review Is Here." *BibleGateway Blog*, December 28, 2015. https://www.biblegateway.com/blog/2015/12/the-top-ten-bible-verses-of-2015-and-more-bible-gateways-year-in-review-is-here/.

Ritzer, George. *The McDonaldization of Society*. 8th ed. Thousand Oaks, CA: Sage, 2015.

Rogerson, John. "What Is Holiness?" In *Holiness Past and Present*, edited by Stephen C. Barton, 3–21. London: T & T Clark, 2003.

Sakenfeld, Katharine Doob. *Faithfulness in Action: Loyalty in Biblical Perspective*. Eugene, OR: Wipf and Stock, 2001.

———, ed. *New Interpreter's Dictionary of the Bible*. 5 vols. Nashville: Abingdon, 2006–9.

Sasson, J. M. "Wordplay in the OT." *IDBSup*, 968–70.

Saussure, Ferdinand de. *Course in General Linguistics*. Translated by Wade Baskin. New York: Columbia University Press, 2011.

The SBL Handbook of Style: For Biblical Studies and Related Disciplines. 2nd ed. Atlanta: SBL, 2014.

Schafer, R. Murray. *The Soundscape: Our Sonic Environment and the Tuning of the World*. Rochester, VT: Destiny, 1994.

Schlimm, Matthew Richard. "The Central Role of Emotions in Biblical Theology, Biblical Ethics, and Popular Conceptions of the Bible." In *Mixed Feelings and Vexed Passions in Biblical Literature: Emotions of Divine and Human Beings in Interdisciplinary Perspective*, edited by Scott Spencer, 43–59. Atlanta: SBL, 2017.

———. *From Fratricide to Forgiveness: The Language and Ethics of Anger in Genesis*. Siphrut: Literature and Theology of the Hebrew Scriptures 7. Winona Lake, IN: Eisenbrauns, 2011.

———. *This Strange and Sacred Scripture: Wrestling with the Old Testament and Its Oddities*. Grand Rapids: Baker Academic, 2015.

Schniedewind, William M. "*Prolegomena* for the Sociolinguistics of Classical Hebrew." *JHebS* 5 (2005): http://www.jhsonline.org/Articles/article_36.pdf.

Schökel, Luis Alonso. *A Manual of Hebrew Poetics*. *SubBi* 11. Rome: Pontifical Biblical Institute, 2000.

Shields, Frederic. "Rahab Hangs the Scarlet Cord from Her Window." Wikimedia Commons. Uploaded by Fæ. https://commons.wikimedia.org/wiki/File%3ARahab_hangs_the_scarlet_cord_from_her_window._Autotype_after_Wellcome_V0034410.jpg.

Smith, Mark S. *The Early History of God: Yahweh and the Other Deities in Ancient Israel.* 2nd ed. Grand Rapids: Eerdmans, 2002.

———. *Poetic Heroes: Literary Commemorations of Warriors and Warrior Culture in the Early Biblical World.* Grand Rapids: Eerdmans, 2014.

———. "Words and Their Worlds." In *Biblical Lexicology: Hebrew and Greek*, edited by Eberhard Bons, Jan Joosten, and Regine Hunziker-Rodewald, 3–31. BZAW 443. Berlin: De Gruyter, 2015.

Smith, Michael K. "Metaphor and Mind." *American Speech* 57 (1982): 128–34.

Spyder Monkey. "The Civil Rights Memorial, Montgomery, AL.jpg." Wikimedia Commons. https://commons.wikimedia.org/wiki/File:The_Civil_Rights_Memorial,_Montgomery,_AL.jpg.

Stewart, John. "Social Construction Panel: 'Five Years Out.'" Position statement presented at the Annual Convention of the National Communication Association, Chicago, IL, November 2009.

Strawn, Brent A. "Teaching the Old Testament: When God Seems Unjust." *Circuit Rider* 36, no. 4 (Aug–Oct 2012): 7–9.

Teilhard de Chardin, Pierre. "Patient Trust." In *Hearts on Fire: Praying with Jesuits*, edited by Michael Harter, 102–3. Chicago: Loyola, 2005.

Theology Working Group. "A Statement on the Prosperity Gospel." *The Lausanne Movement.* https://www.lausanne.org/content/a-statement-on-the-prosperity-gospel.

Thomas, Robert L. *How to Choose a Bible Version.* Rev. ed. Glasgow: Mentor, 2004.

Toorn, Karel van der, Bob Becking, and Pieter W. van der Horst, eds. *Dictionary of Deities and Demons in the Bible.* Leiden: Brill, 1995.

Trible, Phyllis. *God and the Rhetoric of Sexuality.* OBT. Philadelphia: Fortress, 1978.

United Methodist Hymnal. Nashville: United Methodist Publishing House, 1989.

Unseth, Peter. "Sacred Name Bible Translations in English: A Fast-Growing Phenomenon." *BT* 62 (2011): 185–94.

VanGemeren. Willem A., ed. *New International Dictionary of Old Testament Theology and Exegesis.* 5 vols. Grand Rapids: Zondervan, 1997.

Viberg, Åke. *Symbols of Law: A Contextual Analysis of Legal Symbolic Acts in the Old Testament.* ConBOT 34. Stockholm: Almqvist & Wiksell International, 1992.

Voinov, Vitaly. "Troublesome Transliterations." *BT* 63 (2012): 17–27.

Walsh, Carey. "Testing Entry: The Social Functions of City Gates in Biblical Memory." In

Memory and the City in Ancient Israel, edited by Diana V. Edelman and Ehud Ben Zvi, 43–59. Winona Lake, IN: Eisenbrauns, 2014.

Waltke, Bruce K., and Michael O'Connor. *An Introduction to Biblical Hebrew Syntax*. Winona Lake, IN: Eisenbrauns, 1990.

Wardlaw, Terrance R. *Conceptualizing Words for "God" within the Pentateuch: A Cognitive-Semantic Investigation in Literary Context*. LHBOTS 495. New York: T&T Clark, 2008.

Wenham, Gordon J. *Genesis 1–15*. WBC. Nashville: Thomas Nelson, 1987.

———. *Numbers*. TOTC. Downers Grove, IL: Inter-Varsity, 1981.

Westermann, Claus. *Blessing in the Bible and the Life of the Church*. Translated by Keith Crim. OBT. Philadelphia: Fortress, 1978.

———. *Isaiah 40–66: A Commentary*. OTL. Philadelphia: Westminster, 1969.

Whitley, Charles Francis. "The Semantic Range of *Ḥesed*." *Bib* 62 (1981): 519–26.

Wildberger, Hans. *Isaiah 1–12*. CC. Minneapolis: Fortress, 1991.

Williams, James G. "The Alas-Oracles of the Eighth Century Prophets." *HUCA* 38 (1967): 75–91.

Wolde, Ellen van. *Reframing Biblical Studies: When Language and Text Meet Culture, Cognition, and Context*. Winona Lake, IN: Eisenbrauns, 2009.

Wolde, Ellen van, and Robert Rezetko. "Semantics and the Semantics of ברא: A Rejoinder to the Arguments Advanced by B. Becking and M. Korpel." *JHebS* 11 (2011): doi:10.5508/jhs.2011.v11.a9.

Wolff, Hans Walter. *Obadiah and Jonah: A Commentary*. Translated by Margaret Kohl. CC. Minneapolis: Augsburg, 1986.

Wolters, Al. "Wordplay and Dialect in Amos 8:1-2." *JETS* 31 (1988): 407–10.

Wright, Christopher J. H. *The Mission of God's People: A Biblical Theology of the Church's Mission*. Grand Rapids: Zondervan, 2010.

Endnotes

1. Matthew Richard Schlimm, *From Fratricide to Forgiveness: The Language and Ethics of Anger in Genesis*, Siphrut: Literature and Theology of the Hebrew Scriptures 7 (Winona Lake, IN: Eisenbrauns, 2011), 19–34, esp. 19–21.

2. Saint Jerome, *To Pammachius: On the Best Method of Translating (St Jerome, Letter 57)*, trans. Louis G. Kelly (Ottawa: Ecole de Traducteurs et d'Interprètes, Université d'Ottawa, 1976), 8, §6.

3. Martin Luther, "*Sendbrief vom Dolmetschen*," in *An den christlichen Adel deutscher Nation; Von der Freiheit eines Christenmenschen; Sendbrief vom Dolmetschen*, ed. Ernst Kähler, 2nd ed. (Stuttgart: Reclam, 1970), 151–73, esp. 164, translation mine; the original has *tun Abbruch* for "demolish" and *weichen von* for "depart from."

4. Robert P. Carroll, "Cultural Encroachment and Bible Translation: Observations on Elements of Violence, Race and Class in the Production of Bibles in Translation," *Semeia* 76 (1996): 39–53, here 39–40.

5. Two books are especially helpful for digging deeper into Bible translation. The following book offers a useful discussion of what takes place in translation: Gordon D. Fee and Mark L. Strauss, *How to Choose a Translation for All Its Worth: A Guide to Understanding and Using Bible Versions* (Grand Rapids: Zondervan, 2007). The second book is helpful in discussing different translations, though it doesn't discuss more recent translations like the CEB: Robert L. Thomas, *How to Choose a Bible Version*, rev. ed. (Glasgow: Mentor, 2004).

6. See the honest assessment by Rolf A. Jacobson, "Learning Hebrew by Writing in English," *Teaching Theology and Religion* 14 (2011): 125–36, here 125–27.

7. Occasionally, I have selected words that are not especially popular because they illustrate broader points. For example, two of the words mentioned when discussing Isaiah 5:7 aren't popular. Yet, they form a highly significant wordplay with two other common Hebrew words in the verse.

8. See James Barr, *The Semantics of Biblical Language* (London: SCM, 1961); Enio R. Mueller, "The Semantics of Biblical Hebrew: Some Remarks from a Cognitive Perspective," *A Semantic Dictionary of Biblical Hebrew* (Swinton, UK: United Bible Societies, 2000–2009), http://www.sdbh.org/documentation/EnioRMueller_SemanticsBiblicalHebrew.pdf, 9, §2.2. Other examples of works moving beyond Barr include Schlimm, *From Fratricide to Forgiveness*, 28–34; Kurtis Peters, *Hebrew Lexical Semantics and Daily Life in Ancient Israel: What's Cooking in Biblical Hebrew*, BibInt 146 (Leiden: Brill, 2016).

9. Jacobson, "Learning Hebrew," 125–36, provides several useful examples of how knowing Hebrew grammar can enhance one's understanding of the Bible.

10. John C. Poirier, "The Case for Italics in Bible Translation," *Stone-Campbell Journal* 16 (2013): 207–16, here 215.

11. For these reasons and others, it makes sense to heed James Barr's warning about associating Hebrew thought with revelation and Greek thought with human reason (*Biblical Faith and Natural Theology: The Gifford Lectures for 1991, Delivered in the University of Edinburgh* [Oxford: Oxford University Press, 1999], 204–5).

12. See *Qur'an* 12:2; 13:37; 16:103; 19:97; 20:113; 39:27-28; 41:3; 42:7; 43:3; 44:58; 46:12; esp. 26:192-95; 41:44.

13. Ellen Davis, *Reading Israel's Scriptures* [working title], manuscript, quotation from the introduction.

14. Ferdinand de Saussure, *Course in General Linguistics*, trans. Wade Baskin (New York: Columbia University Press, 2011), 67–70; Stephen R. Anderson, *Languages: A Very Short Introduction*, Very Short Introductions 320 (Oxford: Oxford University Press, 2012), 33–34.

15. Saussure, *Course in General Linguistics*, 65–67.

16. Cf. Valérie Kabergs and Hans Ausloos, "Paronomasia or Wordplay? A Babel-Like Confusion towards a Definition of Hebrew Wordplay," *Bib* 93

(2012): 1–20, here 8. For a more technical and expansive classification, see J. M. Sasson, "Wordplay in the OT," *IDBSup*, 968–70.

17. Edward L. Greenstein, "Wordplay, Hebrew," *ABD*, 6:968–71. For a helpful listing of wordplays in biblical Hebrew, see Immanuel M. Casanowicz, "Paronomasia in the Old Testament," *JBL* 12 (1893): 105–67.

18. R. Murray Schafer, *The Soundscape: Our Sonic Environment and the Tuning of the World* (Rochester, VT: Destiny, 1994), 11. Christine Norquest Salinas drew my attention to this work.

19. Ellen F. Davis, *Scripture, Culture, and Agriculture: An Agrarian Reading of the Bible* (New York: Cambridge University Press, 2009), 29. Davis's text was altered slightly to match the system of transliteration used in this book.

20. Matthew Richard Schlimm, *This Strange and Sacred Scripture: Wrestling with the Old Testament and Its Oddities* (Grand Rapids: Baker Academic, 2015), 24–25.

21. For an English translation that interacts heavily with the Hebrew, see Schlimm, *This Strange and Sacred Scripture*, 209–16.

22. Victor Hamilton, *The Book of Genesis: Chapters 1–17*, NICOT (Grand Rapids: Eerdmans, 1990), 352.

23. Jonathan Grossman, "The Double Etymology of Babel in Genesis 11," *ZAW* 129 (2017): 362–75, here 366, 374.

24. Cf. Kabergs and Ausloos, "Paronomasia or Wordplay?" 19. Note also that the Hebrew word for "let us confuse" in 11:7 plays on the Hebrew word for "let us make bricks" in 11:3, as pointed out in Gordon J. Wenham, *Genesis 1–15*, WBC (Nashville: Thomas Nelson, 1987), 236, 239; Hamilton, *Genesis*, 355.

25. Cf. Wenham, *Genesis 1–15*, 234–35.

26. Jesus retells this parable in an interesting way in Matthew 21:33-46 (Brevard Childs, *Isaiah*, OTL [Louisville: Westminster John Knox, 2001], 46).

27. The same Hebrew word used to describe the grapes in Isaiah 5:2 is used to describe the odious smells of Genesis 34:30 and Exodus 5:21; 7:18, 21. Cf. Hans Wildberger, *Isaiah 1–12*, CC (Minneapolis: Fortress, 1991), 182.

28. On the challenges of translating the Hebrew word for "bloodshed," see Wildberger, *Isaiah 1–12*, 185.

29. Some scholars have even posited that in the northern kingdom of Israel, the words for "summer fruit" and "end" would have sounded not just similar but (nearly) identical. See the discussion in Al Wolters, "Wordplay and Dialect in Amos 8:1-2," *JETS* 31 (1988): 407–10.

30. Both the quotation and the numbers come from Jacob Milgrom, *Numbers*, The JPS Torah Commentary (Philadelphia: JPS, 1990), 51. The number of syllables is based on a pre-Masoretic vocalization posited by David Noel Freedman, "The Aaronic Benediction (Numbers 6:24-26)," in *No Famine in the Land: Studies in Honor of John L. McKenzie*, eds. James W. Flanagan and Anita Weisbrod Robinson (Missoula, MT: Scholars, 1975), 35–48, here 35–36.

31. Gordon J. Wenham, *Numbers*, TOTC (Downers Grove, IL: InterVarsity, 1981), 101.

32. Milgrom, *Numbers*, 51.

33. For additional examples of wordplays in the Hebrew Bible, see the excellent work by Luis Alonso Schökel, *A Manual of Hebrew Poetics, SubBi* 11 (Rome: Pontifical Biblical Institute, 2000), 20–33.

34. Biblical Hebrew is a very old language, and we don't know exactly how it sounded in ancient times. We do know that people in different regions pronounced words differently (Judg 12:5-6). Furthermore, the language was initially written without any vowels. Then, to make things even more complicated, many of our English Bible names don't come to us directly from Hebrew but instead reflect a history of translation that included languages such as Greek and Latin. For example, the Hebrew name for Isaac is יִצְחָק, transliterated *yitskhaq*. The English is much closer to the ancient Greek, 'Ισαάκ (transliterated *Isaak*), and identical in spelling to the ancient Latin, "Isaac." However, even with these complicating dynamics, modern readers gain at least a rough approximation of what the original language sounded like.

35. John Dominic Crossan and Richard G. Watts, *Who Is Jesus? Answers to Your Questions about the Historical Jesus* (New York: HarperCollins, 1996), 79.

36. For a detailed explanation of each of these points, see Schlimm, *This Strange and Sacred Scripture*, ch. 2.

37. On occasion, Nathan uses the Hebrew word *natan* meaning "he gives" (2 Sam 12:8, 11). However, this word is extremely common, showing up over two thousand times in the Bible. So, there is nothing particularly extraordinary about Nathan saying *natan* in Hebrew. Many other characters say it as well.

38. These sentences are often used in online book descriptions for J. B. Jackson, *Dictionary of the Proper Names of the Old and New Testament Scriptures, Being an Accurate and Literal Translation from the Original Tongues* (New York: Loizeaux Brothers, 1909), e.g., https://www.barnesandnoble.com/w/a-dictionary-of-scripture-proper-names-j-b-jackson/1001467454. Although some websites claim the sentences are from the book's "Introduction," the original publication does not contain these words.

39. While such a claim has been made, it has its problems. See David M. Howard Jr., "David," *ABD*, 2:41–49, here 41.

40. Hans Walter Wolff, *Obadiah and Jonah: A Commentary*, trans. Margaret Kohl, CC (Minneapolis: Augsburg, 1986), 98–99.

41. Additionally, readers may want to check out Jackson, *Dictionary of the Proper Names of the Old and New Testament Scriptures*, which at the time of my writing is available free through Google Books; see also Alfred Jones, *Jones' Dictionary of Old Testament Proper Names* (Grand Rapids: Kregel, 1990).

42. The underlined words use a longer name for God (*elohim*) than what we have with Bethel (*el*). However, the two appear to have connections and are usually interchangeable (H. Ringgren, "אלהים," *TDOT*, 1:267–84, here 272–73). For an excellent interpretation of the literary artistry of this text, see J. P. Fokkelman, *Narrative Art in Genesis: Specimens of Stylistic and Structural Analysis*, 2nd ed. (Eugene, OR: Wipf & Stock, 1991), 62–64.

43. Outside of worship-related words, a small number of words in English have their etymological roots in Hebrew, such as the English word "sack," which comes from the Hebrew שַׂק, transliterated *saq*.

44. An example of conservativism in worship can be found in Joshua 5:2, a text set in the Bronze Age during which God commands Joshua to circumcise the Israelites with a Stone Age tool (a flint knife).

45. This interpretation is less popular than the one given above. However, the Hebrew word is open to different interpretations. I here assume it is a masculine singular adjective reminding people of God's reliability (or the speaker's

trustworthiness in 1 Kings 1:36; with sarcasm in Jeremiah 28:6). This interpretation works with several texts, including Deuteronomy 27:15-26, where the highest concentration of the word is found. Affirmations of God's character using words from the root אמן abound (e.g., Deut 7:9; Isa 65:16). The word is used in Sirach 7:22 to talk about the reliability of cattle.

46. Alfred Jepsen, "אמן," *TDOT*, 1:292–323, here 320.

47. R. W. L. Moberly, "586 אמן," *NIDOTTE*, 1:427–33, here 428; H. Wildberger, "אמן," *TLOT*, 1:134–57, here 146.

48. E.g., Matt 5:18, 26. John's Gospel often features a double use of "amen," where Jesus says, "amen, amen" (e.g., John 3:3, 5, 11).

49. In Jesus's time, many people spoke Aramaic, a language closely related to Hebrew. It's difficult to tell with complete certainty whether the New Testament's use of "amen" comes from the Hebrew "amen" or the Aramaic "amen." (In Hebrew and Aramaic, "amen" means the same thing and is spelled almost identically.)

The word "Hosanna" shows up in the Gospels. Although there's a closely related Hebrew word used in passages like Psalm 118:25, it's clear that "Hosanna" is an Aramaic rather than a Hebrew word. "Hosanna" means "Please, help!" implying that those speaking need to be saved from oppression or danger.

50. Moberly, *NIDOTTE*, 1:428. Moberly slightly overstates the uniqueness of Jesus's use of this word; a similar usage is found in *KAI*, 200.11.

51. H. Ringgren, "הלל I and II," *TDOT*, 1:404–10, here 406.

52. 1 Chron 16:10; 2 Chron 23:13; 29:30; 30:21; Pss 34:2 [3 Heb.]; 63:11 [12 Heb.]; 64:10 [11 Heb.]; 105:3; 106:5; 113:9; Jer 31:7. See also the etymology given in C. Westermann, "הלל," *TLOT*, 1:371–76, here 371–72.

53. On the interreligious usage of this word, see *OED Online*, s.v. Sabbath | sabbath, *n*.

54. Scholars have debated whether the noun or verb came first, but it's clear the two are related (F. Stolz, "שׁבת," *TLOT*, 3:1297–302, here 1297). Verses with the verb meaning "stop" include Genesis 8:22; Nehemiah 6:3; Job 32:1; Proverbs 22:10; Isaiah 14:4; 24:8; and Jeremiah 31:36.

55. Evelyn L. Parker, "Honoring the Body," in *On Our Way: Christian Practices for Living a Whole Life*, ed. Dorothy C. Bass and Susan R. Briehl (Nashville: Upper Room, 2010), 133–48, here 147. My student Elizabeth Swan drew my attention to this wonderful quotation.

56. Making sacrifices (a key form of worship in the Old Testament) is mentioned on the Sabbath in Numbers 28:9-10; 1 Chronicles 23:31; 2 Chronicles 8:13; 31:3; Nehemiah 10:33 [34 Heb.]; and Ezekiel 45:17; 46:4, 12. The emphasis on cessation of work is found in Genesis 2:2-3; Exodus 16:22-30; 20:9-10; 23:12; 31:14-17; 34:21; 35:2; Leviticus 23:3; Numbers 15:32-36; Deuteronomy 5:14-15; and Jeremiah 17:22-25.

57. Ellen F. Davis, "Slaves or Sabbath-Keepers? A Biblical Perspective on Human Work," *AThR* 83 (2001): 25–40, here 32.

58. John Ortberg, *The Life You've Always Wanted: Spiritual Disciplines of Ordinary People* (Grand Rapids: Zondervan, 2002), 77.

59. Most commentators (e.g., K. Nielsen, "שָׂטָן," *TDOT*, 14:73–78, here 77) agree that Chronicles relies on but alters the text of Samuel so that the Lord doesn't punish David for something that the Lord caused David to do.

60. Unfortunately, some modern translations give a very different impression. The NRSV, for example, translates "the *satan*" of Job 1–2 as "Satan," even though such an approach is unlikely for grammatical reasons. The Hebrew word for "the" isn't usually present when a proper name is in view (C. Breytenbach and P. L. Day, "Satan," *DDD*, 726–32, here 727–28, against *IBHS*, 13.6.a). At most, 1 Chronicles 21:1 may refer to "Satan." However, the grammar of the Hebrew makes it equally likely that the text is talking about "a *satan*" in the sense of "an adversary."

61. Breytenbach and Day, "Satan," 728.

62. This phenomenon happens with a number of transliterated words, as noted in Vitaly Voinov, "Troublesome Transliterations," *BT* 63 (2012): 17–27, here 24–26.

63. Cf. Werner Foerster and Knut Schäferdiek, "σατανᾶς," *TDNT*, 7:151–65, here 7:156–58.

64. See Victor Hamilton, "Satan," *ABD*, 5:985–89, here 988, which suggests that either Persian dualism or the exceptionally harsh realities of the

intertestamental period may have influenced belief in a more developed demonology.

65. Some scholars have suggested the verb instead means "separate," including Ellen van Wolde, *Reframing Biblical Studies: When Language and Text Meet Culture, Cognition, and Context* (Winona Lake, IN: Eisenbrauns, 2009), 184–200; Ellen van Wolde and Robert Rezetko, "Semantics and the Semantics of ברא: A Rejoinder to the Arguments Advanced by B. Becking and M. Korpel," *JHebS* 11 (2011): doi:10.5508/jhs.2011.v11.a9. Others have advanced important counterarguments, e.g., Bob Becking and Marjo C. A. Korpel, "To Create, to Separate or to Construct: An Alternative for a Recent Proposal as to the Interpretation of ברא in Gen 1:1–2:4a," *JHebS* 10 (2010): doi:10.5508/jhs.2010.v10.a3. I prefer the traditional translation "create" in part because approximately 24 percent of verses containing *bara* also include *asah* (meaning "make"), whereas no verses contain both *bara* and a word meaning "separate."

66. W. H. Schmidt, "ברא," *TLOT*, 1:253–56, here 255.

67. It's worth noting that Hebrew verbs can take different patterns. When *bara* appears in the most common pattern (called the Qal pattern), only God is the subject. However, there are other patterns (one tends to be passive, another intensive, another causative) in which *bara* does appear with subjects other than God.

An assumption I'm making in this subsection is that it's more than coincidental that only God is the subject of *bara*. Because the Hebrew Bible is a fragment of a much broader language used in ancient Israel, it's possible that it's just by chance that *bara* only appears with God as its subject. However, many humans are the subject of verbs for making and forming. Meanwhile, in all thirty-eight of its appearances in the Qal pattern, only God appears as the subject of *bara*.

68. Noting that *salakh* does not refer to human pardon or forgiveness, Jacob Milgrom connects *salakh* with reconciliation and God's continuing to fulfill the terms of the covenant (*Numbers*, 392–96, esp. 395–96).

69. According to Karen J. Jobes, "Relevance Theory and the Translation of Scripture," *JETS* 50 (2007): 773–97, here 796, the NIV has approximately 33 percent more words than the combined Hebrew Masoretic text and Nestle-Aland Greek text (twenty-seventh edition). Meanwhile, the NRSV has approximately 64 percent more words than the same.

70. James Barr, "Hebrew Lexicography: Informal Thoughts," in *Linguistics and Biblical Hebrew*, ed. Walter R. Bodine (Winona Lake, IN: Eisenbrauns, 1992), 145. See also Reinier de Blois, "Towards a New Dictionary of Biblical Hebrew Based on Semantic Domains," *A Semantic Dictionary of Biblical Hebrew* (Swinton, UK: United Bible Societies, 2013), http://www.sdbh.org/documentation/Paper_SBL_2000.pdf, §1.2.

71. I'm obviously paraphrasing. On the superiority of Marduk among gods, see Benjamin R. Foster, trans., "Epic of Creation (*Enūma Elish*)," *COS*, 1.111:390–402, e.g., 397.

72. According to Carolyn Leeb, "Translating the Hebrew Body into English Metaphor," *The Social Sciences and Biblical Translation*, ed. Dietmar Neufeld, SBLSymS (Atlanta: SBL, 2008), 109–25, here 109, the heart was first recognized as the body's blood-pumping organ in 1628.

73. In addition to the standard Hebrew reference works, readers may also want to see Michael Carasik, *Theologies of the Mind in Biblical Israel*, StBibLit 85 (New York: Peter Lang, 2006), 104–24.

74. I sometimes hear people say that while the "heart," *lev(av)*, was the center of thinking in the Bible, the guts, *moeh*, were the center of emotion in the Bible. Such a distinction is a false one missing from the Hebrew text. The *lev(av)* had associations with not only thinking (e.g., Deut 15:9) but also emotion (e.g., Neh 2:2; see also *DCH*, s.v. לב). Meanwhile, the guts had associations with emotions, but that likely stems from the transcultural experience of sensing a disturbance in one's gut as a result of significant emotion.

75. A key work popularizing conceptual metaphor is George Lakoff and Mark Johnson, *Metaphors We Live By* (Chicago: University of Chicago Press, 2003). One finds an explanation of precursors to this work in Michael K. Smith, "Metaphor and Mind," *American Speech* 57 (1982): 128–34.

76. Cf. Carol Newsom, "Models of the Moral Self: Hebrew Bible and Second Temple Judaism," *JBL* 131 (2012): 5–25, here 10–11.

77. See 2 Sam 18:14; 2 Kgs 9:24; Ps 45:7 [6 Heb.]; Nah 2:7 [8 Heb.]; Carasik, *Theologies*, 105; H.-J. Fabry, "לב," *TDOT*, 7:399–437, here 411.

78. Fabry, *TDOT*, 7:412; Newsom, "Models of the Moral Self," 10. Fabry's text was altered slightly to match the system of transliteration used in this book.

79. Cf. Leeb, "Translating," 110.

80. David Arthur Lambert, "Refreshing Philology: James Barr, Supersessionism, and the State of Biblical Words," *BibInt* 24 (2016): 332–56, esp. 341–49, argues against the idea that biblical Hebrew reflects a dichotomy between inward thinking and outward action. In this context, he suggests that *lev* does not refer to one's core but rather to "the boundaries of the self" (ibid., 343). This idea is intriguing, but a more thorough-going discussion is needed of the approximately 850 appearances of *lev(av)*.

81. For a more in-depth treatment of the relationship between *nephesh* and "soul," see H. Seebass, "נפש," *TDOT*, 9:497–519, here 508–10.

82. With the word *nephesh* in mind, Brevard Childs writes that the human being in the Old Testament "does not *have* a soul, but *is* a soul (Gen. 2.7). That is to say, [a person] is a complete entity and not a composite of parts from body, soul and spirit" (Brevard Childs, *Old Testament Theology in a Canonical Context* [Philadelphia: Fortress, 1986], 199; cf. Seebass, *TDOT*, 9:511–12).

83. Note especially Leviticus 17:11: "For the life [*nephesh*] of a creature is in the blood" (NIV).

84. Instead of translating the Hebrew word *meod* at the end of Deuteronomy 6:5 as "strength" or "might," I have gone with "*umph!*" The word there is the word commonly translated "very." In other words, it typically intensifies and adds "umph" to things. So, when it is used as a noun in this verse, I find the word "umph" more accurate, even if it's more informal. Bruce K. Waltke, "1395 נפש," *TWOT*, 587–91, here 589, builds on the work of J. McBride to observe that in this verse *levav*, *nephesh*, and *meod* don't emphasize three different parts of the human being (heart, soul, might) but rather the entire human being (our inner drivers [*levav*] and what makes us alive [*nephesh*] to a superlative degree [*meod*]).

85. In the right context, *nephesh* refers to a life that has passed, i.e., a corpse (see Lev 21:1, 11; 22:4; Num 19:11, 13; Hag 2:13). For a useful overview of all the word can entail, see *DCH*, s.v. נפש.

86. Waltke, "1395 נפש," 588.

87. E.g., Lev 11:43; Jer 37:9; Ethan Jones, "Direct Reflexivity in Biblical Hebrew: A Note on נפש," *ZAW* 129 (2017): 411–26, here 423–24.

88. *Elohim* can also be translated "gods" when context indicates it. The Hebrew words אֵל (*el*) and אֱלוֹהַּ (*eloah*) also mean "God," but they are used less often than *elohim*. They often function as divine names (cf. Gen 46:3 CEB; Ps 139:19; see also the discussion in W. Herrmann, "El," *DDD*, 274–80; D. Pardee, "Eloah," *DDD*, 285–88). When *El* is combined with *Shadday* (also spelled *Shaddai*), it likely means "God of the wilderness" or "God of the mountains" (E. A. Knauf, "Shadday," *DDD*, 749–53, here 750). Obviously, mountains are significant religious places in the Old Testament, as we know from both Mount Sinai and Mount Zion. When *El* is combined with *Elyon*, it means "God Most High" (E. E. Elnes and P. D. Miller, "Elyon," *DDD*, 293–99). For a historical study of how *El* eventually became identified with *YHWH*, see Mark S. Smith, *The Early History of God: Yahweh and the Other Deities in Ancient Israel*, 2nd ed. (Grand Rapids: Eerdmans, 2002), 32–43.

89. For a technical examination of these words in the Pentateuch, see Terrance R. Wardlaw, *Conceptualizing Words for "God" within the Pentateuch: A Cognitive-Semantic Investigation in Literary Context*, LHBOTS 495 (New York: T&T Clark, 2008).

90. On connections between *yhwh*, *kurios*, and Jesus, see Richard Bauckham, *Jesus and the God of Israel:* God Crucified *and Other Studies on the New Testament's Christology of Divine Identity* (Grand Rapids: Eerdmans, 2008), 40; cf. Richard B. Hays, *Reading Backwards: Figural Christology and the Fourfold Witness* (Waco, TX: Baylor University Press, 2014), 26. For an explanation of why *adonay* should be translated as "the LORD" rather than "my LORD," see GKC, § 87g, esp. 135q. On *yehvah* (יְהוָה) alerting readers to say not *adonay* but rather the Aramaic word *shema*, meaning "the name," see *HALOT*(se), s.v. יהוה; E. Jenni, "יהוה," *TLOT*, 2:522–26, here 522.

91. A classic articulation of this argument is found in Frank Moore Cross, *Canaanite Myth and Hebrew Epic: Essays in the History of the Religion of Israel* (Cambridge, MA: Harvard University Press, 1973), 60–75. On other possible etymologies, see *HALOT*(se), s.v. יהוה.

92. A recent interpretation of Exodus 3:12-15 favoring this approach is Victor P. Hamilton, *Exodus: An Exegetical Commentary* (Grand Rapids: Baker Academic, 2011), 63–66.

93. See Peter Unseth, "Sacred Name Bible Translations in English: A Fast-Growing Phenomenon," *BT* 62 (2011): 185–94.

94. Terence Fretheim, "Yahweh," *NIDOTTE*, 4:1295–300, here 1297.

95. Abraham Joshua Heschel, *Man Is Not Alone: A Philosophy of Religion* (New York: Farrar, Straus & Young, 1951), 97–98.

96. See also Norm Mundhenk's argument that "Lord" provides an important conceptual link between the Old and New Testaments ("Jesus Is Lord: The Tetragrammaton in Bible Translation," *BT* 61 [2010]: 55–63).

97. The CEB goes the same direction with Psalm 86:13; 88:3 [4 Heb.].

98. Some scholars have developed more elaborate definitions for *sheol,* such as Wächter, "שְׁאוֹל," *TDOT*, 14:239–48, here 242, who writes, "According to the Israelite worldview, Sheol lies beneath the subterranean ocean upon which the earth disk floats." However, it's difficult to be confident of such assessments, particularly when verses like the ones Wächter gives in support (Job 26:5; 38:16-17) are open to other interpretations and come from a book that differs from many other parts of the Bible.

99. *OED Online,* s.v. grave, *n.* 1. As the *Oxford English Dictionary* points out, there are other meanings of "grave" that are less common or unrelated to the meanings discussed here (such as the adjectival meaning "weighty, important").

100. Some texts connect the ungodly with *sheol* (e.g., Pss 9:17 [18 Heb.]; 31:17 [18 Heb.]). However, these texts do not envision *sheol* in terms of hell. Instead, these texts are saying that ungodliness leads to death, an idea found throughout the Bible (e.g., Deut 30:15, 19).

101. Nathan MacDonald, *What Did the Ancient Israelites Eat? Diet in Biblical Times* (Grand Rapids: Eerdmans, 2008), 86; cf. Joseph Blenkinsopp, "Life Expectancy in Ancient Palestine," *SJOT* 11 (1997): 44–55, here 54.

102. In the immediate context, this text emphasizes the death that will come with invading armies. However, other texts make similar remarks about Sheol's insatiable hunger (Prov 1:12-13; Hab 2:5).

103. E.g., Exod 14–15; 1 Sam 17; 2 Kgs 6–7; 18–19; Isa 36–39; 2 Chron 20; Ps 20:7 [8 Heb.]. See also the texts cited in the footnotes of Schlimm, *This Strange and Sacred Scripture*, 68–69.

104. Barr, *Biblical Faith and Natural Theology*, 208.

105. Translating *kherem* is made even more difficult by the fact that sometimes it is used in contexts without explicit reference to military activity (e.g., Num 18:13-15).

106. Schlimm, *This Strange and Sacred Scripture*, 79–81.

107. Ibid.; Brent A. Strawn, "Teaching the Old Testament: When God Seems Unjust," *Circuit Rider* 36, no. 4 (August–October 2012): 7–9, here 8. Cf. Exod 34:10-11; Judg 2:20-23; Zech 14:11.

108. *OED Online*, s.v. hear, *v.*, 8.

109. The NASB, for example, translates the word with a form of the word "hear" or "listen" 981 times and with a form of the word "heed" or "obey" 95 times.

110. When the prepositions *le-* (meaning "to"), *el* (also meaning "to"), and *be-* (meaning "with") follow the verb *shama*, "obey" is usually the intended meaning. Cf. Blois, "Towards a New Dictionary," §1.1.4. However, sometimes "obey" is intended even without those prepositions (e.g., Isa 1:19; Jer 12:17; 35:14; Mic 5:15 [14 Heb.]; BDB, s.v. שׁמע; *HALOT*[se], s.v. שׁמע).

111. In "The Code of Hammurabi," §226–27, one finds a reference to either branding (in the translation by Theophile J. Meek, *ANET*, 176) or haircutting (in the translation by Martha Roth, *COS*, 2.131:349).

112. Åke Viberg, *Symbols of Law: A Contextual Analysis of Legal Symbolic Acts in the Old Testament*, ConBOT 34 (Stockholm: Almqvist & Wiksell International, 1992), 86; Nathan MacDonald, "Deuteronomy," *CEB Study Bible* (Nashville: Common English Bible, 2013), 290 OT (see n. on Deut 15:17).

113. See also Deut 29:4 [3 Heb.]; Isa 6:10; Jer 6:10; Ezek 12:2; Matt 13:15; Mark 8:18; Acts 28:27; Rom 11:8. This point was mentioned in The Bible Project, "Shema," *YouTube*, https://www.youtube.com/watch?v=6KQLOuIKaRA.

114. The word can also refer to what's bad, in a sense divorced from any ethics.

115. For differing ways of interpreting these sorts of remarks in the Bible, see Klaus Koch, *The Prophets*, 2 vols. (Philadelphia: Fortress, 1983–84), e.g., 1:1–6, 64–65, 73–74, and John Barton, *Understand Old Testament Ethics: Approaches and Explorations* (Louisville: Westminster John Knox, 2003), 39–44.

116. The word can also mean "ordinance" as in Deuteronomy 8:11 or "custom" as in 1 Kings 18:28. See also other definitions given in standard lexicons, such as *HALOT*(se), s.v. משפט 1:651–52. I've chosen to focus on "justice" and "judgment" because space limitations disallow a comprehensive analysis of a word like *mishpat*.

117. My student's name is Sara Sutter.

118. Barr, *Semantics of Biblical Language*, 218.

119. "Judgment" also works better than "justice" when the text describes erroneous *mishpat* (Prov 24:23; Hos 10:4; cf. Hab 1:4b).

120. Spyder Monkey, "The Civil Rights Memorial, Montgomery, AL.jpg," Wikimedia Commons, https://commons.wikimedia.org/wiki/File:The_Civil_Rights_Memorial,_Montgomery,_AL.jpg.

121. In Genesis 38:26, *tsadeq* (related to *tsedaqah*) involves a more personal issue (sexuality), as is the case with *mishpat* in Leviticus 18:26. In Psalm 103:6, both *mishpat* and *tsedaqah* involve more societal issues.

As *DCH*, s.v. משפט, explains, *mishpat* can be rendered "justice" or "moderation, restraint, discretion." Meanwhile, *tsedaqah* can be translated as "social justice" or "righteous will" (*DCH*, s.v. צדקה).

122. For a brief but helpful discussion of *ruakh* resting upon, clothing, rushing on, or gripping people, see Newsom, "Models of the Moral Self," 10–11.

123. *OED Online*, s.v. spirit, *n*.

124. *Ruakh* in a verse like Zechariah 4:6 is almost universally translated as "spirit": "Not by might, nor by power, but by my spirit [*ruakh*], says the Lord of hosts" (NRSV). Yet, even here, it's worth wondering whether "breath" or "wind" could be preferable. If so, there's a vivid contrast between worthless human striving and God who simply breathes to flatten mountains into plains (Zech 4:7).

125. Eugene H. Peterson, *Christ Plays in Ten Thousand Places: A Conversation in Spiritual Theology* (Grand Rapids: Eerdmans, 2005), 44–45.

126. Three Old Testament verses speak explicitly about God's "holy *ruakh*" (Ps 51:11 [13 Heb.]; Isa 63:10-11). While Christians naturally think of the third person of the Trinity in these texts, the original audiences didn't. Psalm 51:11 [13 Heb.] can be seen as a prayer that God would not take away God's life-giving

breath. Meanwhile, Isaiah 63:10-11 talks about grieving God's spirit the same way that Isaiah 54:6 describes a forsaken wife grieving.

127. In Hebrew, saying "God's" before something can be a way of emphasizing it. For example, the NRSV translates what Rachel says in Genesis 30:8 as, "With mighty wrestlings I have wrestled with my sister." Literally, she says, "With God's wrestlings I have wrestled with my sister." In Genesis 1:2, the text literally talks about "God's wind," but some scholars have wondered whether the text is actually referring to "a mighty wind" (S. Tengström and H.-J. Fabry, "רוח," *TDOT*, 13:365–402, here 384).

128. Readers who have taken or are taking Hebrew may want to note that although the word appears in the Qal form (as I have listed in parentheses), the Piel form is more common and what's found in Genesis 49:18.

129. Some scholars doubt that there is a connection between "hope" and "cord" (see the discussion in G. Waschke, "קוה," *TDOT*, 12:564–73, here 564–65, 568). Others have suggested that the connection is not what's outlined above, but rather that those who wait and hope are tense like a cord (C. Westermann, "קוה," *TLOT*, 3:1126–32, here 1126).

130. Frederic Shields, "Rahab Hangs the Scarlet Cord from Her Window," Wikimedia Commons, uploaded by Fæ, https://commons.wikimedia.org/wiki/File%3ARahab_hangs_the_scarlet_cord_from_her_window._Autotype_after_Wellcome_V0034410.jpg.

131. Jews similarly await a Messiah, while Muslims also await Jesus's return to judge humanity.

132. Pierre Teilhard de Chardin, "Patient Trust," in *Hearts on Fire: Praying with Jesuits*, ed. Michael Harter (Chicago: Loyola, 2005), 102–3, here 102; Walter Brueggemann, *Prayers for a Privileged People* (Nashville: Abingdon, 2008), 167.

133. Andy Rau, "The Top Ten Bible Verses of 2015 and More: Bible Gateway's Year in Review Is Here," *BibleGateway Blog*, December 28, 2015, https://www.biblegateway.com/blog/2015/12/the-top-ten-bible-verses-of-2015-and-more-bible-gateways-year-in-review-is-here/. This website reflects a remarkable sample size with 1.6 billion pageviews and over 160 million unique visitors in 2015.

134. On the hardships they faced, see Psalm 137.

135. Some scholars interpret this passage as describing the end of a metaphorical death, that is, the end of Israel's exile. While my interpretation is no doubt colored by how the New Testament and subsequently the church has interpreted Isaiah, I see more at work in this text than the simple return from exile. The remainder of 25:8, for example, talks about tears being wiped away from "all faces," which on the basis of 25:7 appears to refer to the faces of all nations. A universal abolishment of death itself is in view, one that brings relief to all of humanity.

136. Some late books like Ezra refer to both "the *torah* of Moses" and "the book of Moses" (Ezra 3:2; 6:18; 7:6). Yet, even with those verses, interpreters debate whether the text has in mind the first five books of the Bible or only parts thereof (F. García López and H.-J. Fabry, "תורה," *TDOT*, 15:609–46, here Fabry, 644).

137. P. Enns, "Law of God," *NIDOTTE*, 4:893–900, here 893. See also Exod 24:12; Deut 17:11; 33:10; Ezra 7:10; Pss 78:5; 94:12; Isa 2:3; Mic 4:2. The matter is, however, complicated because some scholars speculate that a verb meaning "throw" primarily relates to *torah*.

138. See also Psalm 78, which begins by inviting others to hear *torah* and proceeds to tell the story of God's involvement with Israel, not rules or laws.

139. Another reason to obey God's commandments: doing so leads to abundant life, as Deuteronomy 5:33 reminds readers. Obeying God means living in harmony with one's creator.

140. Schlimm, *This Strange and Sacred Scripture*, 122–27.

141. As is true of other chapters, many other examples could be given in addition to the ones listed here. In the case of this chapter, it's noteworthy that the same Hebrew word (*matteh*, מַטֶּה) means both "staff" and "tribe." Numbers 17:1-11 [16-26 Heb.] makes use of this double meaning as each tribe (*matteh*) brings forth its own staff (*matteh*). Another example: it can be fruitful to reflect on how the same Hebrew word (*avodah*, עֲבֹדָה) means both "service" and "worship."

142. There are reasons to be cautious about assuming too much about the relationship between concrete and metaphorical meanings (David J. A. Clines, "The Challenge of Hebrew Lexicography Today," in *Congress Volume: Ljubljana 2007*, edited by André Lemaire [Leiden: Brill, 2010], 87–98, here 90). However, recent work on conceptual metaphor in the field of cognitive linguistics has opened fascinating avenues of research. My work here draws on these newer

avenues of cognitive research. Other biblical scholars taking such avenues include Gary A. Anderson, *Sin: A History* (New Haven: Yale University Press, 2009), esp. 4–6; C. H. J. van der Merwe, "A Cognitive Linguistic Perspective on הִנֵּה in the Pentateuch, Joshua, Judges, and Ruth," *HS* 48 (2007): 101–40, here 105.

143. This professor's name is Gerald Miller. Connecting bubbles with life's temporary nature is not new (cf. discussion of Jean Siméon Chardin, "Soap Bubbles," *The Met*, http://www.metmuseum.org/art/collection/search/435888).

144. The word *hevel* never appears in the same verse as *neshamah*, the life-giving breath mentioned in Genesis 2:7. It only shows up with *ruakh* in Ecclesiastes and one other time (Isa 57:13). Although all three words can refer to "breath," *hevel* is not perceived as positively.

On the word's connections to what vanishes, the word is used to describe the temporary nature of accomplishments (Eccl 1:2-3; 2:4-11, 18-23; 4:4-8), words (Eccl 6:11; cf. 1:8; 5:2-7 [1-6 Heb.]; 12:12), memory (Eccl 2:15-17; cf. 1:11; 9:4-5), possessions (Eccl 2:4-11, 26; 4:8; 5:10-20 [9-19 Heb.]; 6:1-2), human life (Eccl 2:14-17; 3:18-22; 7:15; 8:5-10; 9:9-12; 11:8–12:7; cf. 7:1-4; 9:1-2), justice (Eccl 5:8 [7 Heb.]; 8:10-14; cf. 3:16; 4:1-3; 9:2-3), and good and bad times (Eccl 7:13-15).

145. Milton P. Horne, *Proverbs—Ecclesiastes*, SHBC (Macon, GA: Smyth & Helwys, 2003), 384.

146. Anderson, *Sin*, 13.

147. Thus, when the Israelites beg the Edomites to let them travel through their land, they say, "Please let us pass through [*avar*] your land. . . . We will go along the king's highway, not turning to the right or left, until we pass through [*avar*] your territory" (Num 20:17 NASB).

148. See Num 14:41; Deut 17:2; 26:13; Josh 7:11, 15; 23:16; Judg 2:20; 1 Sam 15:24; 2 Kgs 18:12; 2 Chron 24:20; Ps 17:3; Isa 24:5; Jer 34:18; Hos 6:7; 8:1.

149. After the time of Solomon, the kingdom of Israel was split into two kingdoms: Israel in the north, which lasted until 722 BCE, and Judah in the south, which included Jerusalem and lasted until 587 BCE.

150. On one occasion (Deut 29:12 [11 Heb.]), the Bible uses the word *avar* to talk about "passing *into* a covenant" (i.e., making a covenant) rather than

"violating" or "passing over a covenant." Here, the text may envision passing between the carcasses of slaughtered animals, which (as described in chapter 7) could be part of ancient covenant ceremonies. The verb *avar* can also be used to refer to forgiveness either in the sense of God passing by sin (e.g., Mic 7:18) or when God causes the iniquity to pass away from a person (e.g., Zech 3:4). On these definitions, see H.-P. Stähli, "עבר," *TLOT*, 2:832–35, here 834–35.

151. *OED Online*, s.v. keep, *v.*

152. *DCH*, s.v. שׁמר.

153. Dennis Olson, *Numbers*, IBC (Louisville: Westminster John Knox, 1996), 41, observes, "Psalm 121 is an expanded commentary on the theme of God's keeping of Israel. The verb 'to keep' using God as subject occurs six times in the psalm's eight verses."

154. Anderson, *Sin*, 25.

155. My translation, though a few English translations and some commentaries go in a similar direction. See Anderson, *Sin*, 24–26.

156. This verse is central to the Old Testament's portrait of God. Similar language is used elsewhere (e.g., Mic 7:18).

157. The above section relies heavily on the insights of Anderson, *Sin*, 15–26.

158. "Index of Semantic Fields," *NIDOTTE*, 5:1–216, here 158.

159. The word is used to describe human repentance in texts such as Job 42:6 and Jeremiah 8:6; 31:19.

160. This text is Hosea 14:1-2, 4 in most English translations, but 14:2-3, 5 in the NJPS translation and the Hebrew.

161. See Deut 30:2-5, 16.

162. Here I rely on important distinctions made by Claus Westermann, *Blessing in the Bible and the Life of the Church*, trans. Keith Crim, OBT (Philadelphia: Fortress, 1978), ch. 1. I do recognize that these two modes of divine operation are not mutually exclusive, as pointed out by Christopher Wright Mitchell, *The Meaning of* BRK *"To Bless" in the Old Testament*, SBLDS 95 (Atlanta: Scholars, 1987), 177–79.

163. While the text that follows discusses possible connections between the Hebrew words *berakh* and *berekh*, this discussion is somewhat speculative. Earlier meanings of words do not necessarily have a profound impact on how they are understood in later times (Barr, *Semantics of Biblical Language*, ch. 6, esp. 107–10, 158–60). Thus, the English words "meek" and "mucus" appear to have a related history, but one word doesn't normally make an English speaker think of the other (Robert K. Barnhart, ed., *Chambers Dictionary of Etymology* [London: Chambers, 1988], 648, 683). Here, one cannot even be certain that the Hebrew words for "bless" and "knee" have a common heritage (J. K. Aitken, *The Semantics of Blessing and Cursing in Ancient Hebrew*, ANESSup 23 [Louvain: Peeters, 2007], 93–94, 116). Yet, a passage such as 1 Kings 8:54-56 suggests that Hebrew thinkers associated blessing and knees, whether or not they shared a common etiology. See also William C. Williams, "1384 ברך," *NIDOTTE*, 1:755–57, here 755–56.

164. For more on this practice, see Viberg, *Symbols of Law*, 166–75.

165. For more on curses in the broader ancient Near East and how they function as prayers to the divine world for judgment to befall another person, see Anne Marie Kitz, *Cursed Are You! The Phenomenology of Cursing in Cuneiform and Hebrew Texts* (Winona Lake, IN: Eisenbrauns, 2014).

166. Mitchell, *The Meaning of* BRK, 181–83; Ellen Davis, "Blessing and Well-Being," *The Work of the People*, http://www.theworkofthepeople.com/blessing-and-well-being.

167. Theology Working Group, "A Statement on the Prosperity Gospel," *The Lausanne Movement*, https://www.lausanne.org/content/a-statement-on-the-prosperity-gospel.

168. An excellent reflective treatment of blessing in Genesis is Hemchand Gossai, *Barrenness and Blessing: Abraham, Sarah, and the Journey of Faith* (Eugene, OR: Cascade, 2008), esp. ch. 5. For a thorough treatment of blessing in the Bible as a whole, see Mitchell, *The Meaning of* BRK.

169. Andy Crouch, "The Future Shape of Theological Education," *Catalyst: Contemporary Evangelical Perspectives for United Methodist Seminarians* 39, no. 3 (2013): 1–3, here 2.

170. One of the first translations was the Septuagint, which rendered the text into Greek. Subsequent early translations include the Targumim (into Aramaic just before and during the first three centuries CE), the Peshitta (into Syriac

in the first two centuries CE), and the Vulgate (into Latin around the end of the fourth century CE).

171. It's possible that some biblical authors used archaic Hebrew forms to make particular texts sound older than they were. For example, some claim that the "Song of Deborah" in Judges 5 is among the oldest texts of the Bible. However, it uses a Hebrew construction called the shin-particle (5:7), which usually appears in later texts (e.g., throughout Ecclesiastes). So it is possible that the older features of this text were inserted to make it appear older than it actually is. In any case, we have so few extant classical Hebrew texts that it can be difficult to judge such matters with absolute certainty.

172. We learned the word from Mary Chiapuris Douville, a close family friend originally from Greece. The official Greek command is κοιτάζε from κοιτάζω. However, Mary (now ninety-one years old) recently told me that she didn't pronounce the final syllable because by the time she got to it, whatever you wanted others to see would be gone!

173. Like most words, *hinneh* has multiple definitions. Some of these are less attention-grabbing than others. For example, the word can be used to draw attention to oneself (e.g., "I'm here," 1 Sam 3:16 CEB) or to begin a conditional clause ("If we go...," 1 Sam 9:7 NIV). These examples obviously lack the intensity found when the word occurs alongside a sign or wonder ("Watch out!" Exod 10:4 NLT). For an excellent discussion of the word, see Merwe, "Cognitive Linguistic Perspective."

174. The CEB uses the adverb "supremely."

175. Francis I. Andersen, "Lo and Behold!" in *Hamlet on a Hill: Semitic and Greek Studies Presented to Professor T. Muraoka on the Occasion of His Sixty-Fifth Birthday*, ed. M. F. J. Baasten and W. Th. Van Peursen, OLA 118 (Leuven: Peeters, 2003), 25–56, here 31.

176. On the tendency of *hinneh* to appear in prophetic oracles of judgment, see D. Vetter, "הנה," *TLOT*, 1:379–80, here 380.

177. Jörg Jeremias, *The Book of Amos*, trans. Douglas W. Scott, OTL (Louisville: Westminster John Knox, 1998), 129.

178. American Colony (Jerusalem), Photo Department, "Locust from the Plague in Palestine, 1915.jpg," Wikimedia Commons, uploaded by Maksim,

https://commons.wikimedia.org/wiki/File:Locust_from_the_plague_in_Palestine,_1915.jpg.

179. James Luther Mays, *Amos: A Commentary*, OTL (Philadelphia: Westminster, 1969), 128.

180. Allan Harman, "Particles," *NIDOTTE*, 4:1028–42, here 1032, says of the instances where *hinneh* has a pronoun attached to it that serves as the subject of a participle, "In 94 percent of these cases the subj. is God, and the exclamation concerns a divine threat or promise. They are emphatic particles in that they draw the special attention of the reader to something that is new or unexpected."

181. These two words are frequently treated together by Hebrew scholars, given their similarities in phonetics and (to a lesser extent) usage (e.g., *TDOT*, *NIDOTT*, *TLOT*). However, most sources note important differences between them. *Oy* is much more likely than *hoy* to be followed by the Hebrew words *le-* (meaning "to") or *ki* (meaning "for"). Both words are found predominantly in the Latter Prophets (as noted below), but *hoy* appears there almost exclusively.

182. These Hebrew words, along with the English word "ahoy," appear to be natural expressions (*OED Online*, s.v. hoy, *int.* and *n.*[2]). Similar words are found in Greek, Latin, Russian, and Spanish.

183. On rare occasions, they can have a more positive overtone. See Isa 55:1; Zech 2:6-7 [10-11 Heb.].

184. James G. Williams, "The Alas-Oracles of the Eighth Century Prophets," *HUCA* 38 (1967): 75–91, here 86. Williams's text was altered slightly to match the system of transliteration used in this book.

185. He literally says he is "a man of unclean lips" (Isa 6:5). While that language may suggest he has eaten unclean food (see discussion of "Cleanliness" in chapter 8), it seems more likely that he has, to borrow one scholar's words, "spoken what is impure, untrue, possibly also [what is inappropriate] about God" (Hans Wildberger, *Isaiah 1–12*, 268).

186. *OED Online*, s.v. atone, *v.*

187. Some lexicons (e.g., BDB) emphasize the concrete meaning of this word found in the Qal pattern, meaning "cover over." Thus, the idea would be that Moses hopes to "cover over" the people's sin. I have chosen not to emphasize this potential metaphor in part because of how rarely the verb literally means "to

cover" (Genesis 6:14 is the only appearance in the Qal). Also, I do not wish to give the impression that the Hebrew *kipper* is similar to a "cover-up act," which in English deals with hiding wrongdoing, not reconciliation. The word has also been linked to "ransom" and "wipe away," as discussed in Richard E. Averbeck, "4105/4106 כפר," *NIDOTTE*, 2:689–710, here 691–99. These metaphorical meanings may have been largely lost in the biblical period, even if they once played a larger role in people's imagination (see also F. Maass, "כפר," *TLOT*, 2:624–35, here 625).

188. The end of the verse speaks literally of lifting Jacob's face, which may be a reference to forgiveness (see *nasa*).

189. See the discussion in Schlimm, *From Fratricide to Forgiveness*, 167.

190. The word translated "bribe" in these verses is *koper*, which is related to the verb *kipper*.

191. "The Great Litany," in *The (Online) Book of Common Prayer* (New York: The Church Hymnal Corporation), 148–55, https://www.bcponline.org/GreatLitany/Litany.html.

192. The closest it comes is Micah 4:10. However, that text speaks of going *into* Babylon with the metaphor of birth and then shifts to the image of *deliverance* to describe coming *out* of Babylon.

193. Occasionally, plunder from war is used with this term (e.g., 2 Chron 20:25), as well as particular lands (e.g., 2 Sam 23:12). One also finds references to the deliverance of animals, such as when a shepherd tries to rescue a sheep from a lion (e.g., Amos 3:12).

194. See also Exod 3:8; 6:6; Judg 6:9.

195. Terence Fretheim, "Salvation in the Bible vs. Salvation in the Church," *WW* 13 (1993): 363–72, here 371–72; cf. Joel B. Green, *Why Salvation?* Reframing New Testament Theology (Nashville: Abingdon, 2014); Ellen Davis, *Reading Israel's Scriptures*, introduction.

196. For a further discussion of this topic, see Walter Brueggemann, *Divine Presence amid Violence: Contextualizing Violence in the Book of Joshua* (Eugene: Cascade, 2009).

197. The Church of England, "Prayers and Thanksgivings," *Book of Common Prayer*, http://www.churchofengland.org/prayer-worship/worship/book-of-common-prayer/prayers-and-thanksgivings.aspx, alt.

198. This number pertains to the times the root refers to redemption. A homophone is also used to talk about being defiled.

199. *Local Loan Co. vs. Hunt*, 292 US 234, 244 (1934), cited in Administrative Office of the US Courts on Behalf of the Federal Judiciary, "Process—Bankruptcy Basics," *United States Courts*, http://www.uscourts.gov/services-forms/bankruptcy/bankruptcy-basics/process-bankruptcy-basics.

200. Davis, *Scripture, Culture, and Agriculture*, 158.

201. While farm animals obviously aren't savings accounts, they could be slaughtered and eaten in times of drought. However, in a time before refrigeration, the meat would typically need to be consumed within three days. They thus provided only a short-term solution.

202. In addition to the roles of the redeemer as described here, this nearest relative was also responsible for blood vengeance in a culture without a standing police force (e.g., Num 35:19-27). On another use of this term, see Leviticus 27:13-33.

203. H.-J. Zobel, "צבאות," *TDOT*, 12:215–32, here 232.

204. Heinrich Ewald, *Old and New Testament Theology*, trans. Thomas Goadby (Edinburgh: T. & T. Clark, 1888), 93, https://books.google.com/books?id=OV5BAAAAYAAJ.

205. Martin Luther, "A Mighty Fortress Is Our God," trans. Frederick H. Hedge, *UMH* 110. Although this hymnal has "Sabaoth," I changed the transliteration to *tsevaot*, which matches the system used in this book and is close to the word "Zebaoth" found in Luther's original text.

206. Mark S. Smith, *Poetic Heroes: Literary Commemorations of Warriors and Warrior Culture in the Early Biblical World* (Grand Rapids: Eerdmans, 2014), discusses how warriors were remembered in the biblical world. As he notes, many of these remembrances come from earlier periods, often with God playing significant roles.

207. These possibilities, as well as some of the verses cited, are discussed in T. N. D. Mettinger, "Yahweh Zebaoth," *DDD*, 920–24, here 920.

208. Deut 4:19; 17:3; 2 Kgs 17:16; 21:3, 5; 23:4-5; 2 Chron 33:3, 5; Neh 9:6; Ps 33:6; Isa 34:4; 40:26; 45:12; Jer 8:2; 19:13; 33:22; Zeph 1:5 (BDB, s.v. צבא).

209. Those who know some Hebrew can learn more about this grammatical concept in GKC, §124.

210. Cf. *HALOT*(se), s.v. צָבָא.

211. Cf. A. J. Jacobs, *The Year of Living Biblically* (New York: Simon & Schuster, 2007), 176.

212. Several are on display in Joel 1:4. I say "about" because some of these eight have also been translated "grasshopper."

213. Peters, *Hebrew Lexical Semantics*, 43.

214. I'm deeply indebted to my colleague John Stewart for explaining social construction in such an accessible way, especially his "Social Construction Panel: 'Five Years Out'" (position statement presented at the Annual Convention of the National Communication Association, Chicago, IL, November 2009).

215. Mark S. Smith, "Words and Their Worlds," in *Biblical Lexicology: Hebrew and Greek*, ed. Eberhard Bons, Jan Joosten, and Regine Hunziker-Rodewald, BZAW 443 (Berlin: De Gruyter, 2015), 3–31, here 9, 30, 31.

216. A dated but fairly complete treatment of this word is Brevard S. Childs, *Memory and Tradition in Israel*, SBT (Naperville, IL: Alec R. Allenson, 1962). Childs situates this word in the religious (i.e., cultic) life of ancient Israel. Some of Childs's remarks suggest that this word would fit more in chapter 4 than this chapter, that is, that the word *zakhar* has more meanings than the English "remember," such as "reflect." However, even in cases where "reflect" is obviously in view, the idea of remembering isn't lost. There continues to be a focus on bringing something from the past to mind. For this reason, I treat this word in this chapter.

217. Leslie C. Allen, "2349 זכר," *NIDOTTE*, 1:1100–1106, here 1101.

218. Andrew Bowling, "551 זכר," *TWOT*, 241–43, here 241.

219. Allen, *NIDOTTE*, 1:1101.

220. Wenham, *Numbers*, 149, altered for gender inclusivity.

221. For additional thoughts on *zakhar*, see Carasik, *Theologies*, 72–91.

222. For a differing opinion, see E. Kutsch, "ברית," *TLOT*, 1:256–66, here 260.

223. Scholars have debated whether extrabiblical texts from the ancient Near East shed light on this practice. See Kitz, *Cursed Are You*, 83; Viberg, *Symbols of Law*, 53–57.

224. James L. Crenshaw, *Defending God: Biblical Responses to the Problem of Evil* (Oxford: Oxford University Press, 2005) 55, 213n3.

225. M. Weinfeld, "ברית," *TDOT*, 2:253–79, here 256–57, Weinfeld's italics.

226. *UMH* 607.

227. When people do ride donkeys, it's typically women and children (Exod 4:20; Josh 15:18; Judg 1:14; 19:28; 1 Sam 25:20, 23, 42). In Zechariah 9:9, Jerusalem's king is envisioned on a donkey, an idea the New Testament develops with Jesus. As the next verse of Zechariah shows, the king doesn't ride a horse, which would be an instrument of war. Instead, the king is both humble and peaceful.

228. For useful analyses of this topic, see Philip R. Davies and John Rogerson, *The Old Testament World*, 2nd ed. (Louisville: Westminster John Knox, 2005), 3–22; Frank S. Frick, *A Journey through the Hebrew Scriptures*, 2nd ed. (Belmont, CA: Thomson Wadsworth, 2003), 41–48.

229. Data on this chart comes from several sources, including Davies and Rogerson, *Old Testament World*, 3–14; Oded Borowski, *Daily Life in Biblical Times*, SBLABS 5 (Atlanta: SBL, 2003), 1–6; "Altitudes of Major U.S. Cities," *Red Oaks Trading*, previously available at http://www.altimeters.net/cityaltitudes.html; "Average Annual Precipitation by State," *Current Results*, https://www.currentresults.com/Weather/US/average-annual-state-precipitation.php, which is based on data from the NOAA National Climatic Data Center.

230. This map is altered from Eric Gaba, "Israel Relief Location Map-Blank," Wikimedia Commons, https://commons.wikimedia.org/wiki/File:Israel_relief_location_map-blank.jpg.

231. Some interpreters take a more exclusive approach to this text, seeing it as referring to God traveling alone and not the refugees (e.g., Joseph Blenkinsopp, *Isaiah 40–55: A New Translation with Introduction and Commentary*, AB

[New York: Doubleday, 2002], 181–83). However, given the overall theme of return in Isaiah 40–55, the text at least hints at the refugees having smooth travels home (e.g., Claus Westermann, *Isaiah 40–66: A Commentary*, OTL [Philadelphia: Westminster, 1969], 37–39).

232. Douglas R. Edwards, "Dress and Ornamentation," *ABD*, 2:232–38, here 234.

233. Victor H. Matthews, "Cloth, Clothing," *NIDB*, 1:691–96, here 692.

234. F. J. Helfmeyer, "הלך," *TDOT*, 3:388–403, here 389–90. Helfmeyer's text was altered slightly to match the system of transliteration used in this book.

235. Leeb, "Translating," 109.

236. Oded Borowski, "Horse," *NIDB*, 2:891–93, here 893.

237. *DCH*, s.v. סוס lists a few verses where the word is used to describe transportation. However, a number of these examples either pertain to military situations (e.g., Isa 30:16) or have an unspecified context (e.g., Gen 49:17). An exception would be Ecclesiastes 10:7, but even there, Qohelet expresses the oddity of slaves on horseback.

238. Horses are often mentioned alongside chariots. At times, the Hebrew word for "horse" may even serve as a metonym for "chariot." Assyrian reliefs also depict horsemen wielding spears, bows, and arrows (André Parrot, *Assur* [Paris: Gallimard, 2007], 3, 70–75).

239. Deut 20:1; 1 Kgs 10:25; 22:4; 2 Kgs 3:7; 10:2; 2 Chron 9:24; Prov 21:31; Isa 5:28; Jer 6:23; 8:6; 46:9; 50:37, 42; Ezek 26:11; 38:4; 39:20; Hos 1:7; Amos 2:15; 4:10; Hag 2:22; Zech 9:10; 10:3, 5.

240. Osama Shukir Muhammed Amin, "Assyrian King Ashurbanipal on His Horse Thrusting a Spear onto a Lion's Head: Alabaster Bas-relief from Nineveh, Dating Back to 645–635 BCE and Is Currently Housed in the British Museum, London," Wikimedia Commons, https://commons.wikimedia.org/wiki/File:Assyrian_king_Ashurbanipal_on_his_horse_thrusting_a_spear_onto_a_lion%E2%80%99s_head._Alabaster_bas-relief_from_Nineveh,_dating_back_to_645-635_BCE_and_is_currently_housed_in_the_British_Museum,_London.jpg.

241. See also Pss 33:17; 147:10; Prov 21:31; Hos 1:7; 14:3 [4 Heb.]; Hag 2:22; Zech 9:10; 10:5; 12:4.

242. Brueggemann, *Divine Presence amid Violence*, 55.

243. Van Wolde, *Reframing*, 83, explains that the Hebrew word *shaar* most frequently is attached to a city wall, but sometimes it is connected to the tabernacle, temple, or palace.

244. I created this image based on several plans of city gates found in Borowski, *Daily Life*, 48, Fig. 3.2. This image shows a gate plan similar to that of Hazor, Gezer, Ashdod, and Lachish. Borowski provides a useful summary of city walls and gates that informed the discussion here (pp. 46–49).

245. Amos Ḥakham and Israel V. Berman, *Psalms with the Jerusalem Commentary*, 3 vols. (Jerusalem: Mosad Harav Kook, 2003), 1:178.

246. On the role of gates in community inclusion and exclusion (even in the post-exilic period), see Carey Walsh, "Testing Entry: The Social Functions of City Gates in Biblical Memory," in *Memory and the City in Ancient Israel*, ed. Diana V. Edelman and Ehud Ben Zvi (Winona Lake, IN: Eisenbrauns, 2014), 43–59.

247. Paul D. Wegner, "2416 זקן," *NIDOTTE*, 1:1134–37, here 1135.

248. E. Otto, "שׁער," *TDOT*, 15:359–405, here 397.

249. Ellen van Wolde makes this point in a fairly detailed study of gates in ancient and biblical Israel (*Reframing*, 72–103). For an even more in-depth study focused on archaeology, see Ze᾽ev Herzog, *Archaeology of the City: Urban Planning in Ancient Israel and Its Social Implications*, Nadler Institute of Archaeology Monograph 13 (Tel Aviv: Tel Aviv University Press, 1997), 211–58.

250. William G. Dever, *The Lives of Ordinary People in Ancient Israel: Where Archaeology and the Bible Intersect* (Grand Rapids: Eerdmans, 2012), 185, notes that a few rooms discovered in ancient Jerusalem had toilets.

251. Wood was also used in the construction of houses (e.g., Lev 14:45; Hag 1:4), though it of course does not survive centuries the way that stone does.

252. Helpful analyses of this topic can be found in Dever, *Lives of Ordinary People*, 128–32, 146–89; Borowski, *Daily Life*, 16–22.

253. Chamberi, "Four Room House, Israel Museum, Jerusalem," Wikimedia Commons, https://commons.wikimedia.org/wiki/File:Four_room_house._Israel_Museum,_Jerusalem.JPG.

254. Borowski, *Daily Life*, 20.

255. While animals often stayed inside these houses, they didn't always, as Genesis 33:17 illustrates. MacDonald, *Israelites Eat*, 62, points out that archaeologists are more likely to find the remains of sheep and goats than any other animal.

256. The argument in the textbox involves the canonical shape of the Bible, rather than a diachronical argument about the existence of Leviticus 27 before Judges 11. An exhaustive discussion of the relationship between Leviticus 27 and Judges 11 should furthermore consider Leviticus 27:28-29. Here, I simply observe that while Judges 11 relates to a sacrifice and warfare, it does not use the language of *kherem* found in Leviticus 27:28-29.

257. For more on items inside houses, see Dever, *Lives of Ordinary People*, 148, 159–85.

258. Smith, "Words and Their Worlds," 31.

259. Anthony Pym, *Negotiating the Frontier: Translators and Intercultures in Hispanic History* (New York: Routledge, 2000), 2.

260. *Shalom* has connections with ideas of just retribution, as can be seen here: the obedient receive what's coming to them, namely, peace. However, some authors (esp. G. Gerleman, "שׁלם," *TLOT*, 3:1337–48) have overemphasized the extent to which *shalom* is connected with ideas of retribution. When biblical texts talk about the wicked lacking *shalom* (e.g., Isa 57:21), they aren't saying the wicked lack what's coming to them. To the contrary, the text is saying they are getting exactly what they deserve. *HALOT*(se), s.v. שׁלום, 2:1506-11, here 1507, and F. J. Stendebach, "שׁלום," *TDOT*, 15:13–49, here 18, disagree with Gerleman for additional reasons.

261. Frederick Buechner, *Wishful Thinking: A Theological ABC* (New York: Harper & Row, 1973), 69.

262. While other translations of *leshalom* (לְשָׁלֹם) are possible, the preposition *le-* is fundamentally spatial, a point worth remembering even if *leshalom* is translated as an adverb ("peaceably"). See *IBHS*, 11.2.10.b.

263. Decades ago, James Barr warned biblical scholars against what he called "illegitimate totality transfer," that is, taking everything a word can mean and

assuming all meanings are at work when the word is employed (*Semantics of Biblical Language*, 218).

264. *DCH*, s.v. שׁלום.

265. Davis, "Blessing and Well-Being."

266. *DCH*, s.v. שׁלום.

267. The word does appear in Jeremiah 2:2, which talks about "the *khesed* of your youth." However, the verse refers more to devotion than infatuation, which would make little sense in context.

268. Some definitions even include "strength" (Charles Francis Whitley, "The Semantic Range of *Ḥesed*," *Bib* 62 [1981]: 519–26).

269. Gordon R. Clark, *The Word Hesed in the Hebrew Bible*, JSOTSup 157 (Sheffield: Sheffield Academic, 1993), 267.

270. Milgrom, *Numbers*, 396. Milgrom's text was altered slightly to match the system of transliteration used in this book. Cf. H. J. Stoebe, "חסד," *TLOT*, 2:449–64, here 450.

271. About 5 percent of the time that either word appears in the Hebrew Bible, it's in a verse with the other one. For more on the relationship between these words, see H.-J. Zobel, "חסד," *TDOT*, 5:44–64, esp. 52–53, 60–61, and R. Laird Harris, "698 חסד," *TWOT*, 305–7, which interact with important works like Nelson Glueck, Hesed *in the Bible*, trans. Alfred Gottschalk (Cincinnati: Hebrew Union College Press, 1967); Katharine Doob Sakenfeld, *Faithfulness in Action: Loyalty in Biblical Perspective* (Eugene, OR: Wipf and Stock, 2001).

272. Exod 20:5-6; Num 14:18; Deut 4:31; 5:9-10; 7:9-10; 2 Chron 30:9; Neh 1:5; 9:17, 31; Pss 77:8-9 [9-10 Heb.]; 78:38; 86:5, 15; 103:8, 17; 111:4; 112:4; 116:5; 145:8; Jer 32:18-19; Lam 3:32; Dan 9:4; Joel 2:13; Jonah 4:2; Nah 1:2-3; 4 Ezra 7:132-40. Terence E. Fretheim, *Exodus*, IBC (Louisville: Westminster John Knox, 2010), 302; Crenshaw, *Defending God*, 8, 93, 95, 197n2, 227n42; Hamilton, *Exodus*, 576; Phyllis Trible, *God and the Rhetoric of Sexuality*, OBT (Philadelphia: Fortress, 1978), 1–5.

273. See the sources cited in Matthew Richard Schlimm, "The Central Role of Emotions in Biblical Theology, Biblical Ethics, and Popular Conceptions of the Bible," in *Mixed Feelings and Vexed Passions in Biblical Literature: Emotions of*

Divine and Human Beings in Interdisciplinary Perspective, ed. Scott Spencer (Atlanta: SBL, 2017), 43–59, here 44–45n4.

274. As *HALOT*(se), s.v. עולם, notes, the Hebrew word for "everlasting" can refer to eternal matters, provided that "eternal" isn't understood in a philosophical sense.

275. Rau, "Top Ten Bible Verses."

276. Sakenfeld, *Faithfulness in Action*, 133.

277. Martha Nussbaum, *Upheavals of Thought: The Intelligence of Emotions* (Cambridge: Cambridge University Press, 2003), 202.

278. Richard E. Averbeck, "Clean and Unclean," *NIDOTTE*, 4:477–86, here 478.

279. G. André and H. Ringgren, "טמא," *TDOT*, 5:330–42, here 337, even talks about idolatry and sin as *metaphorical* instances of being unclean.

280. For more on this topic, see Schlimm, *This Strange and Sacred Scripture*, 111–19; Jonathan Klawans, *Impurity and Sin in Ancient Judaism* (Oxford: Oxford University Press, 2000), 3–42.

281. As I note in Schlimm, *This Strange and Sacred Scripture*, 129 n. a, "Hebrew (*qdsh*) and Greek (*hagios*) words relating to holiness appear more frequently in the Hebrew Bible and Greek NT (1,147 times) than Hebrew (*'hb* and *hsd*) and Greek (*agapē* and *phileō*) words relating to love (940 times)."

282. Although many standard dictionaries define Hebrew words for "holiness" in terms of being "set apart," that definition has come under criticism by some scholars such as David J. A. Clines, "Alleged Basic Meanings of the Hebrew Verb *qdš* 'be holy': An Exercise in Comparative Hebrew Lexicography," *Academia*, www.academia.edu/28065748. Note, however, that even *DCH* (which is edited by Clines) includes the definition of "apartness" for *qodesh*.

283. John Rogerson, "What Is Holiness?" in *Holiness Past and Present*, ed. Stephen C. Barton (London: T & T Clark, 2003), 3–21, here 21.

284. Jacob Milgrom, *Leviticus*, CC (Minneapolis: Fortress, 2004), 107. In this quotation, Milgrom's original "*imitatio Dei*" has been replaced with "imitating God" for readability purposes.

285. Christopher J. H. Wright, *The Mission of God's People: A Biblical Theology of the Church's Mission* (Grand Rapids: Zondervan, 2010), 124, suggests that this verse can be translated, "You must be a different people, because YHWH is a different God." See, however, Clines, "Alleged."

286. John Gammie, *Holiness in Israel*, OBT (Minneapolis: Fortress, 1989), 195.

287. Gen 12:10; 41:31; 43:1; 47:4, 13; Exod 8:24 [20 Heb.]; 9:3, 18, 24; 10:14.

288. Exod 7:14; 8:19 [15 Heb.], 32 [28 Heb.]; 9:7, 34; 10:1. On why God played a role in hardening Pharaoh's heart, see Fretheim, *Exodus*, 96–103.

289. Gen 45:13; Lev 10:3.

290. Cf. 1 Chron 16:28; Pss 24:8; 29:1; 62:7 [8 Heb.]; 63:2 [3 Heb.]; 96:7; 145:11-12.

291. Cf. Gen 31:1; 45:13; 1 Kgs 3:13; 1 Chron 29:12, 28; 2 Chron 1:11-12; 17:5; 18:1; 32:27; Esth 1:4; 5:1; Ps 49:16 [17 Heb.]; Prov 3:16; 8:18; 22:4; Eccl 6:2.

292. Josh 7:19; Neh 9:5; Pss 22:23 [24 Heb.]; 66:2; Isa 42:8, 12.

293. Prov 3:35; 12:9; 13:18; Isa 22:18; Hos 4:7; Hab 2:16.

294. Prov 15:33; 18:12; 22:4; 25:27; 29:23.

295. Pss 19:1 [2 Heb.]; 57:5, 11 [6, 12 Heb.]; 97:6; 108:5 [6 Heb.]; 113:4.

296. Gammie, *Holiness in Israel*, 197, ties God's glory to holiness, writing, "Glory is the aspect of the holiness that the divine manifests in some way to human eyes."

297. Exod 40:34-35; Lev 9:23; Num 14:10; 16:19, 42 [17:7 Heb.]; 20:6; 1 Kgs 8:11; 2 Chron 5:14; 7:1-3; Ps 26:8; Ezek 9:3; 10:4, 18-19; 43:4-5; 44:4; Hag 2:7. Imagery of fire and cloud appear in many of these texts as well.

298. In addition to the two reasons listed in the text above, it's worth noting that in some biblical texts, a human being will talk about himself or herself metonymically with the term *kavod*, which may have once referred to the liver (BDB, s.v. כבוד; see, e.g., Pss 16:9; 30:12 [13 Heb.]; 57:8 [9 Heb.]; 108:1 [2 Heb.]; cf.

Lam 2:11). References to the divine *kavod* may thus have been used as a way of figuratively speaking about God's being, analogous to a reference to God's heart.

299. In the following texts, there's an expectation that people could potentially die from seeing God face-to-face: Genesis 32:30 [31 Heb.]; Exodus 3:6; 24:11; Judges 6:22-23; 13:22-23.

300. For more on this topic, see George Ritzer, *The McDonaldization of Society*, 8th ed. (Thousand Oaks, CA: Sage, 2015).

301. There is also a related verb that appears just over twenty-five times in the Hebrew Bible: חָכַם, *khakham*.

302. James L. Crenshaw, *Old Testament Wisdom: An Introduction*, rev. and enlarged ed. (Louisville: Westminster John Knox, 1998), 3.

303. See, e.g., Prov 9:9; 10:31; 11:30; 23:24, which use an adjective related to *tsedaqah*.

304. Cf. Crenshaw, *Old Testament Wisdom*, 10.

305. See, e.g., Prov 10:31-32; 12:18-19; 13:2-3; 15:2; 18:6-7, 20-21; 31:8-9.

306. See, e.g., Prov 3:34; 11:2; 15:33; 18:12; 22:4; 28:26.

307. The Hebrew of Job is notoriously difficult, and it's possible that 38:36 instead speaks of wisdom and understanding among the ibis and rooster, respectively. Cf. NIV.

308. Hebrew also has a verb meaning to "be wise" that (at least in its dictionary form) is spelled and pronounced very much like its word for "wise": *khakham* (חָכַם). That verb is used here.

309. In addition to the passages referenced above, see the Deuterocanonical book Sirach, especially 1:26; 6:37; 15:1; 19:20; 21:11; 34:8; 38:34 [39:1 Grk.].

310. T. S. Matthews, *Under the Influence* (London: Cassell, 1977), 343. My attention was originally drawn to this quotation by Terence E. Fretheim, *The Suffering of God: An Old Testament Perspective*, OBT (Philadelphia: Fortress, 1984), 1.

311. Catherine A. Lutz, *Unnatural Emotions: Everyday Sentiments on a Micronesian Atoll and Their Challenge to Western Theory* (Chicago: University of

Chicago Press, 1988), 18–85; Robert I. Levy, *Tahitians: Mind and Experience in the Society Islands* (Chicago: University of Chicago Press, 1973), 307–8.

312. There's also a Hebrew noun for "fear" that appears nearly fifty times: יִרְאָה, *yirah*.

313. This number includes cases in which *yare* or *yirah* is followed by *yhwh* or (*ha*)*elohim*, either immediately or with the definite direct object marker in between.

314. As H. F. Fuhs, "ירא," *TDOT*, 6:290–315, here 300, describes, a passive form of *yare* ("be feared") appears thirty-six times describing either God, God's name, God's attributes, God's deeds, or God's day of judgment. See, e.g., Exod 15:11; 2 Sam 7:23; Neh 4:14 [8 Heb.]; Dan 9:4; Joel 2:11.

315. Here, most English translations have "respect" or "revere," even though the Hebrew has the verb for fear, *yare*.

316. Lev 19:14; 25:17; Prov 8:13; 10:27; 14:26-27; 15:16; 19:23; 22:4. Some of these verses are mentioned in Fuhs, *TDOT*, 6:311.

317. H.-P. Stähli, "ירא," *TLOT*, 2:568–78, here 575, 577. See, e.g., Deut 31:12; Pss 25:14; 111:5.

318. Judg 6:10; 2 Kgs 17:35-39; cf. 1 Chron 16:25; Pss 27:1; 96:4. In the Bible, there are also cases in which fearing God means essentially to worship God (e.g., Deut 10:12-13; M. V. Van Pelt and W. C. Kaiser Jr., "3707 ירא," *NIDOTTE*, 2:527–33, here 529).

319. Theophanies are cases in which God or God's messenger appears to people. Frequently, God or the messenger will tell the people not to be afraid. See, e.g., Gen 15:1; 21:17; 26:24.

320. Francis of Assisi, "The Prayer of Saint Francis," *UMH* 481. Cf. Ps 56:3-4 [4-5 Heb.].

321. These words were written by John Utz, former director of Duke Divinity School's Center for Theological Writing. In 2003, these sentences appeared on the center's website (https://divinity.duke.edu/academics/center-theological-writing).

322. Dirk Geeraerts and Hubert Cuyckens, "Introducing Cognitive Linguistics," *The Oxford Handbook of Cognitive Linguistics*, ed. Dirk Geeraerts and Hubert Cuyckens (Oxford: Oxford University Press, 2007), 3–21, here 5.

323. A few decades ago, scholars would criticize these sorts of statements, which have continuity with the Sapir-Whorf linguistic relativity hypothesis. More recent developments in scholarship are much more sympathetic to linguistic relativity (William M. Schniedewind, "*Prolegomena* for the Sociolinguistics of Classical Hebrew," *JHebS* 5 [2005]: §2.4, http://www.jhsonline.org/Articles/article_36.pdf; Schlimm, *From Fratricide to Forgiveness*, 28–33).

324. James Barr, *The Concept of Biblical Theology: An Old Testament Perspective* (Minneapolis: Fortress, 1999), 218. Some readers might be surprised to see Barr make this comment, given his critiques of the biblical theology movement (e.g., James Barr, "The Position of Hebrew Language in Theological Education," *International Review of Mission* 50, no. 200 [1961]: 435–44; idem, *Semantics of Biblical Language*). For more on Barr and word studies, see idem, "Semantics and Biblical Theology—A Contribution to the Discussion," in *Congress Volume: Uppsala 1971*, edited by P. A. H. de Boer, VTSup 22 (Leiden: Brill, 1972), 13–19, as well as my more technical discussion in Schlimm, *From Fratricide to Forgiveness*, 28–33.

325. *The SBL Handbook of Style: For Biblical Studies and Related Disciplines*, 2nd ed. (Atlanta: SBL, 2014), 58. Jennifer Pattee gave me the idea of using Star Wars words, and my son, Isaiah Schlimm, helped me come up with some of the examples.

Index of Hebrew Words, Their Common Translations, and Technical Terms

Printed in the USA
CPSIA information can be obtained
at www.ICGtesting.com
JSHW022229300624
65550JS00005B/17

9 781426 799969